AF623940

ENCYCLOPAEDIA OF INDIAN GOVERNMENT: PROGRAMMES AND POLICIES

ENCYCLOPAEDIA
OF
INDIAN GOVERNMENT:
PROGRAMMES AND POLICIES

Vol. 16

Atomic and Non-Conventional Energy

Edited by

Satish Tiwari

ANMOL PUBLICATIONS PVT. LTD.

NEW DELHI - 110 002 (INDIA)

ANMOL PUBLICATIONS PVT. LTD.
4374/4B, Ansari Road, Daryaganj
New Delhi - 110 002

Encyclopaedia of Indian Government: Programmes and Policies
© Reserved
First Edition, 2000
ISBN 81-261-0515-1 (Set)

[Responsibility for the facts stated, opinions expressed, conclusions reached and plagiarism, if any, in these volumes is entirely that of the Editor. The Publisher bears no responsibility for them whatsoever.]

PRINTED IN INDIA

Published by J.L. Kumar for Anmol Publications Pvt. Ltd., New Delhi - 110 002 and Printed at Mehra Offset Press, Delhi.

Contents

Preface

Encyclopaedia of Indian Government: Programmes and Policies contains authoritative information on about fifty departmental policies and their future developmental programmes.

Organised to be completed in 40 volumes, this gigantic work covers Agriculture; Atomic Energy; Chemicals and Fertilizers; Coal; Commerce; Communication; Culture; Defence; Education; Environment and Forests; External Affairs; Finance; Food & Consumer Affairs; Food Processing Industries; Health and Family Welfare; Home Affairs and Internal Security; Human Resources; Industry; Information and Broadcasting; Labour; Law, Justice and Company Affairs; Non-conventional Energy Sources; Ocean Development; Parliamentary Affairs; Personnel, Public Grievances and Pensions; Petroleum and Natural Gas; Planning and Programme Implementation; Planning and Statistics; Posts and Telegraphs; Power; Rural Development; Science and Technology; Social Justice and Empowerment; Space; States Affairs; Steel; Steel and Mines; Sugar and Edible Oils; Surface Transport; Textiles; Tourism; Urban Development; Water Resources; Women and Child development etc.

Based on the information derived from authoritative sources, this work contains authentic facts and figures. I am deeply beholden to all the scholars whose writings are cited or substantially made use of in the present work. I am also thankful to Anmol Publications Pvt. Ltd. for undertaking publication of this encyclopaedia. I am solely responsible for shortcomings in presentation of matter.

Encyclopaedic in nature, this will prove a dependable reference work for scholars and academics besides those appearing for different competitive examinations.

—**Satish Tiwari**

1

Introduction

The threat posed to sustainable development by the increase in greenhouse gas emissions and consequent climate changes occurring globally have understandably caused worldwide concern. According to an assessment by the Intergovernmental Panel on Climate Change, the rise in the average global temperature will be between 1 degree and 3.5 degrees C by the end of the next century i.e. 2100. This represents an average rate of global warming greater than any in the last 10,000 years.

This has undoubtedly serious implications for the survival of not only human beings but also animals and plants. This has led to a series of initiatives at the national and international levels to reverse this trend and take recourse to eco-friendly means to development that would meet the needs of the present without compromising the ability of the future generations to meet their own needs.

Admittedly, the developed nations have contributed a greater share of the emissions of carbon dioxide, leading to global warming. But the current trends in the developing countries are no less alarming and, if allowed unchecked, half of the annual greenhouse gases, it is projected, will be the contribution of developing countries. In India, electric power generation is the largest source of greenhouse gases and accounts for 48 per cent of the carbon emitted. All these underline the urgent need for minimising, if not completely replacing, the reliance on fossil fuels to meet the increasing energy requirements. It is against this backdrop that the non-conventional renewable sources of energy have caught global attention.

The series of global meets in the 1990s from Rio to Kyoto have created a favourable climate for renewable energy development. Following this, not only the multinational corporations but also multilateral agencies like the World Bank, the Global Environment Facility and the Asian Development Bank besides aid agencies in developed countries are vigorously pursuing programmes to develop renewable sources of energy and committing the required funds. The setting up of a Clean Development Mechanism in the coming years will facilitate channelling of funds from the developed countries to support renewable energy development in the developing countries.

India can be said to be a visionary in this respect. For, Indian scientists had not merely thought of tapping the solar energy but even designed the necessary solar devices for water heating and cooking as early as the 1950s. These were technically sound but did not satisfy the principles of sound economics because conventional fossil fuels were in abundance then. Since then there has been a sea-change in the energy scenario.

The increase in population, accompanied by rapid urbanisation and industrialisation led to increased use of fossil fuels. With growing environmental concerns and the dwindling reserves of fossil fuels, recourse to renewable sources of energy became imperative. Even as early as 1955 it was estimated that fossil fuels like coal, oil and gas would not last for more than 150 years if reliance were to be placed entirely on these for energy generation. In India the total potential of renewable energy is estimated to-be 100,000 MW. Recognising the relevance of renewable energy sources, the Government of India set up in 1981 a Commission for Additional Sources of Energy (CASE), on the lines of the Space Commission and the Atomic Energy Commission in the Department of Science and Technology. A year later, a separate Department of Non-Conventional Energy Sources was created in the Ministry of Energy. Ten years later, this was upgraded to the level of a Ministry.

India has thus earned the distinction of being the only country in the world to have an exclusive Ministry for Non-Conventional Energy Sources (MNES) which has been implementing one of the world's largest programmes on renewable energy, spanning the entire spectrum of technologies targeted towards all sections of the society. As part of special initiative to develop the North-Eastern Region, the Ministry has examarked 10% of its domestic budgetary support for the North-East States including Sikkim in its major programmes. It has also approved a scheme for providing central financial assistance to set up and strengthen the State nodal agencies.

A Women's Component Plan has been included in the Ministry's renewable energy programmes such as the National Programme on Improved Chulhas, National Project on Biogas Development, Renewable Energy Parks, Wind Mills Programme, Solar Photovoltaic Programme and Information of Public Awareness Programme.

The policies and programmes initiated over the years have helped in generating public awareness about the advantages of tapping renewable energy sources and bringing about the much-needed shift in the mindset of the people in favour of renewable energy. The devices based on environmentally benign, new and renewable sources of energy (NRSE) are no longer viewed with scepticism. This is evident from the increasing use of NRSE for meeting the energy needs of the rural population and remote areas, the rising share of the renewables in the total power generation capacity and the growing interest evinced by the State Governments, non-governmental organisations and private entrepreneurs in promoting renewable energy projects.

India is fortunate to be endowed with an abundance of renewable energy sources. These include biomass, sun, wind, ocean waters, urban and industrial wastes, hilly hydro and canal heads suitable for small and mini hydel sets etc.

The biomass includes large quantities of cattle dung and human excreta, agricultural residues, bagasse and other by-products of agro-based industries like paper mills etc. The potential of some of these is indeed enormous as indicated in Table 1. During the year under report a number of fresh initiatives were taken, besides continuing the on-going programmes, to exploit the potential to the extent possible.

Table 1

Estimated potential for renewable energy Technologies in India

Sources/systems	Approx. Potential
Biogas plants (No.)	12 million
Improved woodstoves (No.)	120 million
Biomass	17,000 million
Solar energy	20 MW/sq.km
Wind energy	20,000 MW
Small hydro power	10,000 MW
Ocean energy	50,000 MW

There are an estimated 232 million cattle in the country and if one-third of the dung produced annually from these is available for production of biogas and for recycling as farm manure, 12 million biogas plants can be installed. Against this potential, a cumulative total of 27.65 lakh family type and toilet-linked plants under the National Project on Biogas Development and 2360 plants under the Community, Institutional and Nightsoil based Biogas Plants Programme have been installed up to December 1998. This represents just a little over one-fifth of the potential. But still this would lead to a saving of 28 lakh tonnes of fuelwood per year, based on the assumption that one plant saves about 1260 kg of fuelwood per year and 79 per cent of the plants installed are functional, as brought out in a survey carried out by the National Council of Applied Economic Research.

Moreover, these plants produce digested slurry containing nitrogen equivalent to 6.5 lakh tonnes of urea valued at Rs. 260 crore. Apart from the economic benefits cited above, the biogas plants help reduce the drudgery among rural women and girl children engaged in the collection of fuel materials from long distances and cooking in smoky kitchens, minimise the risks of contracting lung and eye ailments by rural women and girl children, and improve the general standard of living. This also helps generate employment and improve sanitation.

Another important programme targeted particularly to rural areas is the promotion of improved chulhas (cookstoves). Besides conserving fuelwood, thereby checking deforestation, this would help eliminate smoke in the kitchen and reduce the drudgery of the rural women folk. Against the estimated potential of 120 million, around 28.5 million improved chulhas have been promoted so far.

The socioeconomic cost-benefit analysis of the programme by the NCAER has brought out that one improved chulha helps save fuel materials equivalent to 210 kg coal/soft coke valued at Rs. 388/- while in terms of kerosene the saving works out to 40 litres per year per chulha valued at Rs. 343/- per household. These tangible benefits and other gains like saving of time in cooking, reduction in lung and eye diseases, generation of employment etc. are clear pointers to the need for a more vigorous pursuit of this programme.

The biomass programme has helped in optimising the productivity of fuelwood tree species in waste lands and marginally degraded lands, besides development and promotion of biomass gasification and briquetting systems. During the year under report, 31 biomass gasifier systems with a total capacity of 3085 kW were installed, of which the largest chunk of 23 systems with a capacity of 2300 kW was in Andhra Pradesh.

In terms of capacity these systems may seem insignificant but in terms of the benefits accrued they are quite significant. These systems have helped in providing electricity to households in remote villages from locally available biomass resources. In Tamil Nadu, biomass gasifier systems are planned to be installed in prisons for cooking purposes. Another significant benefit that can accrue from using biomass based energy systems is reduction in carbon dioxide emissions.

An Itegrated Rural Energy Programme (IREP) has been under implementation as a regular plan scheme since the Seventh Five Year Plan. The programme aims at developing the planning and institutional capabilities in the States/UTs and implementing area-founded integrated energy projects in a most cost effective manner with a mix of all types of energy sources. The programme has been extended to 860 blocks, which represents about

16% of the total number of blocks in the country. The programme offers the most cost effective options of various energy sources for meeting the basic energy needs of cooking, heating and lighting especially for the weaker sections of the society.

The programme also ensures active participation of local people in the planning and implementation of various activities promoted under the programme through the involvement of local bodies, panchayats and other institutions, wherever feasible. In order to augment the impact of the programme, the States and UTs have been requested to provide a budget of Rs. 5 lakh per IREP Block per year under the State budget outlay and mobilse the financial resources from other Rural Development Programmes for providing energy input in IREP Blocks by integrating block level IREP plans with block developmental plans.

While these are mainly targeted to meet the needs of rural and remote areas, the solar photovoltaic (SPV) programme seeks to cater to the requirements of both the rural and urban areas. India receives solar energy equivalent to over 5000 trillion kWh/year which is far more than the total energy consumption of the country. The daily average solar energy incidence varies from 4 to 7 kWh/sq.m. depending upon the location. The SPV programme has resulted in significant technological developments, besides widespread field demonstration and utilisation of devices for various applications.

A strong R& base and production capabilities in the entire area starting from silicon cells to PV modules and complete systems have been created. The SPV systems that are being promoted include solar lanterns, home lighting systems, solar home systems, street lighting systems, SPV power plants etc. During the year, 20,484 solar lanterns, 15,206 home lighting systems/ solar home systems, 437 street lighting systems and 57 kWp capacity SPV power plants were promoted up to December 1998. As the targets pitched were quite high the implementing agenciès have been given time till June 1999 to reach the target. Ten regions in the country have been designated as High Focus Areas for implementation of the SPV programme.

So far, SPV systems with an aggregate capacity of 35 MWp have been deployed for different applications. For water pumping applications, SPV systems, windmills, small aerogencrators and wind-solar photovoltaic hybrid systems are being prcmoted. A cumulative total of 2787 SPV water pumping systems, 515 windmills and small aerogenerators; with aggregate capacity of 35 kW have been installed up to December 1998. From all accounts, the SPV programme has caught on and many organisations have begun using SPV systems for a variety of applications which include provision of power for rural telephones, railway signalling, low power transmitters, cathodic protection, water desalination etc.

Another major programme relates to promotion of solar thermal technologies. Among these, solar water heating systems occupy an important place. Hot water is needed for a number of applications at homes, in offices, institutions, hotels, hospitals, industrial units etc. The Ministry's promotional efforts have resulted in the installation of 4,50,000 sq.m. of solar water heating collectors which can heat more than 22 million litres of water to a temperature of 60-70 degrees C every day. This is no small achievement and the technology of solar water heating is now fairly mature even though there may be scope for some improvements.

The advantages of using solar water heating systems are quite obvious. Use of 1000 domestic solar water heaters of 100 litre capacity each will contribute to a peak load shaving of 1 MW. Use of large systems can result in substantial saving of electricity or other commercial fuels like coal, wood, furnace oil etc. Besides this, carbon dioxide emissions into the atmosphere can be prevented. According to a conservative estimate, the potential in our country for deployment of such systems is around 30 million sq.m of collector area, against which 4.5 lakh sq.m of collectors have been installed. This brings out the enormous scope that still exists in this area of renewable energy. In recent years, the manufacturing base of solar water heating systems has improved substantially and there are 37 approved manufacturers with production capacity of 100000 sq.m of collector area per year.

Large-scale promotion of solar water heating systems, through a number of financial and fiscal incentives, has been taken up. Besides the Indian Renewable Energy Development Agency (IREDA), five banks have come forward to provide soft loan for those interested in going in for these systems. Quite a few industrial units have installed solar water heating systems. A model code/building bye-laws to make use of solar water heaters mandatory in government buildings is being formulated. Meanwhile, half a dozen State Governments have taken the lead in making installation of solar water heating systems mandatory in government buildings.

The solar thermal programme also covers solar cookers, solar air heating systems and solar architecture. During the year, 5000 solar cookers have been sold till December 31, 1998 making a total of 4,62,000 sold since the inception of the Ministry. There are 25 manufacturers of box type solar cookers. The Ministry has taken the initiative to introduce solar cookers for community use. In this context, the concentrating type community cooker developed by ULOG group of Switzerland is being evaluated.

A unique feature of this device is that with this it is possible to cook food with solar energy within the kitchen itself. Solar air heating systems for drying of farm produces are making a foray and during the year a Tamil Nadu company has installed an air heating system for drying coriander. The solar architecture concept is slowly catching on and two buildings with solar-efficient design have been constructed in Himachal Pradesh. Meetings with architects have been organized to promote this concept.

Through demonstration and pilot projects the Ministry has been promoting solar thermal technologies for different applications.

The rapid urbanisation and industrialisa tion have led to huge quantities of garbage and industrial effluents piling up in cities and towns, causing pollution and environmental degradation. In recent years, technologies have been developed to extract energy from urban and industrial wastes and the Ministry has taken a number of initiatives to promote "waste to energy" projects. It is estimated that 1000 MW of power can be generated from urban and municipal wastes and 700 MW from industrial wastes in our country. Besides the national programme, a UNDP/GEF assisted project has been launched to develop high-rate biomethanation processes as a means to reduce greenhouse gas emissions. A number of fiscal and financial incentives are being offered to attract private sector investments in "waste to energy" projects. A few projects have come up and more are in the pipeline.

One of the major objectives of the various programmes of the Ministry is to increase the share of renewable sources of energy in the total power generation capacity in the country. Thanks to the initiatives taken by the Ministry, there has been a steady growth in power generation based on renewable sources and 1378 MW, representing 1.5 per cent of the total grid capacity, is now based on renewable sources. Solar, wind, biomass and small hydro are the main sources of renewable energy used for power generation.

The solar power programme has two components, one based on the photovoltaic (PV) route and the other on the thermal route. Under SPV power programme, 11 projects with an aggregate capacity of 815 kW, commissioned earlier and during the year under report, are in operation. One more project of 100 kW is expected to be commissioned before the year end.

Twelve projects with an aggregate capacity of 750 kW are under different stages of installation. Under the solar thermal power programme, a 140 MW integrated solar combined cycle power plant with solar thermal power component of 35 MW at Mathania near Jodhpur has been proposed. This project has been approved by the CASE and a number of other clearances have been obtained. The detailed project report has been prepared for the project to be implemented by Rajasthan State

Power Corporation Ltd. with Central assistance of Rs 50 crore and an equity of Rs 50 crore by the State Government. The Global Environment Facility (GEF) has agreed to provide a grant of US $ 49 million and the German Government will provide, through KfW, a loan of DM 250 million. Once this comes up, it will mark an important milestone in the country's march towards sustainable development based on renewable energy sources.

Meanwhile, the country has made a mark in the wind energy sector and now ranks fourth in the world with a total wind power capacity of 992 MW. The growth has been phenomenal because at the beginning of the Eighth Plan the capacity created was a mere 40 MW which rose to 900 MW by the end of the Eighth Plan and to 992 MW by December 31, 1998. The wind power projects have generated over 3.7 billion units of electricity so far. The initial estimate of 20,000 MW of wind power potential is being revised. The technical potential, currently estimated at 9000 MW, is also likely to go up. The wind power programme has been geared to tap the nature's bounty by undertaking extensive wind resource assessment and identifying potential locations. As many as 160 locations having a potential of 5000 MW have been identified in 13 States.

A notable feature of the wind power programme has been the interest evinced by private entrepreneurs in setting up commercial wind power projects. In fact, of the 1000 MW capacity created so far, 950 MW has been established in commercial projects while the remaining 50 MW has been contributed by demonstration projects. IREDA has set up a revolving fund to finance commercial projects and has received/ likely to receive assistance by way of sizeable credit from multilateral and bilateral aid agencies like World Bank, GEF, DANIDA, KfW, and OECF (Japan).

A number of other financial institutions like IDBI, ICICI and IFCI, besides power finance companies like REC and PFC provide finance for wind power projects. Private sector financing and leasing companies too have come forward to support this sector. On its part, the Government of India has announced a package of fiscal concessions to promote wind power projects. There are 15 manufacturers of wind turbine equipment with annual production capacity of 500 MW.

A number of companies have tied up with foreign wind turbine firms for joint venture/licensed production of wind electric generators (WEG). The annual turnover of wind industry had reached Rs 1500 crore during the Eighth Plan and Indian-made wind turbines are now being exported. It can truly be stated that India has gained sufficient experience, both technological and operational, and is now on the threshold of "take off' in wind power.

Biomass as a source of electricity holds considerable promise. It is estimated that 405 million tonnes of crop residues are produced every year, a large portion of which goes waste or is used inefficiently. By using only the surplus biomass materials available more than 16,000 MW of power can be generated. In this context, bagasse-based cogeneration has assumed significance. An estimated 3500 MW of additional power can be produced if all the 430 sugar mills in the country switched over to modern techniques of cogeneration.

The Ministry has initiated programmes to promote continuous technological innovations in cogeneration. Besides bagasse, a number of other biomass materials like straw, stalks, stems, and agro-industrial processing residues like shells, husks, deoiled cakes, forestry residues And woody biomass are being promoted for power generation. As many as 28 biomass power projects with an aggregate capacity of 141 MW have been commissioned as on December 31, 1998 and another 27 with an aggregate capacity of 180 MW are under construction.

During the year under report, a Programme Partnership Initiative (PPI) in bagasse-based cogeneration programmes was launched to enthuse, motivate and assist sugar mills to take to cogeneration. Encouraged by the response evoked by the PPI in cogeneration, it has been proposed to widen the scope of PPI to cover other potential areas like paper industry, rice milling industry, cotton, coconut, tea processing etc.

It is worthwhile to note that the Infrastructure Leasing and Financial Services Ltd. has come out with an innovative model to tap the cogeneration potential available in the cooperative/public sector sugar mills. The Tamil Nadu Government has approved the formation of a joint venture company with the IL&FS, cooperative/public sector sugar mills and a partner firm in order to establish 10 cogeneration projects with an aggregate capacity of 200 MW at a total estimated cost of Rs 560 crore. The Governments of Andhra Pradesh, Gujarat, Haryana, Maharashtra, Punjab and Uttar

Pradesh have evinced interest in adopting the Tamil Nadu approach to promote cogeneration. The thrust areas for technology development in the field of power generation based on bagasse and other biomass materials have been identified by the Technology Development Committee constituted by the Ministry. During the year under report, the Preparatory Assistance (PA) Mission for developing the full project document for the "India Biomass Power Generation Project" for GEF funding commenced its preparatory work. Discussions were held with the EC-Asean Cogeneration Programme authorities with a view to developing a component for biomass power project in India especially aimed at the establishment of small-sized (1 MW) units. The investment-cum-technical assistance component is likely to be about 6 million Euro Currency.

Small hydro resources have the potential of generating 10,000 MW of power. The Ministry is giving a major thrust to the promotion of small hydel projects in the Ninth Plan as they are economically viable and environmentally benign. Hitherto, the MNES had the mandate of promoting small hydel projects up to 3 MW capacity. It has now been decided to transfer to the MNES the responsibility of promoting small hydel projects of capacity ranging between 3 and 25 MW. The MNES has developed data base of 3349 potential sites with an aggregate capacity of 2852 MW for projects up to 3 MW and 662 sites with aggregate capacity of 5519 MW for projects in the range of 3-15 MW capacity. So far, 225 small hydel projects up to 3 MW capacity aggregating to 173 MW have been completed and 185 projects with aggregate capacity of 188 MW are under construction. The MNES is also implementing a project with technical assistance from UNDP/GEF for optimising the development of small hydro resources in Himalayan and Sub-Himalayan regions.

There are quite a few other eco-friendly energy sources and tapping them requires technology development. These include fuel cells, hydrogen, geothermal energy, ocean energy, etc. The Ministry has been supporting research and technology development efforts in these areas through research institutions. The public sector enterprise BHEL has been actively participating in this programme by developing and installing x power plants. Notable progress has been recorded during the year in the development of these new technologies, including the development of electric vehicles and other alternate fuels for surface transport.

The renewable energy development programme of the MNES has evoked considerable interest at the international level with the result that multilateral and bilateral development aid agencies have come forward to provide financial resources for a number of projects. India has also been actively participating in various international conferences on renewable energy and sharing her experience and expertise with other developing countries.

The Indian Renewable Energy Development Agency (IREDA), which is the promotional and financing arm of the Ministry, has been quite effective in mobilising resources and promoting commercial ventures in the NRSE sector. The Solar Energy Centre set up in Gurgaon on the outskirts of Delhi and the Centre for Wind Energy Technology being set up in Tamil Nadu provide technical support to the Ministry in the implementation of solar and wind energy programmes.

The Solar Energy Centre continued to perform as per the objectives laid down for it. Testing of solar cookers, solar flat plate collectors, solar PV lanterns, home lighting systems, street lighting systems, luminaires, water pumping systems and PV modules was carried out. Training programmes were conducted for bank officers, UN university students, technicians from State nodal agencies, practising air-conditioning engineers and architects and photovoltaic engineers.

Consultancy and advisory services were formally initiated and two assignments were carried out. Open Days were observed for the general public and school children from 3rd to 5th February, 1999 to increase awareness about various solar technologies. A National Essay Competition is being organised for school children and teachers. Besides these, a National Institute of Renewable Energy (named after late Sardar. Swaran Singh) is being established at Jalandhar in Punjab which would cover the entire spectrum of NRSE and cater to research and human resource needs of the NRSE programmes. As one of the main constraints to the promotion of renewables is their high initial cost, the R&D efforts are being directed to achieve cost reduction without compromising on quality.

As the success of any programme depends upon its wide acceptance by the users, the Ministry has mounted a vigorous campaign of information dissemination and awareness generation bringing out the cost advantage's of NRSE devices in the long run, besides the environmental benefits of using them. Apart from the print and electronic media, the Ministry has been relying on exhibitions to reach the target groups. In addition, a scheme of Energy Parks has been launched which envisages display and demonstration of NRSE devices in educational institutions and public places.

Encouraged by the positive response evoked by its various programmes, the Ministry has taken up the formulation of a National Renewable Energy Policy which seeks to address the various issues that influence the successful implementation of NRSE programmes.

As a part of this policy a medium-term renewable energy programme is being chalked out to ensure that by 2012 the share of renewable sources in the total power generation capacity increases to about 10 per cent from the present level of 1.5 per cent. This calls for new perceptions, attitudinal changes, strong international action and national commitment. By the end of the first decade of the 21st century it would be cost-effective to generate and supply electricity based on renewable sources aggregating to several thousand megawatts. The reason is that fossil fuels will by then reach their maximum potential and their prices will become higher than the renewable energy options.

2

Research and Development Organisations

Bhabha Atomic Research Centre

Nuclear tests at Pokhran

India conducted five nuclear tests during the period May 11-13, 1998 at the Pokhran range in Rajasthan desert. The first three detonations took place simultaneously at 15.45 hrs. IST, on May 11. These included a thermonuclear device, a fission device and a sub-kiloton device. The fission device was much smaller in size and weight as compared to the one used for the May 18, 1974 explosion.

The thermonuclear device had two stages, the primary stage was a fusion-boosted fission device and the secondary was a thermonuclear device. The two nuclear devices, fired on May 13 at 12.21 hrs. IST, were in the subkiloton yield range. The detonations were very successful and predictions of the yield of the three devices were very accurate. The yield of the thermonuclear device was chosen to minimise the seismic damage to surrounding villages. The depths of emplacements were fixed so that the explosions were contained with no surface radioactivity after the tests and test sites. Detailed seismic analysis using 160 global stations and close-in acceleration measurements have since been carried out which confirms the estimated combined yield of May 11 tests to be around 60 KT.

Research reactors

Research reactors Apsara and Dhruva continued to be operated for production of radioisotopes and for providing facilities for neutron beam experiments and testing of neutron in-pile detectors. Their performance at required power levels was satisfactory. After extensive ageing studies, reactor CIRUS was taken up for refurbishing to extend its useful life.

Reactor design and development

Advanced heavy water reactor (AHWR)

Design, development, analytical and experimental activities were vigorously pursued. Fuel design and experimental studies to improve fuel performance were done. The prototype 52 pin fuel cluster was installed in the Flow Test Facility at Engineering Hall 7 for pressure drop and endurance testing. Vibration measurements on dummy fuel assembly were carried out to evaluate performance during high, moderate and low flows.

Thermal hydraulic studies

Experimental loops for carrying out tests on steady state thermosyphon and stability of two phase natural circulation were commissioned and preliminary test runs were started. Preliminary sub-channel analysis of fuel bundle was carried out. Steady state heat transfer analysis of the polycarbon blocks of AHWR moderator system was carried out. An experimental setup was fabricated to study 2-phase flow pattern transition using neutron beam radiography in APSARA reactor.

Component/systems design

Design of coolant channel was completed. A 3D model of AHWR building was completed. A detailed specification for pyrocarbon blocks was prepared. ECCS accumulator with fluidic device was designed using a specially developed computer code.

Reactor engineering

Integrated Garter Spring Repositioning system was assembled and qualified for reactor work at MAPS-I site. Repositioning of the garter springs was taken up in five coolant channels. The design of Instrumented fuel pin for testing of PHWR fuel pin under Loss of Coolant Accident (LOCA) conditions was finalised. A diagnostic method for detection of turbine blade vibration was developed with data input from the reactor sites. Development of a passive hydrogen combiner device was completed and the system was commissioned.

All the operating facilities/loops *e.g.*, Integral Teat Facility, Flow Test Facility, 3MW boiling water loop, fuelling machine test facility were satisfactorily operated for conducting a variety of experiments, testing of components and data generation.

Reactor safety

Design and procurement related activities were carried out in respect of the Instrumentation and Control System for Containment Studies Facility (CSF). Quantification of human reliability based on Operator Action Tree Sequence and I-IRA Event Tree Model was done. Preliminary design of the PHT model vessel was carried out for the proposed Containment Studies Facility. Seismic re-qualification analysis for the identified structures and components of CIRUS was continued. The fatigue monitoring system at HWP, Kota was found to be working satisfactorily.

The data base development for implementing the same to HWP, Tuticorin has been completed. A facility, 'Nuclear Synergism Simulator' was set up and commissioned at PANBIT to test components under combined environmental conditions for studying the interaction effects of temperature, radiation, humidity and operating electrical stresses. A procedure for the qualification of components has been prepared. For life extension of Heavy Water Plant, Kota, a preliminary seismic re-evaluation of process tanks, dump tanks and their supporting structures was completed.

As a part of the cooperative contaminant research programme jointly sponsored by the USNRC and NUPEC, a pre-test analysis of 1:4 Scaled model of an existing Japanese pressurised water reactor (PWR) prestressed concrete containment vessel had begun and a set of preliminary results were obtained. The accident analysis of TAPSBWRs, for the case of recirculation Line Break and Main Stream Line Break was completed.

Reactor control instrumentation

The work on design and development of advanced computer/microprocessor based Instrumentation and Control (I&C) systems for forthcoming PHWRs at Kalga-1&2 and RAPP-3&4 was continued. Work was also carried out in other areas such as development of in-service inspection tools, design and development of software Verification and Validation (V&V) tools, hardware and systems reliability assessment and so on. An electrical supervisory Control and Data Acquisition (SCADA) was developed to monitor and c electrical equipment for RAPP-3.

The complete SCADA system was integrated and tested for the specific functions of monitoring, interlocks control and the system was installed site. The development of microcomputer based system for reactor power regulation for use in Kaiga- 1&2 and RAP 3&4 was completed. Reliability analysis of microcomputer based hardware circuit modules used in various safety and safety related I&C systems designed for 1&2 and RAPP-3&4 was completed.

The development of Coolant Channel Inspection System, BARCIS M III With special features to suit Fuel

Machine vault layout at NAPS was completed. A four axis drive mechanism suitable for mounting on Fuelling Machine bridge was developed. A quad CCTV system for remotised alignment remotised calibration checking linear and rotary displacements inspection heads and surveillance Fuelling Machine vault was implemented.

A facility for on-line calibration checking of ultrasonic transducers was incorporated. The successful completion of this system has resulted substantial savings in foreign exchange. An on-line Fatigue Monitoring tern was developed to assess the structural degradation of components.

One such unit had been installed and commissioned at Heavy Water Plant, Kota. A computerised control system a KOMAGE hydraulic press for uranium oxide fuel pellet fabrication commissioned at Nuclear Fuel Complex and the field trials have been satisfactory. This will be a significant imp substitution.

As per MOU signed with IOC an Instrumented PIG for oil pi lines, was developed and trial progressed. The design, development, commissioning and testing of microprocessor based Traction Control System for 25 KV AC, 4200 HP, Locomotives of Indian Railways was concluded after successful full-load line trials of a retrofitted Locomotive at Bhusaval.

This project was a collaborative, effort among BARC, DOE and RDSO. The thyristor convertors were manufactured at ECIL as per design by BARC and RDSO. The hardware and software for the control system was jointly developed by BARC and RDSO. BARC has been actively involved in the FALCON RPV programme of DRDO and had designed and commissioned three tracking antenna control systems for the vehicle mounted 6' diameter antenna, in partnership with ECIL.

Refuelling technology

In-head calibration plug for BARCIS Mark-II has been successfully used in MAPS for calibration of ultra- sonic sensors. An automatic clamping mechanism was designed for wet INGRES delivery system. It will reduce time and men-rem consumption during garter spring repositioning in the reactor. Channel Isolating Plug for maintenance of end fitting seal face of PHWR has been developed and delivered to NAPS and successfully tested.

Nuclear fuels

Production of fuel pins with Mark II mixed carbide fuel composition for FBTR was recommenced. Fuel pins for sub- assemblies were fabricated and necessary DHRUVA fuel clusters were delivered Fabrication of fuel pins for the 11th&12th MOX subassemblies for TAPS were continued at Advanced Fuels Fabrication Facility (AFFF), Tarapur.

As a part of the development work on annular fuel pellet fabrication for PFBR a large number of acceptable quality annular pellets were fabricated at AFFF using a new tooling developed in-house. Work on the commissioning/operation of Computer Controlled Sol-Gel Plant was continued at AFFF, Tarapur. An indigenous microwave furnace designed and fabricated at the plant was commissioned for carrying out dry recycle work on MOX fuel pellet scrap.

Fuel reprocessing

Project KARP (Kalpakkam Reprocessing Plant), designed for reprocessing capacity of 100 Te per annum, was initiated into commissioning runs involving processing of spent fuel from MAPS on establishing satisfactory design safety case for regulatory authorisation by the Atomic Energy Regulatory Board. The Reprocessing Plant was dedicated to the Nation by the Prime Minister on the September 15, 1998.

The site clearance work for the on- going Project ROP, Tarapur was nearing completion. The process design has been put to peer review. Design Basis Reports for the primary containment storage tanks and secondary and tertiary barriers in stainless steel and the RCC vault housing the storage tanks for the IX Plan Project—AWTF, Tarapur were prepared. Investigations were also carried out on the applicability of dried banana pith (inner stem) for the sorption of various radionuclides which are generally present at trace level in Purex process waste effluents.

Nuclear waste management

BARC is responsible for safe management of all types and categories of radioactive liquid and solid wastes generated at Trombay, Tarapur, Rajasthan and Kalpakkam. During the year all the waste management facilities operated satisfactorily. The low and intermediate level liquid wastes were provided suitable treatment and bulk of the radioactivity was retained in the form of sludge concentrates.

The authorised limits for discharge of radioactivity through liquid route were reduced by AERB. However activity discharges to the environment were kept well below authorised limits. The solid wastes were collected, segregated, suitably treated and conditioned before disposal in engineered facilities. At Trombay, the organic liquid waste was transferred to newly augmented storage facility.

At Tarapur, the intermediate level liquid waste treatment plant was restarted after carrying out necessary modification and maintenance. Application was submitted to AERB for licensing the facility at Tarapur for storage of vitrified high level solid waste. Waste Immobilisation Plant at Trombay, was in the last phase of mechanical completion. For the first time in BARC, an indigenously developed and manufactured Servo Manipulator in collaboration with M/s.

HMT Bangalore was installed inside the vitrification cell and its performance was being evaluated for design intent. A Multi barrier design of active trench for safe transfer of high level liquid waste from source to the plant had been completed earlier, execution of this work was underway. Multi-zone medium frequency induction furnace for vitrification of high level waste, developed for the first time in the country was successfully commissioned.

A state-of- the-art Data Aquisition & Control System (DACS) was developed in collaboration with M/s. ECIL. The system was under installation at the plant site. Construction of main process building of Waste Immobilisation Project, Kalpakkam was nearing completion. Procurement of process equipment continued. Detailing of various systems and layouts was under progress. Studies on 'Recovery&Recycle of long lived actinides from high level liquid waste' and 'Vitrification of high level waste' were carried out as part of the process development for HLW management.

Management of spent solvent of reprocessing origin was demonstrated on a full scale. After successful runs based on 'alkaline hydrolysis' of TBP an active plant was in advanced stages of erection&commissioning. As an alternative to direct fixation in polymer matrix for spent lon-exchange resins, a strategy involving combination of oxidation process for complete destruction of spent organic lon- exchange resins were evolved and was under test on laboratory/pilot scale.

Vitrification studies were carried out on toxic waste streams arising during processing of beryllium from beryl ore. Based on these studies, details are being worked out for setting up of full scale vitrification facility at

Beryllium Plant, Vashi. Development and use of specific sorbents/lon exchangers for removal of Cs, Sr and other radionuclides from different waste streams were carried out Repeated loading-elution-regeneration cycles carried out have established their successful performance. Preliminary work on the synthesis of magnetic sorbents for decontamination of low and intermediate liquid waste were initiated. Investigations were in progress for selection of suitable site for disposal of immobilised waste products in geological repositories in association with various national agencies.

Detailed geological and geophysical studies were completed at one site and were in progress at another site. Services were provided to all the units of DAE for *in situ* testing of air cleaning systems to minimise the release of gaseous activity to the environment. Special air filters for personal protection and air cleaning systems were designed, assembled and supplied to various users of DAE. Spent radiation sources from hospitals, educational institutes, industries and DAE units were collected and suitably stored/disposed in the engineered containment systems. Health, Safety&Environment Protection of plant personnel, public in general and environment against radiation continued to be the prime activity of BARC. Following were the activities:

Radiological safety and surveillance

Radiological safety support for nuclear power plants, research reactors other nuclear fuel cycle facilities, BRIT, VECC Calcutta and CAT Indore was provided on a routine basis. Environmental surveillance at nuclear power plant sites, fuel cycle facilities and Trombay was also provided. Personnel monitoring services were provided radiation workers from industrial, medical, research and DAE institutions Whole body counting of plant personnel for internal contamination was continued at the various Environmental Radiological Laboratories (ERLs) a other facilities.

Health physics coverage was provided to in-service Inspection (ISI) 66 coolant channels in MAPS-2; turbine overhauling work, shutdown MOV replacement, recirculation loop MOV stern replacement, core spray loop 11 and reactor clean up system return line replacement work and core shroud inspection work in TAPS-2; complete core unloading of CIRUS reactor and major refurbishing activity at PP, Trombay and PREFRE, Tarapur.

Environmental Radiological Laboratory at Kaiga was inaugurated on June 22, 1998 and a manual entitled "Environmental Radiological Laboratory Procedure Manual" and a brochure "Environmental Radiological Laboratory, Kaiga" was released. Kakrapar ERL was identified by the World Association of Nuclear Operators (WANO) Group as an area where good practices were being carried out and the Group expressed its desire to share the ERL experience.

Installation of new systems

A low cost Digital Pocket Radiation Dosimeter (DIGI DOSE) was developed based on semi conductor detector with continuous digital read out over a range of 1 Sv to 999999 Sv. Semi automatic TLD badge readers were developed and were put into use for Personnel Monitoring Service. PC add-on cards for ADC and data acquisition were designed and fabricated for aerial gamma spectrometer. Eight such systems are being developed for DAE and the Defence Services.

A compact wall mounted environmental dose monitor with LCD display and with an infrared trans-receiver based 1/0 communication facility was developed. High range gamma dose rate monitor was developed for mapping gamma radiation fields inside coolant channels of power reactors and these were used at RAPS and MAPS.

A software package was developed for the postal dose intercomparison of different radiotherapy centres in the country. A dose management software for personnel monitering programme was implemented. It was working successfully at KAPS, RAPS, MAPS& Dhruva reactions. A novel method of internal dose assessment based on the determination of thorium in the blood serum of occupational workers of a thorium Plant was developed and applied to estimate the internal dose to a few occupational workers at OSCOM.

The analysis of the samples and subsequent dose calculations showed that the annual committed effective dose due to thorium, to these subjects, was below the permissible limit. Individual values of fluence to ambient dose equivalent conversion factors were calculated for various radio active neutron sources used in calibration of radiation monitors.

Safety studies

Studies on "Leachability evaluation of Beryllium" from redmud and that stabilized with cement in different proportions using standard leachability protocols reveal that the effective diffusion coefficient of Be in the stabilized matrix was 7 to 8 orders of magnitude lower than the molecular diffusion coefficient of Be in the water, indicating the effectiveness of stabilisation. A probabilistic safety assessment model was developed for the long term safety assessment near surface radioactive disposal facilities. A comprehensive quality assurance protocol was developed to test various parameters that affect image quality in mammography.

A dosimetric protocol was established for the retirement of melanoma using eye plaque incorporating 1251 seeds. Dosimetric and safety studies on stents incorporating 32P/192Ir/188Re were carried out for evaluating their suitability for the treatment of resenosis following angioplasty.

Investigations on dosimetry of low energy electron beams were carried out thermoluminiscence phosphor was developed which is useful for environmental monitoring and studies in medical physics. Computerised glow curve deconvolution programme was developed for resolving complex TL glow curves. Comparative radiation safety evaluation of medical cyclotrons for selection of a unit for Radiation Medicine Centre (RMC), shielding requirement assessment of 500 keV, 20 mA electron beam accelerator at Vashi; Shield augmentation for storage ring Indus-I and biological shield design and ventilation requirements for the proposed POTON irradiator were carried out.

A complex model for generating wind fields was developed for application to non-homogenous terrains such as those in Trombay and Kaiga continued countrywide radon/thoron mapping. Studies on the daily human intake of heavy metals and their retention times in blood were carried out. Lead levels in human blood samples formed an indicator for lead levels in the atmosphere.

Services

Authorisations for movement of industrial radiography sources, no objection certificates for procurement and use of radioactive materials for industrial radiography and advisory services on safe transport of radioactive materials were provided on a routine basis. Safety analysis and type approval tests were carried out on colour and black&white TV monitors, X-ray baggage inspection systems, metal halide lamps incorporating 85 Kr and thorium frills, industrial radiography X ray machines, models of nucleonic gauges and a few consumer products incorporating radioisotopes, medical accelerators, a simulator, cobalt 60 radiotherapy units and remote afterloading units.

As a part of Accident Prevention Programme, a comprehensive safety status report was prepared and this contains information on accident statistics, special safety surveys, training on safety, first aid, fire fighting, medical examinations and emergency drills carried out. BARC won AERB safety shield for the fifth year in succession under the category of R&D Units. Analytical services for radiochemical analysis were provided to pharmaceutical companies. Passive monitoring for thoron and its daughters, in gas mantle industries, using SSNDT was carried out.

Isotope technology

The R&D activities at BARC were focused on development of processes for the production of isotopes, isotopic radiation sources and applications of radioisotopes and radiation which are of relevance to Indian industry and society. These activities include development of procedure for the production of fission produced molybdenum, 1251, 153Sm, 186Re, development of 32P and 1251 radiation sources for endovascular and eye brachytherapy, suitable radiopharmaceuticals for medical diagnosis, development of radiation process for cable polymer industry and utilization of isotopes and radiation sources for better harnessing of natural resources and as a diagnostic tool for industrial trouble shooting.

The development of trained professional for utilizing unique benefits of radioisotope applications in the industry and medicine forms another important activity. In the field of nuclear medicine, development of therapeutic radiopharmaceuticals continued. A laboratory for monoclonal against Prostrate Specific Antigen (PSA) antibody production was set up. A polymer based on grafting of acrylic acid on carboxymethyl cellulose was prepared using Co-60 gamma irradiation.

Hydrogels were prepared by grafting acrylamide on carboxymethyl cellulose using Co-60 gamma radiation. These hydrogels are capable of selective absorption of basic dyes from aqueous solutions. Studies on radiation shielding integrity of thick multilayered components, made of lead, steel and concrete were carried out. In continuation of the isotope study in the Puma river basin in Maharashtra to understand the origin of salinity of the groundwater, samples collected from the area were analysed.

A series of radiotracer experiments were carried out in a trickle bed reactor with three different types of catalyst to understand liquid phase hydrodynamics. Electron Beam (EB) irradiation of diamonds was carried out at full beam power on commercial basis. An irradiation throughput of 40,000 ring was achieved by employing 17 spindles in the conveyor system. Radiation crosslinkable PE and P based EPR formulations for wire/ cab insulations in the form of sheets cables from Shriram Institute for Industrial Research, Delhi were irradiated various electron beam dose ranging from 25 kGy to 500 kGy. Twenty nos of nuclear explosion detectors used in battle tanks we gamma trigger tested in PANBIT Army based workshop, Pune.

Gamma scanning of Depropaniser column of M/s. Reliance Industrial Ltd., Hazira, was carried out for trouble shooting. The approval of radiation processing for several additional food items expected to provide the necessary impetus for commercialization of preservation process by the food industry. Water samples from Priyadarsh and other lakes in Antarctica which were collected during an earlier Indian expedition, in Jan-Feb.

1997, were analyse for environmental stable isotopes tritium.

Fuel and radiochemistry

Uranium-plutonium mixed oxide microspheres with 3% plutonium were prepared by the Sol-gel method. For the preparation of UO_2 fuel pellets Sol-gel microspheres pelletization Auto Sol-gel plant, an auto feeder vessel was designed and was in operation for the production of UO_2 microspheres.

To study fuel-clad and fission products interaction, use thermodynamic and X-ray data were obtained on certain alloys and compounds. Evaluation of extraction data PU(IV) using macroporous bifunctional phosphinic acid resin has shown feasibility of removal of plutonium from oxalate waste. Gamma ray spectrometric method was developed for the determination of plutonium content in the solid matrix and used routinely. Analytical services continued to be provided for the determination of metallic and nonmetallic constituents for the chemical quality control of Mark II FBTR fuel.

Work in the area of radiochemistry covered research in the field of nuclear fission, nuclear reactions, nuclear spectroscopy, development of NDA and neutron activation analysis. In the area of the actinide chemistry several new procedures were developed for the separation actinides and fission products. A large number of amides and diamides were studied with a view to their applications in separation of actinides from irradiated fuels (Th, U) as well as recovery of actinides from HLW.

In the area of spectroscopic analysis new methods were developed for determination of trace level impurities in ThO_2 matrix. The routine analysis of a large number of samples of fresh batch for FBTR fuel are being carried out. Use of EPR, PAS and fluorescence technique was done to understand some of the interesting solid state properties of actinide doped compounds.

Studies on fragment angular momentum in odd Z fissioning system 241Am (n,f) were carried out. Calibration of hull monitor set up at KARP based on fission product monitoring using HPGe detector was completed. Neutron activation analysis was used for determination of Au&Pd in samples of atomic minerals. Estimate of uranium in granite samples were carried out.

A procedure for the decontamination of alkaline intermediate level liquid wastes (ILLW) from plutonium and americium using hydrous iron oxide (HIO) was standardised. Analytical spectroscopy work was focussed on the ongoing efforts to find a suitable chemical separation procedure for determination of impurities in U/Pu by ICP-AES.

Chemical technology

Heavy water upgrading

All the tower internals for 1 4 sections of the 1050 mm diameter column of the upgrading plant for Kaiga-I were fabricated, activated, tested and dispatched to site. Fabrication of tower internals for Kaiga-II was completed and testing progressed. BARC successfully completed the analysis & certification work of heavy water exported to M/S Korean Electric Power Corporation, South Korea by Heavy Water Board. To meet the requirement of Neon-22 isotope of Defence Organisation, a thermal diffusion column was set up and operated. The results obtained were very encouraging.

Based on this data, a prototype column of suitable capacity was designed and was under fabrication. Another test assembly having five columns was set up to study the interstage flow -parameters. An advanced electrolyser plant for oxygen production was set up at BARC and successfully commissioned.

Desalination

6300 m3/d Combined MSF-RO Nuclear Desalination Demonstration Plant (NDDP), Kalpakkam : The detailed design of the MSF and RO plants were carried out and the proposal for taking steam, sea water and power from MAPS was prepared. The MSF and RO pilot plants set up at the BARC were operated to study the behaviour of high temperature operation of RO plant and the transient behaviour of the MSF plant. This data will be useful for coupling of the NDDP with MAPS. R&D work on synthesis of new polymers and membranes and development of compact spiral module system were successfully completed.

Chemical engineering

BARC has been engaged in developing specialised materials required the Atomic Energy Programme. The three pilot plants *viz.*, "Processing magnesium fluoride lining material "Facility for enrichment of Boron by ion exchange" and "Development 1500 Ampere prototype fluorine c and 5 tonnes/year sulphur hexafluoride" were set up. Setting up of the two plants under IX five year plan *viz.*

Development nuclear grade thorium oxide a Lithium metal pilot plant continued was vigorously pursued. The design of the plants was completed and procurement, infrastructure and other related matters were in progress. Specialised scintillation chemical and were being supplied to TIFR their Ooty project for gamma-rays detection and to other division in B for making scintillation counters. The other activities include development carbon anodes for fluorine cell, fused salt electrolysis for preparation of a metals and other R&D activities.

Materials science

This process was developed at optimised to obtain an

adherent coating of boron on aluminium and stainless steel substrates, required for the fabrication of neutron sensing elements ion chambers and counters used reactor control. For hydrogen mitigation during accidental release of hydrogen gas a nuclear power station, a process was developed to fabricate a suitable catalyst using palladium and platinum coated alumina powder.

Technology development for YVO4: Eu3+ for high pressure metal vapour lamps and metal halide lamps was completed. At the request of IRE, investigation were carried out on the separation better than 99% pure neodymium permanent magnet applications and process was developed for the portion of pure neodymium. A process was optimised for the recovery of the heavy rare earths, in particular yttrium, from the indigenous xenotime concentrate. Over 99% leaching recovery was obtained by the sulphuric acid process. Separation of individual elements was carried out by dual cycle solvent extraction.

Production of uranium metal ingots was adequate to meet the complete requirements of research reactor fuel fabrication. Sustained in-house R&D efforts have led to the production of better quality ingots which has resulted in considerable improvements in fuel performance. Setting up of a plant for augmentation of uranium metal production has progressed considerably.

The technology for the synthesis of diethyl phosphoric acid (D2 EPHA), an important metal extractant in the organophosphorus series, was transferred to Heavy Water Board. Setting up of a pilot plant reached an advanced stage and the commercial production was scheduled to start in May/June, 1999 at HWP, Talcher.

The product from this plant will be able to meet the requirements for base metal industries, for uranium extraction from phosphoric acid and for separation of uranium from some ore bodies. A process for the separation and recovery of cobalt, nickel and other elements from the leach liquor of oceanic polymetallic nodules was developed at BARC for the Department of Ocean Development (DOD). Based on the processes developed at BARC for separation and at RRL, Bhubaneswar, for leaching, DOD and Hindustan Zinc Ltd., Udaipur, have planned to set up a pilot plant during the ninth plan to process about 500 kg of ocean nodules per day.

A development programme was initiated to prepare carbon shapes for use as scatterer in AHWR. Preliminary studies were carried out to fabricate carbon spheres in the size range of 10-25 mm diameter, followed by pyrolytic carbon coating. Development activities were continued on the preparation of refractory metals, alloys and intermetallic compounds. Pure vanadium metal was prepared by fused salt electro-refining using a vanadium-nitrogen alloy as a soluble anode.

A corrosion monitoring method, based on the analysis of electrochemical noise generated from corroding specimens was developed for laboratory and field use. The technique was undergoing test for use in monitoring the integrity of containers during long term storage of radioactive wastes. Alloy 718 will find extensive use in the KAVERI engine of the light combat aircraft (LCA). Following an understanding with Gas Turbine Research Establishment (GTRE), Bangalore, studies on some specific problems related to the fabrication of parts from this alloy were carried out and remedial measures suggested.

Aeronautical Development Agency (ADA), Bangalore, plans to use Ni-TiFe shape memory Alloy clips in the Agency's aircraft development project. A R&D

programme has been undertaken to develop a tool for the expansion of the Ni-Ti-Fe clips and for characterization and eusability assessment of dimensionally recovered clips. An expansion tool that can carry out the deformation of the shape memory alloy component in a liquid nitrogen environment was designed and fabricated. A 29- kg ingot of Ni-Ti shape memory alloy of near equiatomic composition and good shape memory characteristics was prepared by double consumable vacuum arc melting at NFC. Several Ni-Ti-Fe alloys were prepared by non- consumable vacuum arc melting.

Kinetics of hydride blister growth was studied in relation to hydrogen concentration, cold spot/bulk specimen temperature and cold spot geometry. Specimens of aluminium, copper, porous nickel and titanium were successfully diffusion-bonded to stainless steel. A variety of advanced materials namely, intermetallics and composites were synthesized by the self-propagating high temperature synthesis (SHS) technique.

Single phase crystalline hematite (a-Fe_2O_3) particles of 0:.3 mm median diameter and a narrow size distribution (100% < 1 mm) were prepared by gel crystallization technique resulting powder was found accept for radioimmunoassay applications ANTARIKSHA which is a part Indian Space Research, Organisation (ISRO), entered into an agreement M/s. Hughes Space and communication Centre, USA to supply 20 sets beryllium shafts and flange assemblies conforming to their design drawing and specifications. These assemblies were produced by precision machining at BARC. The final components were given a critical finishing touch.

Gadolinium is used as a "burnable" poison in the nuclear reactors to c the reactivity of fresh reactor fuel assembly. Preparation of $GdAlO_3$ carried out by citrate get route. The process is simple and recovery, other th handling losses, is highest.

Rare earths development

High purity neodymium oxide used for manufacture of neodymium (Nd) metal, which finds applications the making of neodymium/iron/boron alloy for permanent magnets. The process developed by REDS was successfully tested at IREL, Alwaye and tonnage quantities of product of internationally competitive quality were produced. IREL is further planning a joint venture for large scale neodyinium met plant. Pure Nd prepared by the BARC process was tested by Japanese users was found to be of high quality.

Ore dressing

Studies were carried out on Tummalapalle uranium ore using MGS with rougher tails as feed with the objective of improving recovery at the rougher stage. Mineralogical studies on uranium and associated metals along SSZ were continued.

Detrital and remobilized types of uraninite and brannerite formed by pronto-reaction are identified in Narwapahar ore samples. Autoradiographic studies were carried out to confirm the brannerite formation. Experiments were continued on the multi-metallic preconcentrate sample from Kyrgyzstan in order to improve grade and recovery of the tungsten and tin concentrates. Alkali roasting followed by leaching with water of the combined concentrate is being tried to evolve a generalized metallurgical flow-sheet to process the combined concentrate. Beneficiation studies were initiated on lead-zinc-copper ore samples from Sikkim.

In the Jaduguda Uranium ore, occurrence of detrital assemblage of chromite and uraninite was identified. Mineral chemistry and structural formula calculations on the tourmalines from Jaduguda indicated that they are Ai-poor belongings to Ca-poor metapelites and metapsamites with dravite compistion.

Remote handling and robotics

Research and development programme at BARC is oriented towards development of need-based and custom designed technologies in the areas of Intervention Robotics, Advanced Automation and Remotisation for beneficial substitution of manual tabour for a variety of task in nuclear facilities characterised by constraints such as hostile environment, limited work-space and inaccessible work areas limiting direct human intervention. The Bilateral Master Slave Servo manipulators which materialized through fruitful collaboration between BARC and HMT, Bangalore are under installation for field trials and commissioning at WIP, BARC site at Trombay.

With the completion of minor modifications in the mechanical subassemblies of the Co-60 Teletherapy unit and reassembly thereof, progressive integration of the control systems and interlocks was underway. Design of mechanical, electrical and control systems for the commercial scale irradiator (POTON) for sprout inhibition of onions and potatoes was finalised; fabrication of certain components and subsystems was underway. Development of certain custom-made robotic/remote handling systems for power reactor maintenance progressed. Detailed design of the proposed inspection system for Moderator Heat Exchanger at NAPS reached the final stage and the necessary components are being procured.

Development of certain application oriented Robot configurations and mobile mechanisms was in progress. Based on the performance of the scaled down version of the Autonomous Guided Vehicle (AGV) for fuel rod handling, the basic design was under improvement to facilitate integration of the sensors and control system and direct scale up after final demonstration of the improved model.

Preliminary design of a Mobile Robot for inspection of PFBR main vessel was completed. Computer Aided Robot Programming (CARP) environment—an interactive graphic environment with several advanced features through multiple window GUI—was developed for the 6 DoF Robot and the functional system was demonstrated. Full 3D simulation of the robot motion under control was demonstrated. Methods were implemented for intelligent collision avoidance and robot locus generation from source to target objects for the 6DoF Robot. Necessary software and hardware were being developed for intelligent grasp control for the Robot Gripper. Other significant programmes currently under different stages of development include the 3 piece Mechanical Master Slave Manipulator, Power Manipulator for KARP, Periscope for FBTR and a comprehensive system for total automation of transfer package for BRIT.

Central workshops

Central Workshops of BARC continued to contribute towards design, development and manufacture of sophisticated equipment for R&D work as well as Power Reactor Programme. Assignments include manufacture of equipment for projects with international collaboration. Some of the major jobs undertaken included, AHWR Fuel Spacer Development, Replacement Tube Bundles for CIRUS, Seal & Sheild Plug Assemblies for DHRUVA, R.F. Cavity for superconducting Cyclotron, Steam Generators for FISBE, Detector frames for PHENIX, USA, Development of Roundway Bearing single &'V' type for 500 MWe PHWR, CRDM Components, Beam line equipment for 6.65 spectrometer, Antenna for Aditya Tokmak, Inclined

Fuelling Transfer Machine, High temperature X-ray diffractometer, MACE Telescope, Hot neutron source, Liquid scintillator, Vacuum furnace for crystal, Universal calibration machine, Special purpose winch, Leak before break specimen, Laser based surface finish: measuring instrument and so on.

Electronics and instrumentation

Computer

Processing power available on 6-node ANUPAM Alpha Super Computer was further enhanced by adding another 4-node, thus presently giving a sustained performance of 1.5 giga flops for large scientific jobs, with a peak speed of 8 giga flops. An exercise was carried out to ascertain the feasibility of replacing dual CRAY-X/MP super computer, being used for medium range weather forecasting at National Centre for Medium Range Weather Forecasting (NCMRWF), DST, Delhi, with an ANUPAM Alpha super computer.

It was observed that an ANUPAM Alpha (1+4 node) can replace the presently operational dual CRAY-X/MP which is an obsolete machine and requires enormous resources for operation and maintenance. A new super computer ANUPAM PII using Pentium II personal computers and a fast 100 Mbps Ethernet switch, was developed. A 4 node ANUPAM PII, using Pentium II microprocessors @ 266 MHz gives a user performance of 248 MFLOPS, with a peak speed of I giga flop. ANUPAM PII can be easily scaled upto 128 nodes, giving a sustained speed of 14-15 giga flops. The image processing software being developed was further enhanced to support Shape Analysis, Adaptive thresholding and Fame processing. This software was used for evaluating hydride plated content in Zircaloy-2 pressure tubes, Analysis of Fracture Propagation in Materials and high temperature creep studies in Materials.

Electronics

Modernisation of the nuclear instrumentation of Fast Breeder Test Reactor at Kalpakkam was successfully commissioned and reactor attained criticality on June 25, 1998. As the core gamma at RAPS-2 during Ist approach to criticality was greater than 104 R/hr, elaborate tests were carried to measure the gamma tolerance the Boron-10 lined counters. Based on the results these detectors were replaced with Fission counters. The startup instrumentation was modified to interface with Fission counters

Prototype detectors were developed for neutron and gamma measurement in power reactors. A prototype boron- 10 lined proportional counter was developed for reactor start up instrumentation. An ion chamber was developed for Beam Spill Monitoring application at the synchrotron facility at CAT, Indore Seven neutron flux monitors incorporating 3He proportional counters were supplied to VEC, Calcutta for area neutron monitoring.

Eight numbers of "Rod Monitoring Units" were fabricated and tested by QS, NPCIL for shipment to RAPS 3 and 4 site. The sample unit was success fully subjected to seismic and climatic tests at ECIL. The on-line Turbine shaft expansion measurement unit for RAPS I & 2 are developed and supplied to site. These units are working satisfactorily. A battery operated portable MCA was designed around CHAMELEON (credit card PC) based CPU card with 8K nuclear ADC, programmable gain Pulse amplifier and programmable high voltage cards with ISA Bus.

Other significant achievements during 1998 included: Advanced Ultra sonic Imaging Systems (ULTIMA 100+) supplied to BHEL (Hyderabad); First model of Single Board PC Add on 200 MSPS Transient/ Repetitive waveform digitizer was developed. ADSP 2100

(DSP) based PC Add-on board was developed for high speed processing of ID/2D digital data such as digitized waveforms and images.

ANUGAMI-S because of entire dependence on host PC had low cost and hence had been accepted by IAEA for the Agency's Upgradation program. Eighty-one ANUGAMI-S cards were supplied to different countries under IAEA program. Second version of interface card ANUAGMI-P with on-board processor (TRANSPUTER) and memory is more versatile for acquisition of nuclear medicine imaging data and was installed at two institutes at Delhi—All India Institute of Medical Science (AIIMS) and at Institute of Nu clear Medicine and Allied Sciences (INMAS). MTMPS is a high performance PC-CAMAC data aquisition system developed by BARC for Accelerator based nuclear physics experiments.

Electronic systems

A computer based inspection system to highlight the internal disorders of mangoes has been developed and the installed in BARC. For fracture mechanics experiment, on piping components to carry out leak before-break studies, an image processing system with 4 CCD camera input was developed for simultaneously monitoring crack growth and crack mouth opening at specified displacement/load values. A PC based CCTV System with digital video storage facility was developed for video alarm assessment. A contact condition monitoring system to monitor up to sixteen door sensors and a micro-controller based distress alarm system were developed.

A dual channel acoustic emission analyse was developed to capture signals from piezoelectric sensors. The system was used successfully to detect simulated leaks in the seal plugs at fuelling machine test facility at BARC. A DSP card based Multi Frequency Eddy Current

(MFEC) System hardware was commissioned at BARC. A compact pre-amplifier for direct mounting on the integral assembly of NaI(TI) scintillation detector coupled by photomultiplier tube was developed for use in linear profile scanner at RMC (BARC), Parel for detecting functional metastates of the thyroid patients.

Physical sciences

Nuclear physics

The 14 MV Pelletron accelerator was used to carry out a large variety of experimental studies using the medium energy heavy ion beams from the accelerator. Extensive Theoretical studies were carried out in Intermediate Energy Physics and Relativistic Heavy Ion Collision. Several features of absorptive tunnelling through complex potential barriers were investigated in relation to the heavy ion fusion process.

An exact statistical model code for the calculation of fission fragment angular distributions with inclusion of projectile, target spins and K-dependent transmission coefficients was developed for the analysis of the data of heavy ion induced fission reactions. The installation and commissioning of Folded Tandem Ion Accelerator (FOTIA) continued. The gas handling system designed and fabricated was fully commissioned. The accelerator column section was raised to a voltage of 3.4 million volts. The pelletron machine was operated round the clock with an efficiency of 75% up-time, and was used by the experimental groups of BARC (NPD, Metallurgy, Radiochemistry), TIFF, SINP, VECC and IUC.

Superconducting LINAC booster project was progressing well. Detector parts for the muon tracking system of the PHENIX detector were fabricated in central workshops and delivered to LANL, USA. Further fabrication work was in progress for both the south and north arms of the muon detector. Collaboration experiments continued at the Legnaro National Laboratory, Italy and RIKEN, Japan. The experiment at RIKEN involves the study of giant dipole resonance in neutron rich nuclei using the radioactive ion beam facility.

Accelerator pulse

A 500 keV industrial electron accelerator developed indigenously by BARC was commissioned for its first phase of operation by the Hon'ble Prime Minister of India Shri Atal Bihari Vajpayee on August 10, 1998. Collective acceleration of Fluorine and Carbon ions to 28.5 MeV and 18 MeV respectively with ion current around 25 A peak was attained on KALI-200 generator. The KALI-5000 pulse power system having die ratings of I MV, 80 kA, 60 ns, was in the advanced stage of assembly.

NRL-HARL

BARC has a long-term programme of establishing a new astronomy facility, GRACE, in the country at Mt. Abu, Rajasthan, fat front-ranking research activities in the field of gamma-ray astrophysics. India's first imaging gamma-ray telescope, the principal component of the TACTIC telescope array, has already been successfully commissioned at Mt. Abu and was in use for regular observation campaigns. This year, the mechanical structures of three additional telescopes of the TACTIC array were installed at Mt. Abu and their special-design duplex cameras were fabricated.

Observations were carried out recently with an upgraded 169-pixel Imaging camera on several well-known gamma-ray sources, including 2 BL-Lac objects and a supernova remnant (the Crab Nebula). A path-breaking result was that Cerenkov images, produced by gamma-ray and cosmic-ray nuclear progenitors, exhibit a fractal character. This realization has resulted in a more robust event characterization scheme.

Another interesting investigation carried out concerns the utilization of the cognitive power of an Artificial Neural Network for real-time reconstruction of the arrival direction of a high energy primary seen by a wide-angle Cerenkov array. This result will have important consequences on the design of the MYSTIQUE telescope planned to be built at Mt. Abu during next few years. A highlight result in the area of theoretical astrophysics was the generation of a catalogue of potentially promising target sources of galactic and extragalactic genres for the experiments being set up at the GRACE facility.

Theoretical physics

BARC is engaged in the physics problems of reactor design, safety and operation. It also carries out research in many areas of physics and applied mathematics, such as transport theory, radiation hydodynamics, non-linear equations, numerical methods, classical and quantum chaos, and quantum optics. A new simulator code was developed for providing fuel management service to Boiling Water Reactors at Tarapur. For PHWRs, studies were conducted for the first approach to criticality for RAPS-2 reactor after shut down as a result of replacement of coolant channels. For Kaiga-1 & 2 reactors, reactivity devices were simulated for fuel bum up and cold and hot core conditions.

Physics design manual for Kaiga-1& 2, preliminary safety analysis report for RAPP-3 & 4 were reviewed. A core model based on modal kinetics method was developed for real time reactor simulator for 220 MWe PHWRs, to be used for training purpose. Design of AHWR/PHWR critical facility was worked out, especially for studying physics of 500 MWe PHWR lattices. Studies on efficient numerical methods used for the solution of neutron diffusion and transport equations were started.

Reasons for the failure of spherical harmonics expansion method for solving neutron transport problems in spherical geometry were identified. In the field of quantum optics, nonlinear optical properties of atoms in a laser cooled harmonic trap were studied. This problem is of interest in physics of trapped atoms and ions.

Laser and plasma technology

A variety of technically superior, cost effective plasma sprayed duplex structures consisting of a metallic undercoat and a, top ceramic coat was developed for in-house nuclear applications. During the year, air-operated, vortex-cum magnetically stabilized hollow electrode plasma torches with power capacities upto 100 KW were developed. An injection seeded, single longitudinal mode Neodymium: YAG laser has recently been installed.

Laser & Plasma Technology was working on gamma ray attenuation method for void fraction measurement in two phase liquid metal flows. Recently a seven detector system to receive gamma rays passing through various chords of the flow in a 75 mm circular pipe was installed on a rotating platform. This unique system was in use in collaboration with IIT Kanpur to develop and validate several scheme of tomographic algorithms and void fraction profiles.

Technical physics and protoope engineering

Several Ion-implanted Si detectors of varying sizes, developed, and a number of silicon surface barrier detectors for nuclear research were produced. Fabrication of improved direct reading dosimeters for the dose range 0-500 mR and showing natural charge leakage within

1% per d1ay was another significant indigenous achievement. The suitability of Pt/Pd thin films as catalysts for H_2 mitigation facility was studied and commendable progress was made on the development of ruggedised H_2S gas sensors, as well as H_2 gas sensors covering extended concentration range (0 - 8%).

Development of $CdWO_4$ crystal scintillator was carried out both for industrial computer tomography as well as dosimetry applications. BaB_2O_4 crystals were grown for non-linear optical applications and a detailed investigation on the effect of sodium doping was also performed. For a variety of applications, crystals of NaCl, KCI, LiF, CsI, CaF_2, BaF_2 and $CdWO_4$ were supplied in large numbers to users in BARC, NPC and DRDO. In the area of glass technology, preparation of silicate glass powder, arsenic chalcogenide glass windows was carried out. Another major activity was the development of packages for hybrid microcircuits in which Department of Space was involved.

Development work on building a compact RF generator capable of giving upto 2.5KW power at 27.12 MHz and its integration with inductively coupled plasma torch assembly was completed and this unit was also integrated with ICP-AES system developed for KARP. Precision magnet current regulators for particle accelerators were developed *viz.*, 50OAmp,75V for Folded Tandem Ion Accelerator (FOTIA), being commissioned at Trombay and 100Amp,40V for Beam Line Magnet being set up at Calicut University.

A special high voltage medium frequency power supply for electrochemical etching for CR-39 detector was fabricated. A variable temperature insert and a six tesla superconducting magnet were fabricated for magneto-resistance measurement and short sample test facility required for evaluating superconducting NbTi cable. In-house fabrication of UHV components and other mechanical assemblies/ subsystems required for the development of mass spectrometers, high resolution electron spectrometer and total gas analysers was carried out. Ascanning Auger electron spectrometer having spatial resolution of 5 mm was developed.

A needle valve based compact sample introduction system for D/H mass spectrometer was developed. In the area of superconductive basic investigations were carried out of the influence of disorder on the behaviour of flux line lattice under different magnetic histories, effect of surface barrier on magnetization relaxation and vortex lines in high temperature super conductors.

Condensed matter physics

A molecular dynamic (MD) simulation under pressure was carried out $MgAl_2O_4$ to clarify about disorder amorphisation and phase change. A modified Michelson interferometer was set up as VISAR. Radiation transport calculations ICF target designs need accurate opacity tables for a variety of materials a wide range of density and temperature.

Molecular dynamics studies of seismic wave velocities and density variations involving various phase transition of the geophysically important mine enstatite $Mg_2\ Si_2O_6$ were undertake These are the first calculations of seismic velocity at high pressures and temperatures and have enabled an atom level interpretation of phase transition of mantle constituents and resultant seismic discontinuities. Using a lattice dynamical approach, we have calculated the phonon frequencies and equation of state of $CasiO_3$ pervoskite at Earth's lowest mantle pressures. The calculated equation of state was in good agreement with experimental data. Neutron diffraction experiment were carried out on a number of compounds to study the atomic and magnetic ordering. A new technique of Three Dimensional Neutron CT scan (313 C Scam) has been developed. It is now possible to obtain not only conventional CT scan in slices but also to visualise the inner parts of any object in its three dimensional view by stacking of various CT scans one over the other. Two scientists from BARC were the first international users of any public beam line in SPRING-8, the third generation synchrotron facility in Japan. They collected diffraction data for a number of protein crystals.

Seismology

All routine monitoring channels at the Gauribidanur seismic array (GBA) and Delhi Seismic Unit (DSU) functioned satisfactorily without interruption. Enormous efforts were made to set up at various places including sites in the Pokhran region a host of on-line seismic monitoring systems operating round-the-clock with capability to acquire high-quality seismic data from probable underground nuclear test explosions.

Designed and developed indigenously, the seismic systems incorporated different types of triaxial ground motion sensors to provide digital data in high dynamic range covering a wide band of signal frequency from close-in to distant observations from source.

All the above temporary as well as permanent seismic installations did indeed successfully record the Indian nuclear tests at Pokhran (POK-II) on May 11 and 13, 1998. Among the ongoing R&D activities, further work on seismicity investigations in the peninsular Indian shield, artificial neural network and parametric modelling of microseismic noise in the array space progressed well. The code duration magnitude scale developed earlier was re-examined and regression analysis performed on a much larger data set of regional earthquakes providing fresh inputs to the shield seismic study.

Spectroscopy

Highly efficient broad band anti-reflection coatings were designed, developed and optimised for Nd-Yag laser application. A high reflectivity intracavity for Ruby laser has been fabricated for ISRO. Several multilayer beam splatters were successfully developed for laser cooling experiment with R/T splitting ratio of 30/70 and 10/90 over the wavelength range 650 to 800nm.

Chemical sciences

Analytical chemistry

Analytical service support to various of BARC and other units of DAE were continued. The number of samples analysed during the year were about 3000 involving 7200 determinations. Different types of samples like metals and alloys, organic and inorganic compounds, biological and environment materials as well as solution sample were analysed using various technique like spectrochemical, electro-analytical chromatographic and nuclear analytical methods. Basic research in analytical chemistry was continued. Ion exchange behaviour of Nafion membrane for the removal of impurities from bulk Ga/Al solution or for the facilitated transport of alkali metal ions was investigate cyclic voltammetry of antimony and palladium was studied.

The reduction behaviour of lanthanum was studied us in various electrochemical techniques. Kinetic and thermo-chemical parameters for the reaction of the oxide and titanium dioxide were investigated. Thin layer activation techniques was employed for the study of surface wear in zircaloy. Analytical procedures were developed for the analysis of palladium antimony and selenium by electrochemical techniques. Trace impurities in high purity lead and of cadmium in uranium were analysed electrochemical procedures.

A method for the determination of trace level boron by spectrophotometry using both batch and flow injection was develop Charged particle activation analysis procedure for the determination of bulk hydrogen in nuclear materials was developed. Procedures were also developed or modified for the analysis mercury in zinc concentrates, arsenic in groundwater, high purity arsenic m and oxides, high purity reagents and various other materials.

Separation procedures were worked out for the determination of palladium and gold in geological materials using polyaniline as a novel ion exchange material. A gas chromatographic procedure for the determination of carbide carbon in inorganic materials was developed. Collaboration with CFSL, Hyderabad was continued in order to effectively use nuclear methods for forensic work. Irradiation facilities were offered to GSI and other academic institutions. An Ultra Trace Analysis Facility (UTAF) was refurbished at HRDCentre for the analysis of high purity materials like arsenic and gallium.

Applied chemistry

Chemical decontamination of C/U system of TAPS Unit 2 was taken up. This consists of two phases. Phase-1 involved reaching a system temperature of 360-365 K and a dissolved oxygen content of < 120 ppb and this was accomplished. Preliminary experiments of Phase-2 involving actual decontamination were initiated. A modified feasibility report incorporating both the phases has been made ready.

Pulse radiolysis technique was used to find more stable Cr(II) complexes which have applications in LOMI decontamination technique. In connection with the Task Force constituted to look into thermodynamic and transport properties of thoria based fuels to be used in Advanced Heavy Water Reactors, bulk thermal expansion of pure ThO_2, $BaThO_3$ and $SrThO_3$ were investigated by Dilatometry from room temperature to 1073 K. The detailed phase relations in MF_2-YF_3 (M=Ba, Sr, Ca) were studied. Several new phases were reported for the first time.

A number of strategic materials, rare earth oxyfluorides, superconducting oxide $LaBa_2Cu_2CoO_{7+d}$ were investigated for bulk thermal expansion and volume thermal expansion by Dilatometry and High Temperature XRD from room temperature to 1073 K. Studies on the vaporization behaviour of alkaline earth thorates such as $BaThO_3$ $SrThO_3$, Cs_2ThO_3 Rb_2ThO_3 were initiated. The work on BaTh03 was completed and there was good agreement in the thermodynamic properties of this compound as derived from both transpiration and Knudsen method. A new experimental facility for the study of release behaviour of volatile and gaseous fission products from nuclear fuels was set up and will give useful data on their diffusion coefficients.

Bio-organic chemistry

The research activities are directed towards the border line between organic chemistry and life sciences. Both applied and basic aspects of bio-organic chemistry are undertaken. Antioxidants have aroused great interest in recent years because of their chemopreventive importance in many of the degenerative diseases and about 40 naturally occurring compounds belonging to different classes (flavanoids, xanthones, terpenes and so on) were screened for their lipoxygenase inhibitory activity.

The anti-lipoxygenase activities of ginger and garlic were evaluated and a bioactive compound was isolated from ginger. Immunomodulators have aroused recent interest as many of these are promising anti-cancer and radioprotecting agents. A new polysaccharide possessing immunomodulatory activity has been isolated from an Indian medicinal plant and its partial structure was established. Preliminary results show that it has radioprotective action as well. A provisional patent has been filed on its active.

Using a low valent titanium based protocol developed in BARC, synthesis of several vicinal diamines, was accomplished. The protocol was used for the preparation of compounds which may find application in nuclear medicine. A provisional patent has been filed for this novel low valent titanium reagent. Polypeptides are the emerging high-value chemicals which find applications as pharmaceuticals, food-additivies as well as radiopharmaceuticals. Using the available expertise, polypeptide ligands, were synthesised via a solid phase technique. The technique was being extended for the synthesis of somatostatin and its analogs.

The utility of the methodology was under development in making a combinatorial library of biomolecules. In continuation of the ongoing programme on Integrated Pest Management (IPM), work was targetted to some cash and agricultural crops. Using synthetic pheromones, mass trapping has been carried out in collaboration with Central Cotton Research Institute, Nagpur. The pheromone treated fields produced an enhanced yield (30%) of high-value marketable cotton. As a part of the MOU signed between BARC and Central Tuber Crop Research Institute (CTCRI), Thiruvananthapuram, field evaluation of the sweet potato weevil (SPW) pheromone was continued.

In view of very encouraging results, the pheromone treatments were incorporated for the All India Coordinated trials on SPW. The potentialities of the biological processes for the preparation of organic compounds are being increasingly realised. Biocatalysts (enzymes), the cornerstone of modem biotechnology are likely to contribute significantly it the future chemical industry. Towards this end, efforts were directed to design novel asymmetric synthesis of high-value, low-volume bioactive compounds such as pharmaceuticals and agrochemicals. As part of our efforts in the development of clean technology, effort were directed to design novel asymmetric synthesis of high-value, low-volume bioactive compounds such as pharmaceuticals and agrochemicals.

A plan based biosorption strategy was explore for the decontamination of some radionuclides. Encouraging results were obtained using the plant, Sesuvium portulacastrum. Good uptake of several metal ions *viz.*, Th, Eu, Cs, U and Sr present individually and as mixtures were observed with the biomass. Microbial biomass has also been used for bioremediation.

Chemistry

The other activities in the field of Chemistry were primarily in basic sciences in the thrust areas of radiation and photochemistry, chemical dynamics, catalysis, solid state chemistry, interfacial sciences, high Tc superconducting materials, nanoclusters of metals, inorganic and organometallic chemistry. BARC has also been actively engaged in R&D work on hydrogels, catalyst development, thin films, ultrapurification of materials, and so on. Some of the significant achievements of these investigations are highlighted below:

Research work was initiated on femto second transient absorption studies using the recently developed Femto Second Laser Spectrometer. Solvent effects on the relaxation of electronically excited laser dye LDS-821 and subsequent vibrational cooling, relaxation of excited benzil molecule, photoprocesses of fullerenes and their aggregation in solution phase were investigated.

The free radical intermediates resulting from a number of drug and antioxidant molecules and biomolecules were characterized by pulse radiolysis studies, and significant results were obtained. The reaction of NO and NO_2 with organic molecules, a thrust area in environmental research was being actively pursued. Metal nano-particles species of several systems were synthesized by radiolysis technique and their physical properties were established.

A new process for the preparation of polyvinyl alcohol-based hydrogen by irradiation was developed in collaboration between Chemistry and BRIT. The material was undergoing clinical trials for wound dressing on patients with bum injuries in local hospitals.

The commissioning and testing of Cluster Generation Machine set up earlier as part of the VIIIth plan project were completed. Multiphoton ionization studies were carried out on ketones. The clustering behaviour in bimetallic clusters was correlated with electronegativities of the constituent elements.

Transient electric bireffingence studies on micelles, and investigations on growth of micelles in cationic-anionic mixtures gave interesting results. Studies on self-assembled monolayers and surface activity were initiated. It was found that the poor selectivity of Amberlyst-15 ion exchange resin could be attributed to the state of water in the resin.

Heated Filament Chemical Vapour Deposition was scaled up and optimised for uniform diamond deposition on substrates covering up to 4.0 inch diameter, both planar as well as three dimensional. Diamond coated tungsten carbide tool inserts have shown more than a 100 fold improvement in high speed machining of aluminium based alloys, and a very good surface finish.

Methodology was developed for making upto 1.0 inch diameter self- supporting diamond windows.

The metal and polymer-based catalysts developed for removal of hydrogen from the containment areas of nuclear reactors under postulated severe accident conditions were successfully tested in an engineering scale test reactor set up by Reactor Engineering. Advances were made in the chemistry of monomeric and binuclear palladium/platinum complexes with organochalcogenide ligands.

A mode-coupling theory based microscopic approach to the dielectric friction on an ion was developed to explain conductivity of electrolyte solutions, and for application to charge transfer reactions in solutions. A new perturbative density functional theory was formulated for the study of absorption of in homogeneous complex fluid mixtures on surfaces, and porous materials.

Water and steam chemistry laboratory

Analytical methods were developed for monitoring the chemical cleaning process. Decontamination studies were carried out on the failed HX of MAPSI and cut specimens from HX of MAPS-II. A new analytical method for the estimation of MPA and ETA was developed. Electrochemical corrosion studies on carbon steel in process cooling water were carried out. It was observed that >20 ppm N_2H_4 accelerates corrosion of CS in the presence of sea water.

Commissioning of high Temperature high pressure (HTHP) loop has reached an advanced stage. The carbon steel surge tank and the primary and secondary loops were commissioned and hot conditioned. The system parameters functioned as expected during the high temperature operation.

Investigation on the prevalence of Balanus reticulatus in the process water heat exchangers of MAPS was carried out. The effect of bacterial exopolysaccharide, alginic acid and agarose on Balanus reticulatus was studied. The results of acute thermal shock on barnacle larvae indicated that the response of larvae was dependent on the time and temperature of chlorination.

Bio-sciences

Nuclear agriculture and biotechnology

The pigeonpea culture TT97-48 was promoted to advanced yield trial (AVT) on the basis of its yield performance in the Southern zone by the All India Coordinated Research Project on Pigeonpea. Trombay groundnut cultures, TG 32, 33, 34 and 35 were promoted to AVT in different zones for different reasons. The possibility of using salt tolerant plants for phytoremediation of radio- cesium was studied using callus tissue and seedlings of Chenopodium.

The potential of the lactose utilising yeast Kluyveromyces fragilis biomass as a biosorbent for Cr (VI) was investigated. A process for the extraction of industrially important enzymes *viz.* catalase, invertase and alcohol dehydrogenase from yeast biomass was scaled up to treat over 10 kg of yeast. In signal transduction studies on potatoes, treatment with low concentration of jasmonic acid has shown enhanced expression of calmodulin indicating the importance of jasmonic acid as a signalling molecule in signal transduction.

Food technology

Based on the research and developmental work undertaken at BARC, the Government of India through a Gazette Notification in April 6, 1998 have cleared radiation processing of several additional food items for domestic marketing and consumption. These include rice, wheat products (atta, sooji, maida), dried fruits (raisins, dates, figs), mango, ginger, garlic, shallots, meat, chicken and its products. Earlier in August 1994 the Government had approved irradiation of onions, potatoes and spices. Additional clearances for irradiation of pulses and sea foods were recommended by the Central Committee for Food Standards, Ministry of health at its meeting held on 14th December 1998.

Application of radiation technology for preservation of food items can benefit both the farmer and consumer by reducing wastage. Recent laboratory Studies have shown that irradiation can extend the shelf-life of Mushrooms, strawberry, cakes and ensure microbial safety in traditional milk based sweet meats like 'Pedha'.

Irradiation enhanced the nutritional quality of legumes (pulses) by rapidly degrading the flatulence causing oligosaccharides (complex carbohydrates) into its constituent simple sugars during germination. BARC has taken steps to commercialize the technology. A commercial demonstration irradiator for the treatment of onions was under construction in Lasalgaon, Nashik district of Maharashtra. A commercial, demonstration irradiator for spices was nearing completion in Navi Mumbai.

Molecular biology and agriculture

Research in molecular biology and molecular agriculture emphasizes elucidation of basic mechanisms involved in cellular response to radiation and other stresses, genotyping in plants and humans, and introduction of the latest concepts and techniques in the biological research programme of BARC.

A multienzyme complex which can repair irradiated DNA in test tube was purified and characterized; specific site mutations in the human gene encoding carbonic anhydrase were made with a view to establishing the identity of the amino acids directly involved in the activity and folding of this protein; extensive computer analysis based on software developed in house led to an elegant Darwinian explanation of recently reported bacterial mutations with apparently Lamarckian characteristics; several image processing software useful in agricultural research were developed in collaboration with the Computer and Electronic Instrumentations; two bacterial proteins involved in regulation of cellular response to radiation and cold stress were purified for structural studies in collaboration with the X-ray crystallography group of CMPD; DNA-based techniques were used for diagnosis of genetic diseases and genotyping of human population groups; several new plant proteins induced by dessication were identified and cDNA encoding them was sequenced, and a new project for developing DNA markers for genotyping & genetic analysis of legumes was initiated.

Cell biology

The presence of oxygen is known to enhance radiation damage in several biological systems including cells in culture in vitro. Using rat liver and brain mitochondria, calf thymus DNA and plasmid pBR322 DNA, we have examined the mechanisms of damage induced by gamma-radiation in the presence and absence of oxygen as well as its modulation by these three compounds. Our results reveal that presence of oxygen greatly enhances damage in mitochondria as well as in plasmid DNA but not in calf thymus DNA and that caffeine has differential effects in the presence and absence of oxygen.

Studies were carried out to see the cytogenetic changes caused by in vitro treatment of human lymphocytes with 5-Azacytidine *in vitro*. Studies on the effect of low dose radiation exposure (LDR) on immune response were continued. Experimental conditions were standardised for the amplification of cDNA, representing DCNI(P22), the most basic protein of all the polypeptides that were investigated to be induced under conditions of prolonged desiccation in *Portulaca grandiflora.*

Work on Modulation of clastogenic activity of Mitomycin C (MMC) by absorbic acid was continued with human peripheral blood cultures. The result further confirmed that clastogenic effect of MMC in human lymphocytes was potentiated by Ascorbic acid. Analysis of chromosomal aberrations in peripheral blood lymphocytes of adult subjects of high background radiation areas of Kerala was done and metaphase spreads were analysed.

Radiation Medicine Centre (RMC)

Radiation Medicine Centre a involved in three major spheres of activity *i.e.*, research and development in health sciences primarily using radionuclides, patient related services involving diagnosis of many a disorder as well as treatment using radiopharmaceuticals and human resource development in nuclear medicine through formal teaching and training programmes for students.

Efforts were initiated to procure a state-of-the-art in-house medical cyclotron for the production of very short-lived radionuclides of physiological interest, *viz.*, ^{18}IF, ^{11}Cz, ^{13}IN, ^{15}O with half lives of 110, 20, 2 min. respectively during the IX Five Year Plan period. It was envisaged that associated computer-driven, remote-controlled, shielded,and automated chemistry reaction modules would be installed for the rapid synthesis of large amounts of physiological active biomolecules like ^{18}F-2Fluorodeoxyglucose ^{11}C-methionine. ^{13}N-NH_4 + 15O substrates, and so on, employing the above radionuclides. The detection of the positron-emitting radionuclides in the human body would be achieved using Positron Emission Tomographic (PET) systems.

The use of these was likely to have a far reaching impact on patient management (diagnosis, prognosis and treatment) in the field of oncology, neurology, cardiology, infection, and so on. The facility would be first of its kind in the country and perhaps in S.E. Asia. The 'turn key' project was in an advanced stage of planing. A sophisticated dual-headed, variable angle SPECT gamma camera with fan beam collimator was acquired. The instrument has advanced capabilities, and would help to obtain two views of patients at one tune and thus speed up the throughput of patients. Further, it has a facility for networking, and would be a great boon to patients.

An old General Electric analog camera was upgraded to digital one by using indigenous P.C. based technology single layer acquisition card facility for on-line energy, linearity and uniformity correction, as well as SPECT acquisition and analysis. A Nude Mice Housing Facility was established at RMC. This would facilitate the development of experimental models of various types of tumours of human origin and would be useful for the study of agents that could be targetted to tissues, and help development of diagnostic/therapeutic agents.

Twelve batches of radio-therapeutic agent 1311-mIBG was prepared in-house for the treatment of patients of neuro- endocrine tumours like neuroblastoma, pheochromacytoma, and so on. In addition an equal number of diagnostic batches were also made. Presently this is the only laboratory in the country making this expensive, and relatively unstable radiopharmaceuticals. Aqueous kits of a variety of Sn(II) ligand and other kits were made indigenously using in-house developed technology, and stored at 45°C. These kits having superior properties were used to formulate radiopharmaceuticals for patients.

About 90,000 mCi amounts of 99mTc radio-pharmaceuticals of various descriptions—for brain/ cardiac/liver/ hepatobiliary/renal-glomerular filtration and anatomy/lungs/tyroid/salivary/thyroid and so on were formulated, dispensed and used. Procedures for coating antibodies to polystyrene tubes was validated. A RIA kit for microal-buminuria especially to detect diabetic nephropathy was extensively tested. A RIA kit for T_4 using antibody coated magnetic particle separation has been formulated for BRIT.

The therapeutic efficacy of Chlorin, a porphyrin derivative and a photosensitiser has been studied in mice with transplanted fibrosarcoma and mammary tumours. Following irradiation with Cu vapour + pumped dye laser (fibre optic needle based technique) it was found that there was necrosis in the respective tumours (proven by histopathology) study performed in collaboration with CAT, Indore.

Different types of tests for the diagnosis of tuberculosis at small health care centres/hospital based immunological assays/sensitive and specific PCR assays were validated. An I.A.E.A sponsored programme on molecular typing of mycobacterial strain in multi-drug resistant tuberculosis was under way. About 8000 radiodiagnostic investigations involving various organs / tissues/neoplams were carried out during the year.

Technical services

Apart from providing technical support and services to the R&D activities, major work for augmentation and upgradation of in-house services for BARC under IX Plan were taken up. A major upgradation programme which involves augmenting the capacity of central air-conditioning plant upgradation of major electrical works at Central Air-conditioning Plant, electrical substations, centralised supervisory control system (SCADA) for substations, interconnection of South and North Site substations, upgradation of South Site service water lines and so on was started. BARC continued with its energy conservation programme which resulted in considerable saving of power.

Indira Gandhi Centre for Atomic Research

The Indira Gandhi Centre for Atomic Research (IGCAR) at Kalpakkam, Tamil Nadu, is engaged in the development of sodium cooled fast breeder reactor technology, related fuel cycle and safety. The Fast Breeder Test Reactor (FBTR) is its major facility. Advanced laboratories for carrying out research and development work in the fast breeder reactor technology have been set up. The Centre is developing a 500 MWe Prototype Fast Breeder Reactor (PFBR).

Fast reactor programme

Fast breeder test reactor (FBTR)

The reactor was operated successfully during the year, reaching a burn-up level of 45,000 MWd/t. The performance of the carbide fuel was found to be excellent. A major refurbishing was done to improve the plant availability and fire safety and a programme of irradiation of zirconium-niobium alloy, used in PHWRs was initiated.

KAMNI reactor

Regular operation of the reactor upto the rated power of 30 kW was continued. Irradiation of various samples and activation analysis of various structural and nuclear materials were carried out. Neutron radiography, an important application of this reactor, was also done. The reactor is ready for taking up the neutron radiography of FBTR fuel assembly. Prototype Fast Breeder Reactor (PFBR) The Site Evaluation Report was under review by AERB. Significant progress was made in the design components and systems of Nuclear Steam Supply System (NSSS) and conventional systems.

Preliminary Safety Analysis Report on reactor assembly, Heat transport system and on component handling were prepared and the first phase of the experiment project in this fields of core seismic design and main vessel integrity under hypothetical core disruptive accident were completed. The document for the material properties to be used in the design, was piled; the technology development the manufacture of the main vessel PFBR was completed; activity towards the technology development for Inclined Fuel Transfer Machir Grid Plate, Sodium Service Valves were initiated, and material specifications tube sheets of heat exchangers we prepared for initiating production.

FBR R&D and engineering

Engineering development

The operation of the Large Component Test Rig (LCTR) was continued heat transfer experiments. The fabrication of the full scale model of the control plug of PFBR was in an advanced stage of completion. The piping and the auxiliary for the experimental facility for sodium water reaction studies are expected be commissioned shortly. The experimental study on the likely sodium deposition in the narrow long annulus of Control and Safety Drive Mechanism (CSRDM) was up in a small sodium set up. A contract was concluded with M/s. KBL for the development of new hydraulic design, using 1/3 scale model, for a compact primary sodium pump.

The dynamic behaviour of the primary pump rotor was being studied experimentally in a full scale test section-in house. The initial results of the tests were satisfactory. A development contract was in progress at the Fluid Control Research Institute, Palghat for validation tests on slip joints of both primary and secondary sodium pumps. The former reached an advanced stage of fabrication and testing.

A DC conduction pump was designed and was under construction for use in failed fuel identification model of PFBR. The dash pot for the CSRDM was tested in full scale, and based on the test results, modifications continued. A high temperature electromagnet was assembled and its load carrying capacity and response time for the Diverse Safety Rod Mechanism (DSRDM) were verified. The results were encouraging.

A project for the development of Temperature Sensitive Magnetic Switch developed for measuring sodium flow in FBTR fuel subassemblies. The models for the study of the secondary flow distribution in intermediate heat exchanger were installed in FCRI, Palghat and the experiments progressed.

The experimental setup, for conducting the flow induced vibration studies on a prototype instrumented sub-assembly, was fabricated. A 1/5th scale model of the core outlet region of PFBR was constructed for the study of thermal striping near the control plug region and tests were in progress. The tests were carried out for the improvement of the performance of Sodium Ionisation Detectors (SID). Feasibility of using SID as a sodium leak detection system in the presence of flue gases from a fired heater was being explored.

Work on the Steam Generator Tests Facility (SGTF) progressed well. Detailed design of the sodium loop E components gained momentum and orders for the components were being placed. The detailed engineering design of the buildings was completed and the technical bids for the steam water system of the facility were progressed and recommendations were 4 finalised. The installation of the various components of the Isotope Separation Plant made significant progress and the contract for the plant piping works was awarded. The engineering experiments on pilot scale progressed.

Reactor physics

Periodic calibration of control rods, measurement of temperature coefficients of reactivity and monitoring of the reactivity loss due to burnup were carried out for FBTR. The probabilistic safety analysis for blockage of flow in FBTR fuel subassemblies and their detection were completed. The kinetic experiments for the verification of delayed neutron parameters and also the isothermal temperature coefficient measurements for KAMINI reactor, were completed. Experiments to irradiate various samples were conducted to fine tune the system. The PFBR core physics design was approved by the Project Design Safety Committee (PDSC). The document for safety analysis and shielding wen completed for approval of PDSC.

Materials chemistry

A radio-nuclide trap made of Reticulated Vitreous Carbon (RVC) for removal of radioactive cesium from sodium was successfully tested and found suitable for reactor application, Studies were conducted on the compatibility of zircaloy with sodium. A sophisticated direct reading spectrometer was commissioned for qualitative determination of the constituents of stainless steels, ferritic steels and incoloy used in nuclear applications. Fundamental studies for understanding the role of diluents in the solvent extraction process in fuel reprocessing were carried out.

Thermal ionisation mass spectrometric studies were conducted on dissolver solution of the spent fuel pallet of FBTR to assess the burn-up level. Electrochemcial hydrogen meters and carbon meters were designed, developed and installed in FBTR secondary sodium circuit. A meter based on diffusion of hydrogen through nickel coil and detection by thermal conductivity detector, was installed and commissioned for monitoring hydrogen in FBTR cover gas (argon). Various experiments to enhance the sensitivity of SnO, based sensors for detection of hydrogen were carried out.

Fuel chemistry

One of the samples of FBTR fuel pin was dissolved in nitric acid and the bumup of the fuel was measured by determining the concentrations of uranium, plutonium and selected rareearths in the dissolver solution. The feasibility of using the indigenously developed bifunctional phosphinic acid resin for recovering uranium from raffinate streams was successfully demonstrated, at NFC, Hyderabad, The synthesis of the resin on large scale was taken up with a local manufacturer. The resin was also found to extract zirconium and hafnium.

Basic studies on solvent extraction were continued. A commercially available aminophosphonic type resin was evaluated for actinide recovery. It was found to extract uranium from a variety of acid media. Studies were undertaken to develop inorganic sorbents for extraction of Cesium from high active waste solution. A new combustion synthesis route was established for the preparation of thoria powder, which could be sintered to theoretical densities more than 95% at relatively low temperatures. This method using citric acid as the fuel was found to have many advantages over the conventional route.

Electronics and instrumentation

Client-server based Maintenance Management Information System was developed for FBTR to take into account the maintenance schedule, performance history, spares and and so on, a Mobile Data Acquisition system for MAPS, PLC based control system for Structural Mechanics Laboratory of IGCAR and Distributed Data Acquisition System for RAPS-II were developed and implemented.

Metallurgy and materials technology

Low Cycle Fatigue (LCF) properties of indigenously developed modified 9 Cr-I Mo steel was characterised over a temperature range of 773 to 873 K to assess its suitability for PFBR Steam Generator (SG) applications. Detailed investigations on LCF behaviour of austenitic steel 316 L(N) weld metal and 316 L(N)/316 L(N) weld joints and creep fatigue tests on 15 Cr- 15 Ni-2.2 Mo titanium modified austenitic stainless steel (D9 alloy) with titanium to carbon ratio of 4 in solution annealed and cold worked conditions were carried out for PFBR.

Alternative technology was developed for aluminising of inconel 718 and its welding for PFBR SG. 316 L electrodes with controlled nitrogen content was developed in collaboration with an Indian firm. A technique based on ultrasonic velocity measurement was standardised to characterise the annealing behaviour of D9 alloy. Theoretical and experimental works were carried out to determine the temperature distribution in plates during welding by Shielded Metal Arc Welding process and a correlation was established, for predicting the residual stresses in weldments.

Investigations on stress corrosion cracking of 316 LN samples in sodium hydroxide were carried out to assess the behaviour of the components during cleaning, after their exposure to liquid sodium in a fast reactor. A novel method of "heat correction' was used to develop multiple heat stress, rupture correlations for a large number of ferritic and austenitic structural steels. Repair welding procedure for type 410 stainless steel for low pressure turbine blades of KAPS was established using 316L electrodes.

Materials research

A facility installed for laser treatment of surfaces was used in the systematic study of microstructural changes in 2–1/4 Cr –1 Mo steel on laser treatment. Precise and accurate vapour pressure measurements were made and enthalpy of sublimation was estimated in cesium iodide by horizontal thermal analyser as a transpiration apparatus. Studies on depth profiling of defects were conducted in thin film interfaces and colossal magneto resistance films by using the indigenously built Low Energy Positron Beam (LEPB) Facility.

An ultra-high vacuum compatible facility commissioned for analysis of mass spectra of evolved gas at high temperatures, was used to characterise the structural and stoichiometric transformation in nuclear fuel cycle materials. An integrated flux locked loop electronics for linearising the output of the indigenously built SQUID was designed, fabricated and tested successfully.

Post-Irradiation Examination (PIE)

The PIE was carried out on three experimental subassemblies irradiated in FBTR showed that no appreciable amount of swelling had taken place and the reduction in the gap between the fuel and the clad was only marginal. Further, no changes in the microstructure were observed in the fuel after irradiation and there was no effect of fuel-clad interaction. Experiments on irradiation of pressurised capsules made of zircaloy tube and zirconium - niobium alloy, to study the in-reactor creep rate, were started and the first two capsules were discharged from FBTR and PIE progressed. This will help in determining the useful life of the coolant tubes and planning of their replacement in PHWRs.

Non-destructive testing and evaluation

A MOBile SCANner (MOBSCAN), having a travel of 15 metres and a stroke of 500 mm, with a provision for mounting a camera, was designed and developed for non-destructive examination of large plates. A Remotely Operated Power MANipulator (ROPMAN) provided with six degrees of freedom and with a gripper, was designed for hot cell applications. It is capable of upgradation to a full-fledged robotic arm. The design and development of a walking robot for in-service inspection of steam generators was completed.

The system can automatically deploy ultrasonic, eddy current and vision probes. It is adaptable to various types of heat exchanger configurations and can also scan large plates. This can also be modified to carry a manipulator arm, a closed circuit TV camera and so on, for maintenance/surveillance applications. Experimental studies were carried out to characterise the secondary phases in cold worked AISI 304 SS specimens using SQUID. These measurements were successful even with 10 % volume fraction as compared with 20 to 27 % for other methods.

The technique of laser scattering was developed and successfully applied for the study of corrosion pits in stainless steel, monitoring the roughness of machined surfaces and the characterisation of laser induced surface modification. A laser based etching technique was also established for non-contact etching of metallic and ceramic specimens. An impact echo test method was developed for reliable examination concrete structures.

This method overcomes the limitations in the non-destructive examination of thick structures by using low frequency ultrasonics. IGCAR extended its expertise in the areas of NDT and failure analysis to other DAE units and also to a large number of strategic /core sectors of Indian industry.

Computing facilities

Enhancing the computing facilitied at IGCAR continued. Work progressed for establishing an ATM Optical Fibre backbone for networking of their various facilities of IGCAR. Commissioning of the Firewall system was on hand for improving the network security for the internet facility. Various modules for the computerisation of IGCAR administration and the Hospital Management System were developed and their testing progressed.

Health and safety

A bubble detector was indigenously developed and calibrated. It was used for evaluation of neutron shielding properties of borated compressed wood and also for evaluation of neutron dose to patients undergoing high energy X-ray and electron radiotherapy. Design of major components of a Compton profile spectrometer and the development work on the Intense Pulsed Neutron Facility had made significant progress. An Electron Cyclotron Resonance X-ray source was designed and constructed for use as a portable medical imaging unit.

A miniature pocket dosimeter, with audible alarm for every preset cumulative dose increase and overall cumulative dose was designed and fabricated. A continuous gamma dose logger for site environmental monitoring was also developed as an import substitution. An indigenous modelling code for the estimation of the activity release, transport and deposition of corrosion products as a function of time and distance in the primary sodium circuit of FBTR, was developed and validated successfully.

A 2-dimensional numeric code, handling the hydrodynamics of a simulated Core Disruptive Accident was developed. Stress-strain correlation under dynamic pressure loading was studied at room temperature.

Efforts were on hand to correlate the shock energy and strain energy of the deformed specimen. A 100 U condenser bank was set up to generate transient pressures. This will be used in fast reactor safety studies related to containment capability.

A programme to model the fuel behaviour in reactor accidental situations was initiated. To assess the consequences of damage suffered by concrete in contact with sodium, experiments were conducted. Two experimental trials were carried out to study the air-cleaning of sodium fire containments. The aerosol trapping efficiency of the beds was found to be above 95 %. Fabrication of some of the components for the sodium fire test facility was started.

Safety surveillance inspections were carried out at all the facilities at Kalpakkam. Safety educational programmes and first aid training were also conducted, as a part of industrial safety. All incidents and occurrences were investigated in detail and a database software for the same was developed.

Coastal Atmospheric dispersion studies by employing tethered balloon, tower and mini-sodar were continued at Kalpakkam. A new thermo-luminescent phosphor, capable of measuring radiation dose of 5 mR was developed. Criticality safety evaluation of the process vessel for RAPS, shielding calculations for beam port of KAMINI reactor and testing of the shielding integrity of blisters, shield doors and hot cells of KARP were carried out. A LAN for the safety related activities was established.

Fuel reprocessing

FBTR fuel reprocessing

The Safety Report for the Lead Mini Cell (LMC) was cleared by Safety Committee and is under the scrutiny of SARCOP. The installation of the facility reached an advanced stage of completion. The cold commissioning of LMC, for reprocessing FBTR fuel on laboratory scale, is targeted for July 1999.

Fast reactor fuel processing plan

The site works for the air-conditioning and ventilation and service piping were completed. Tender for the fabrication of the process vessel was issued. Specifications for the cell piping works were prepared and the drawings for one of the cells were taken up. Most of the reconversion boxes were received at site. Preliminary design of radiation shielding glass frames was worked out for the radiation shielding windows received at site. U-233 refurbishing of system for recovery from thorium rods.

Commissioning tests for the second campaign of uranium-233 recovery from irradiated thorium rods, were completed. With the clearance obtained from Safety Committee, the hot operations were continued.

R and D activities

A solvent extraction method was developed from acetic acid medium was employed in the recovery of U-233. Methods were also developed which will replace the use of hazardous formaldehyde, resulting in lesser waste volume. Extracto-spectro-photometric determination of uranium and plutonium was developed for fuel reprocessing application.

Engineering and technical services

Civil engineering

The civil engineering group handled all aspects of civil engineering., services right from conceptual, structural, architectural and public health, designs, estimates and contracts, quality control and construction of all projects in IGCAR, CWMF, KARP," WIP and also preliminary design work connected with PFBR. Design and construction of the housing, other public buildings and so on, in DAE Township were, also carried out. Consultancy services: for architectural and structural designs: were rendered to MAPS, BARC some of the aided institutions.

The extension building for the Fuel Reprocessing Development Laboratory was completed. Towards the infrastructure development in IGCAR, civil works related to the construction of security building, compound wall, widening of roads at IGCAR entrance and so on, were taken up.

The civil works for the IX plan projects such as mechanical maintenance and vibration building, substation building for steam generator test facility, structural mechanics lab, electronics and instrumentation laboratory and Quality assurance building and so on, were taken up. The construction of 112 quarters in the new township at Anupuram was progressing well and will be completed shortly. The IX plan works related to housing and infrastructure development were initiated at Aunpuram.

Construction of sixth battery of 49 tile holes for CWMF, inflammable stores building for KARP and main process building of WIP were completed. Special investigation works to assess the static and dynamic parameters and liquefaction potential of PFBR site were completed.

The bore hole studies for 90 metres depth for soil investigation made progress. The contract on the studies related to shore line stability for Kalpakkam was awarded to National Institute of Oceanography and the work progressed. Studies towards the development of special concretes for PFBR commenced.

Engineering services

Operation and maintenance of electrical, air-conditioning

and ventilation and communication systems continued. Various energy saving measures were implemented for the electrical distribution and lighting systems in the Township. Specification for procurement of energy efficient 500 TR centrifugal chillers were finalised, and procurement of substation equipment for SGTF progressed. Internal electrification works made progress for various quarters at Anupuram. Technical support was provided to other organisations.

Quality engineering

Quality Assurance and NDT services were provided for various projects such as FRFRP, Technology Development works related to PFBR, Boron Enrichment Plant and others, and Quality surveillance, pre-service and in-service inspection support were extended to Heavy Water Plants at Manuguru and Kota, TAPS, IAF and so on. A development study to evaluate the influence of welding parameters on impact and fatigue properties of weld joints of boiler materials for PFBR was completed.

Management services

Significant progress was made in the implementation of the Phase I of the Purchase Management System at Madras Regional Purchase Unit, Chennai. A system for the feedback information to the indenters in respect of various tenders and purchase orders was developed and introduced.

A sophisticated system for monitoring the expenditure of all the capital projects of the Centre was implemented successfully. A system for preparation of budget proposals for capital projects was designed & developed and the same was under release. Procurement of the servers and client nodes for the LAN for interconnecting the Project Monitoring/Purchase Management Systems progressed.

Central workshop

Central Workshop caters to the manufacturing and R&D needs of various facilities and projects at Kalpakkam. It also serves for the technology and process development for the manufacture of nuclear components, which will be transferred to the Indian industries for execution. The Workshop developed a sleek miniature TIG welding torch. A mockup study for the development of high temperature brazing for joining copper conductor with SS 316 LN duct was in the final stage of adoption for the DC conduction pump for PFBR.

Technologies under evaluation for transfer included production of Yttrrium Vanadate phosphor for use in mercury lamps, and technology for Lascan Dia Gauge. For NPCIL, development of ISI equipment for Moderator Heat Exchanger and RAPS type steam generator continued.

Patening/copyright activity

Three patents were given in acceptance and five patents were filed with the Patent Office, Mumbai.

Exoprts

BARC supplied Second lot of 500 Thoria buttons to General Electric, USA; Bulk reagents for Radio-immunoassay (RIA) to EGYPT; Liquid injection system and gas apparatus for radio-tracer experiments to Bangladesh; TLD Badges with provision of TLD badge reader services to Saudi Arabia; Gamma-Camera-Interface-Cards to Latin American, Asian and African countries through IAEA.

Management services

Project monitoring: The project coordination activities for all projects for which financial sanction was received, continued. Databases containing information on all the projects under R&D, I&M, and Power Sectors in BARC were created for project monitoring. Action was initiated for procurement of a variety of items. A statistical report on the retirement profile of scientific and technical staff for the period 1998-2002 was prepared to define future recruitment policy.

Centre for advanced technology

The Centre for Advanced Technology (CAT) at Indore, Madhya Pradesh spearheads the national efforts in research and development of lasers, accelerators, high vacuum technology, cryogenics and technology for manufacture of large magnets. The Centre is setting up a Synchrotron Radiation Sources (SRS) Facility which will be an unique research setup in the country.

Laser programme

A semiconductor laser-pumped, intracavity-doubled, laser giving 300 mW cw power at 532 nm was developed at CAT. This laser without intracavity doubler also gives 750 mW of IR power at 1064nm. These figures correspond to 40% conversion efficiency with intracavity doubling.

An industrial model of high power transverse flow CW CO_2 laser which gives 3.5 kW laser power in multi-mode and 2 kW in a lower order mode was also developed. This is coupled with a CNC work-table and is being used regularly for industrial applications such as material processing applications *e.g.*, as cutting of metallic and nonmetallic sheets, welding of various kind of steel, titanium *etc.*, and surface transformation hardening, surface re-solidification, alloying and cladding.

Laser cladding of Stellite-694 over Nickel super alloy was demonstrated for refurbishing worn-out gas turbine blade. An engineered version of this laser system was also developed and will be delivered to Jadavpur University under national lase program. On excitation by ultraviolet light *e.g.*, nitrogen laser, uranyl salts fluoresce with characteristic emission. A laser fluorimeter was developed at CAT earlier, using this principle. This instrument finds applications for the Atomic Energy Programme in prospecting and mining of uranium, reactor fuel fabrication facilities and nuclear waste management. A new improved version of this laser flourimeter has now been developed at CAT.

This has a modular design with a laser module consisting of sealed off type Nitrogen laser, an optical module and a processor module. Its salient features include PC connectivity, back lit LCD display, programmability, software on PC for data acquisition and processing *etc.* An unstable Q-switched Nd:YAG laser using variable reflectivity mirror (VRM) was developed at CAT.

Unstable laser resonator configuration supports high mode volume in active medium while giving diffraction limited beam, thereby capable of delivering higher energies. Since, this configuration has shorter resonator length, it is also capable of delivering shorter pulse width. The main features of this laser is higher output energy and shorter pulse width, hence high peak power, compact laser head and short temporal pulse. One such system, model RD-YG-300, was supplied and commissioned at Atomic Energy Commission Syria, Damascus. A laser marker system was developed using a Nd YAG laser. The laser beam traces a programmed path, with the help of galvanometric mirror assemblies, to mark text, logos and pictures on hard surfaces.

This PC based system consists of a X-Y galvanometric mirror assembly, a video digitizer, CCD (charged coupled device) camera, mirror driver cards and a PC add-on interface card. The software developed accepts plot files generated by 'Autocad' software or a picture captured by video camera and marks it on the target. One laser marker system for scribing a set of straight lines on solar cell is supplied to M/s Eco-Solar System, India Pvt. Ltd., Pune. They have started regular production of solar cell.

Medical application of lasers

In one of the research projects under the National Laser Programme, effect of nitrogen laser on bum wounds and non-healing ulcers was studied using nitrogen lasers developed at CAT. Studies have shown that it has a bactericidal effect and can be used in healing of chronic/ acute infected wounds.

A prospective study has been done on a variety of indication *viz.*, traumatic wounds, bums, varicose ulcers, diabetic foot, pressure sores and skin soft tissue infections. Particularly, with organism resistant to all antibiotics, it has shown significant wound sterilization effect along with improvement in microvascularity and epitheialisation. Leading to faster healing and reducing hospital stay. There is also pain relief in ischaemic wounds. About 400 cases with Nitrogen laser with very good results are already treated. Special laser scanner is developed by CAT to facilitate laser radiation of large wound areas.

Cryogenics

Further improvements were carried out in the design of the closed cycle cryocoolers being developed at CAT. A second model of single stage unit is giving a cooling power of 3 watts at 50 K, whereas the overall size is smaller than the first model which had a cooling power of 250 mw at 50 K.

Applied and basic research

An x-ray crystal spectrometer with 2D-spatial imaging and on-line operation was set up for studies of x-ray emission from laser produced plasmas. The spectrograph was used for measurements of x-ray line intensity enhancement of transitions in highly charged ions of laser produced plasmas expanding in different background gases.

Variable energy cyclotron centre

The Variable Energy Cyclotron Centre (VECC) at Calcutta is a national research centre in nuclear field. The variable energy cyclotron at the Centre delivers beams of nuclear particles for research in nuclear physics and nuclear chemistry, and produces radioisotopes for various applications. The Centre is setting up a superconducting cyclotron.

Superconducting cyclotron

The superconducting cyclotron project of VECC made significant progress. Fabrication of major component advanced significantly. All major steel forgings for the main magnet frame were completed and they were found to be excellent quality. The machining of various parts of magnet frame will begin shortly. The quality of the superconducting coil winding made satisfactory progress. All the fabrication drawing were critically examined and approved. The set up will be assembled at VECC in the middle of 1999 and the actual coil winding made satisfactory progress.

All the fabrication of superconducting coil winding will begin in August 1999. Formalities for placement of fabrication contract for the complex cryostat assembly, which will house the superconducting coils, were completed. Progress was also made at BARC, towards fabrication of the superconducting cable for the coil. Purchase order for the main liquid helium plant was placed on a French firm. The plant is expected to start producing liquid helium in July 1999. A 90 litre capacity liquid nitrogen plant is already operating satisfactorily. After procurement and planning, fabrication of the radio-frequency (RF) resonator structure started at BARC.

Several major parts of the RF resonators were also contracted out for fabrication. The electronic part of the RF system was under fabrication at the centre. Detailed design work on several units for the system was completed. A 300 Ampere power supply was fabricated as a prototype for the main magnet of the superconducting cyclotron. Design work was also carried out to extend the operating current level to 1000 Ampere.

Several prototype power supplies for the RF system of the superconducting cyclotron were also fabricated and tested. A number of prototypes for magnet power supplies were also fabricated. Design of an advanced Electron Cyclotron Resonance Ion source operating at 14.5 GHz was finalized. Construction of the building for the new accelerator was to commence shortly. All the tendering formalities for carrying out specialize jobs were completed

Heavy ion acceleration in variable energy cyclotron

On August 26,1998, a new milestone was set at VECC when for the first time 115 MeV 0(5+) heavy ion beam was successfully extracted out of the cyclotron (VEC). This ushered in a new era of research opportunities for the scientists. Other new beams will also be available from the cyclotron. In early 1998, 0(6+) beam was successfully accelerated up to an energy over 200 MeV within the cyclotron—the highest ion energy ever achieved in the country. VEC had been utilized since 1981 for basic research and applications in the field of nuclear and allied sciences. So far, only the proton, deuteron and alpha beams were accelerated with VEC. With this success, the VECC now stands at par with the best cyclotron centres in the world.

The heavy ion acceleration programme was undertaken a few years ago. In this program the first major milestone was successful operations of the indigenously developed Electron Cyclotron Resonance (ECR) heavy ion source in May 1991. This is an advanced heavy ion source, ideally suited for cyclotron injection.

The change over to heavy ion injection was delayed due to users' pressure to finish their experiments with light ion beams.

Major modifications in the cyclotron and its systems had to be carried out for satisfactory acceleration of heavy ions. The central region of the cyclotron was considerably altered. Vacuum level in the cyclotron and beam lines was improved. Magnet power supplies, radio-frequency and LCW systems were upgraded.

The newly extracted 0(5+) beam was transported to the experimental area where several tests on the beam were carried out by a group of scientists from VECC and SINP. To enhance the versatility of the cyclotron to accelerate heavy ion beams, a 14.5 GHz ECR source was under installation. This heavy ion source will deliver ions of solid species also. Detailed design and layout of the injection line for the new source were worked out.

Radioactive ion beam project

The availability of Radioactive Ion Beams (RIBs) will signal the dawn of a new era in heavy-ion science. RIBs will not only provide answers to many important questions, it would also open up many basic and applied research topics in the fields of condensed matter physics, biology, chemistry and medicine. VECC has undertaken the task of building a RIB facility. A significant amount of progress could be achieved in terms of completing the design of various state-of-art accelerators and accelerator subsystems in the last one year. The design of a low velocity heavy-ion Radio Frequency Quadrupole (RFQ), the design of a two ion-source stand, the design of a high B-mode ECR ion source and that of a low velocity heavy-ion IH LINAC were completed. Efforts to initiate intense R&D programme for the development of thick targets were underway.

Recovery and analysis of helium

The recovery of helium from the natural gas available in thermal springs at Bakreswar commenced and a pilot plant for helium extraction was set up there. Set up for final purification of helium was in progress. Setting up of raw gas entrapment facilities at Tantloi (Bihar) also commenced, and gas analysis and survey work to augment sources around Tantloi were in progress.

Computational facilities

Computer facility was installed and a powerful server was commissioned to carry out computational and simulation works for the superconducting cyclotron. A major part of the campus-wide networking was implemented. A PC/CAMAC based control of vacuum subsystem on ECR ion source was tested successfully and CAMAC routines were developed.

Beam profiler system of cyclotron was updated to work around MS-Widows. Cyclotron beam view and property acquisition and distribution system was developed with image acquisition hardware and in-house developed software. An administrative data base system was being implemented around ORACLE.

Ouark -gluon plasma

VECC was involved in commissioning of photon multiplicity detectors (PMD) for experiments at the European Centre for Nuclear Research (CERN) in Geneva as well as at Brookhaven National Laboratory (BNL) in New York.

These detectors were designed to look for signals of the Quark-Gluon Plasma (QGP) phase transition. First generation of these detectors using plastic scintillators, and CCD camera read out were installed in WA93 and WA98 experiments at the SPS at CERN.

Basic research in physics

Phase transition in nuclear matter

The equation of state is important for the studies of nuclei and also objects of astrophysical interest. The equation of state of finite nuclei showed some peculiar properties. Such properties were studied in a mean field model.

Chaos in nuclear dynamics

The one-body dissipative force that operates in macroscopic nuclear dynamics arises essentially due to the random nature of the intrinsic nuclear motion. A theory for one-body dissipation was developed. This theory termed as chaos weighted wall formula (CWWF) extended the applicability of one-body theory to a wide range of systems with nearly regular to strongly chaotic intrinsic dynamics.

OCD phase transition

A study on the properties of hadrons at finite temperature and density was performed. The effects of reduction in hadronic masses and widths on the electromagnetic ejectiles (photons and dileptons) originating from ultra-relativistic heavy-ion collisions were investigated. Unstable particles to play in low mass dilepton production resulting from heavy-ion collisions and this has been a subject of several investigations. These features were investigated by using the rho and omega mesons as illustrative examples.

The temperature and density dependence of the rho-omega mixing amplitude was studied from a purely hadronic model. It was observed that the mixing amplitude changes substantially at high temperature and density. This result may have a strong bearing on the QGP diagnostics. The cosmic first order phase transition from quarks to hadrons, occurring a few microseconds after the Big Bang, would lead to the formation of quark nuggets. Studies done on these quarks nuggets gave interesting results. Quark nuggets as possible candidates for baryonic dark matter are being investigated. Studies were also conducted relating to the framework of relativistic Fokker Planck equation, to dynamical equilibration of the hot quark gluon matter formed in ultrarelativistic heavy-ion collisions, and the time evolution of the system.

Regional radiation medical centre

A 4 Mev linear electron accelerator had a successful run for radiation treatment of cancer patients. More t thousand five hundred patients treatment successfully. Apart from therapy the work for accurate diagnosis of cancer tumours were quite successful as well. With the help of an interest free loan from the Kingdom of Belgium to Government of India, SINP with VECC, Government of West Bengal, West Bengal Industrial Development Corporation and IBA—Belgium continued the sitting up of a captive Cyclotron of hio current 30 MeV proton for production of radio isotopes such as thallium for heart ailments.

Atomic Minerals Directorate

The Atomic Minerals Division entered 50th year of its existence on July 29, 1998. On the occasion of its Golden Jubilee Celebrations the Division was renamed as the Atomic Minerals Directorate for Exploration and Research (AMD).

Uranium investigations

The airborne gamma-ray spectrometric system (AGRS) newly fabricated by AMD was test flown and was found to perform well. Satellite data interpretation, digital image processing, photogeological studies, data integration and critical studies on various potential areas were carried out. Noteworthy uranium mineralisation was located near Miryalguda (Andhra Pradesh) as a result of follow-up ground checking. Radiometric reconnaissance survey over 9,780 sq. km and detailed surveys over 450 sq. km were carried out which resulted in locating/delineating new uranium anomalies.

Geophysical surveys were carried out in selected areas of Madhya Pradesh, Rajasthan, Meghalaya, Haryana and Karnataka. These surveys helped in narrowing down target areas. Magnetic surveys at Tosham-Nigana, Haryana indicated presence of anomalies which could be due to metallic mineralisation. Regional magnetic surveys carried out east of Juba, Raipur district, Madhya Pradesh indicated presence of fracture zones.

TEM surveys around Gogi Karnataka indicated a conductor axis coinciding with Basement -Bhima basin contact. Geochemical surveys (water, soil and stream sediments) were carried out over 12,165 sq. kin in different parts of the country. These helped in narrowing down the target areas and delineating their trends in parts of Cuddapah, Kurnool, Guntur and Prakasham districts of Andhra Pradesh for undertaking further detailed surveys.

Exploratory drilling aggregating to over 30,000 metre was carried out to probe/delineate the subsurface continuity of uranium mineralisation in different promising sectors. Correlatable ore grade uranium mineralised intercepts of the order of 0. 10% U_3O_8 and above were obtained at Gogi (Karnataka); Wahkyn (Meghalaya); Peddagattu and Koppunuru (Andhra Pradesh) and Ghateshwar (Rajasthan). Lesser grade (<O. 10% U_3O_8) uranium mineralisation was also intercepted at some places in Uttar Pradesh, Andhra Pradesh, Bihar and Rajasthan.

3

Policy, Planning and Public Awareness

India has the distinction of being the only country in the world to have an exclusive Ministry dealing with new and renewable energy sources. The relevance of increasing use of renewable energy sources in the transition to a sustainable energy base was recognised in our country even in the early 1970s. Since early 1980s a significant thrust has been given to the development, trial and induction of a variety of renewable energy technologies for use in different sectors. To begin with, these endeavours were steered and overseen by the Commission for Additional Sources of Energy (CASE) set up in 1981 in the Department of Science and Technology.

Subsequently, in 1982, a separate Department was created in the Ministry of Energy, entrusted with the charge of promoting nonconventional energy sources. A decade later this was upgraded and a separate Ministry was created to handle all areas of renewable energy development.

Charter of MNES

Under the Allocation of Business Rules, the Ministry has been assigned charge of the following:

— Commission for Additional Sources of Energy (CASE)

Integrated Rural Energy Programme (IREP)

— Research and development of biogas and programmes relating to biogas units

— Programmes relating to improved chulhas and research and development thereof

— Small hydel projects

— Geothermal energy

— Solar thermal devices

— Wind energy

— Solar photovoltaic devices, including their development, production and application.

— Tidal energy, wave and ocean thermal energy.

— Indian Renewable Energy Development Agency,

Structure of the ministry

CASE

The Commission for Additional Sources of Energy (CASE) was established in 1981, on the lines of the Atomic Energy Commission and the Space Commission, to oversee the development of new energy sources in the country. The Commission functions under the Chairmanship of the Secretary, NINES and has the following responsibilities:

— Formulating policies and programmes for the development of new and renewable sources of energy;

— Coordinating and intensifying research and development activities in new and renewable sources of energy;

— Ensuring implementation of Government's policies in regard to all matters concerning new and renewable sources of energy;

The Commission held two meetings during 1998-99 to consider and approve the policies, programmes and schemes of the Ministry and to review the progress of implementation of various programmes.

The Ministry's activities are being carried on under six broad groups viz. 'Rural Energy', 'Solar Energy', 'Power from Renewables', 'Energy from Urban and Industrial Wastes', 'New Technologies', and 'Administration and Coordination'. Each group is headed by a Senior Adviser/Adviser or a Joint Secretary. In addition, the Ministry has an Integrated Finance Division which functions under a Joint Secretary and Financial Adviser. The Ministry is classified as a Scientific Ministry.

The Ministry has 9 regional offices located at Ahmedabad, Bhopal, Bhubaneshwar, Chandigarh, Guwahati, Hyderabad, Patna, Lucknow and Chennai. These offices carry out monitoring and inspection of projects and maintain liaison with the concerned State Governments and State nodal agencies and other implementing agencies.

The Solar Energy Centre, which functions as a division of the Ministry, is located in its own campus at Gwalpahari in Gurgaon district of Haryana. A Centre for Wind Energy Technology (CWET) is being established in Tamil Nadu. This will serve as the technical focal point for wind power development.

IREDA

The Indian Renewable Energy Development Agency (IREDA) is a financial institution set up to provide loans and other assistance to the manufacturers and the users of renewable energy systems. IREDA administers several programmes on behalf of the Ministry and is located in New Delhi.

Sardar Swaran Singh National Institute of Renewable Energy

The need for a national level institution devoted to the entire spectrum of renewable energy sources was felt and articulated during consultations held in connection with the formulation of a national renewable energy policy. In response to this, after detailed discussion and approval by the Commission for Additional Sources of Energy (CASE), a National Institute of Renewable Energy named after the late Sardar Swaran Singh is being established by the NINES at Jalandhar. It was felt that the Institute should especially focus on new areas which are not being taken up in the existing Centres supported by the Ministry, such as biomass energy, energy recovery from wastes and new technologies. It was also felt that the Institute should focus on human resources development and international cooperation, supplement the activities of the existing Centres and provide coordination as an apex institution in the area of renewable energy.

The Governing Council of the Institute has been constituted with the Secretary of the Ministry as Chairman. A Search Committee has been constituted, under the Chairmanship of the Secretary of the Ministry, to identify suitable candidates for appointment as the Director of the Institute. The Project Report covering location and land requirement, administrative and organizational setup, manpower requirement, cost estimate and financial management of the Institute has been prepared.

A meeting of the Governing Council was held on June 19, 1998, and in pursuance of the decisions taken therein, a Scientific and Technical Advisory Committee (STAC) and a Building and Infrastructure Development Committee (BIDC) were constituted. The first meetings of both these Committees were held on August 17, 1998. The Commission on Additional Sources of Energy is currently examining the scope, structure, content, interrelationship of the Institute with the sister institutions, infrastructure and financial aspects.

Renewable energy policy

The Ministry is in the process of formulating a comprehensive policy on renewable energy and the necessary supporting legislation. The Policy aims at augmenting the grid electricity supply with power from renewable sources, ensuring for the rural areas electricity and energy based on renewable sources, substitution of fossil fuels with renewable sources for decentralised power generation and reduction in environmental pollution caused by excessive use of fossil fuels. The Policy seeks to address issues relating to institutional arrangements, mobilisation of financial resources, promotion of renewable energy industry, and development of human resources necessary for large-scale adoption of new and renewable sources of energy.

A medium-term programme is being chalked out as part of the Policy, which aims at achieving 10 per cent share for renewable energy in the total installed capacity of grid electricity generation by the year 2012. The Policy seeks to ensure "Electricity for All" by promoting power generation based on solar, biomass, small hydro, and wind energy sources and providing electricity to all the villages which have no electricity now. It further aims at improving the quality of energy supply to rural areas to bring about their all round development through the Integrated Rural Energy Programme, which is proposed to be extended to all the blocks in the country by 2012.

The Policy seeks to bring about a smooth transition from the present economy based almost in totality on the fossil fuels, whose reserves are limited, towards a sustainable economy based on renewable sources of energy which are unlimited, thereby achieving the goal of "Energy for All.".

Planning & coordination

The Planning & Co-ordination Division is the focal point for co-ordinating all the activities of the Ministry. This Division also prepares and coordinates the Annual Plans and Five Year Plans. During the year, the Draft Ninth Five Year Plan and the "Special Action Plan for Rapid Expansion and Improvement of Physical Infrastructure including Non-Conventional Energy Sources during the Ninth Five Year Plan" were finalised in consultation with the Planning Commission.

Sub-plan for women

The Ministry has incorporated a Sub-Plan for Women in the various renewable energy programmes such as biogas, improved chulha, water mills, solar photovoltaic, publicity and awareness. The Women Component Plan of the Ministry envisages women's role in renewable energy sector not only as a beneficiary of, but also as a contributor to, this sector.

North-east initiative

During 1998-99, the Ministry allocated 10% of its domestic budgetary support for taking up programmes and projects in the North-Eastern States and Sikkim, mainly on biogas, improved chulha, integrated rural energy, small hydro power and solar photovoltaics. The Ministry has introduced a new scheme for providing Central financial assistance for the setting up and strengthening of State nodal agencies (SNAs) in North-Eastern States and Sikkim during 199899. The scheme will be operative during the Ninth Five Year Plan.

The basic objective of this scheme is to support State Governments in their efforts to create and strengthen the State nodal agencies working exclusively in the area of non-conventional energy so that the planning, coordination, implementation and monitoring of non-conventional energy programmes and schemes in the North-Eastern States and Sikkim can be strengthened. The scheme provides for grants-in-aid to the State nodal agencies/State Governments to partially meet the recurring and non-recurring expenditure during the Ninth Plan Period.

The Ministry organised a meeting at Guwahati on October 14, 1998 of State Secretaries and Chief Executives of State nodal agencies of all North-Eastern States and Sikkim to discuss and review various policy issues relating to funding of non-conventional energy programmes/projects and their implementation and monitoring. A target of 2265 biogas plants and 1,04,000 improved chulhas was set for the region during 199899. The targets set for solar lanterns and home lighting systems were 6100 and 1350 respectively.

The costs of various NRSE devices/systems are higher in North-Eastern States due to difficult terrain and logistic problems. It has therefore been decided that the subsidies provided by the Ministry under the various programmes may be re-worked based on the difference in costs between the North-Eastern States and other regions of the country so that the cost to the user in the NE States would be the same as that in other parts of the country. Higher subsidies are being provided to the North Eastern States during 1998-99 under biogas, improved chulha, solar water heating system and small hydro power programmes. In order to tap the small hydro sources of the region a special scheme of 50% capital grant is being provided to take up small hydro schemes

Annual meeting of state secretaries/nodal departments.

The Ministry held the annual meeting of State Secretaries and Chief Executives of State nodal agencies for non-conventional energy sources on 9th & 10th February, 1999 in New Delhi. The meeting reviewed the progress of renewable energy programmes and considered the initiatives and strategies for a national policy on renewable energy sources for the coming years. The meeting was inaugurated by Sri P.R. Kumaramangalam, Union Minister of Power, Parliamentary Affairs and Non-Conventional Energy Sources. He also gave away the Awards for excellence in performance in the promotion of non-conventional energy sources.

Human resource development

Human resource forms a critical input for socioeconomic and technological development. Capacity-building is especially relevant in a new and emerging area like non-conventional energy where technologies are gradually stabilising and are being perceived as reliable and cost-effective. During the year, 19 officers were nominated for participation in 13 training programmes on subjects such as financial management, office management, environmental management, administrative behaviour, etc. This is in addition to the technical training programmes under which seven officers participated in three training programmes, seminars and symposia.

Progressive use of Hindi

During 1998-99, a number of measures were taken for accelerating the pace of implementation of the Official Language Policy in the Ministry. Inspection of the Regional Office at Bhopal was conducted regarding the use of Hindi. Special emphasis was laid on improving the percentage of correspondence in Hindi with officers/individuals in Region 'A' and 'B'. As a result, notwithstanding the scientific and technical nature of the work of the Ministry, 33 per cent of the correspondence was done in Hindi. As per the provisions contained under section 3(3) of the Official Language Act, 1963, all specified documents were issued bilingually. Besides, the Rule 5 of the Official Language Rules 1976 was adhered to fully by replying in Hindi all the letters received in Hindi. There has also been an increase in Hindi noting/ drafting in the official work.

In order to increase the use of Hindi in the programmes for promotion of non -conventional energy sources, the Ministry has started organising seminars etc. in Hindi. The first such seminar was organised at Chinhat (Lucknow) under the auspices of NEDA on April 4, 1997 and the second one was organised at Bhopal under the auspices of MPUVN on December 29, 1998. The entire proceedings in these seminars were conducted in Hindi.

During the year under review, action was initiated for reconstituting the Hindi Salahakar Samiti of the Ministry. In addition, the departmental Official Language Implementation Committee held its meetings regularly and reviewed the quarterly Hindi progress reports of the Ministry and its regional offices/undertakings. Based on this, measures to correct the deficiencies, if any, were suggested.

With a view to creating awareness and accelerating the pace of use of Hindi, a 'Hindi Fortnight was observed in the Ministry from September I to 15, 1998, during which September 14 was observed as 'Hindi Day' and a number of Hindi competitions were conducted to mark this occasion. A Hindi workshop was also held for the officers of the Ministry. A total of 47 officers/staff, belonging to Hindi and non-Hindi categories who had excelled in their performance were given cash prizes.

To encourage original writing of books in Hindi and translation in Hindi of books in English on topics relating to new and renewable sources of energy, the Ministry has been implementing a "Prakritik Urja Puraskar Yojana". Under this, the book entitled 'Anant Urja Srota-Bhutapiya Urja', written by Sri. Shyam Sunder Sharma was awarded during 1998-99 the first prize of Rs. 15000/- along with a certificate for the calendar year 1996. Besides, the incentives scheme to encourage noting/drafting in Hindi was continued during 1998-99 and prizes were given to five officials of the Ministry.

Technology information forecasting, assessment and data bank

Information technology (IT) has, over the years, emerged as a vital tool for bringing about a transformation in every facet of human life and ushering in a knowledge-based society to meet the challenges of the 21st century. In view of this, a series of recommendations were made by the National Task Force on Information Technology and Software Development set up by the Prime Minister for effective use of IT in the governance of the country.

As a follow-up of this, the Ministry of Non -Conventional Energy Sources has created "Technology Information Forecasting, Assessment and Data Bank (TIFAD)" Division for widespread use of IT to promote renewable sources of energy. During the year, this Division took a number of steps including provision of updated computer facilities, creation of centralised as well as decentralised databank, provision of Internet and E-mail connections, establishment of Local Area Networks (LAN) and Renewable Energy Network (RENET), creation of NINES Web Page and structured database in renewable energy and training to officers and staff in the use of computers. All these have helped in increasing the use of 'Information Technology' in the Ministry, its Regional Offices and the Solar Energy Centre. These are detailed in the succeeding paragraphs.

Provision of computer hardware & software

Independent workstations with PCs and printers have been provided in all the Programme Divisions for officers from the level of Section Officers. As many as 121 desktop/laptop computers along with the required number of printers, UPSs/CVTs, Modems, colour scanners, Server, external CD Writers, external CD ROM Drives, internal CD ROM Drives and Multimedia kits have been procured and installed in the Ministry.

The Ministry has provided 9 computer systems, comprising of a desktop computer, a LaserJet 6L Printer, a Modem, a UPS and a Fax machine to each of the nine Regional Offices at Ahmedabad, Bhopal, Bhubaneswar, Chandigarh, Chennai, Guwahati, Hyderabad, Lucknow and Patna.

Eight computers, along with the required number of Printers, and C-200 VSAT system have been installed in the Solar Energy Centre at Gwalpahari, Haryana. All these computer systems are largely utilising MS-Windows'95 as Operating System Software and MS-Office'97 as application software with some other software.

In the earlier years, the National Informatics Centre (NIC) had installed UNIX-based computer terminals in both the buildings in which Ministry is located. There is one NIC-Computer Centre in each of the two buildings, equipped with two Xenix-based 386 systems and one Unix-based 486 system. These are being currently used primarily for the preparation of payrolls and other related works. Two Windows NT-based Pentium systems have also been installed to work as Web Servers. With the installation of independent, intelligent and high speed desktop-based Computer workstations, the Unix-based Systems have become obsolete and are being phased out.

Local Area Network (LAN)

The NIC has agreed to provide at its cost Local Area Networks for integrating all the PCs in the Ministry to provide inter-connectivity and access to various divisions for the computerised information. Accordingly, laying and wiring of circuits for LAN in one of the buildings (Block-14), covering 30 systems, have since been completed. The work on setting up LAN to connect the remaining computer systems in Block-14 and in the other NINES offices in the Paryavaran Bhawan is in progress and is expected to be completed before the end of 1998-99.

Renewable Energy Network (RENET)

In order to have 'On -line' electronic flow of data and information between the Ministry and the State nodal agencies, the State Governments, R&D and technology institutions and non-governmental organisations associated with the renewable energy sector, it has been decided to establish a Renewable Energy Wide Area Computer Communication Network called RENET. The MNES is providing grants-in-aid to the State nodal agencies up to the extent of 50% of the total cost, subject to a maximum of Rs. 3.00 lakh per State nodal agency for the installation of VSAT communication link.

Data base and data bank

The basic infrastructure and software development for data management has been created in the Ministry which is being routinely used for storage of data, its processing and report generation for various programmes. This includes finance budgeting, accounts and preparation of payrolls of the Ministry officials, monitoring of public grievances, Diary and State-wise and programme-wise report generation for renewable energy installations. Computerised information/database for various programmes of the Ministry is currently being maintained by different Programme Divisions with the help of independent workstations available with the concerned Divisions. In order to provide access to the computerised information within the Ministry and to outstation users, it is proposed to create structured databases/databanks based on pre-designed input and output formats and customised software.

The State nodal agencies have also been requested to send the formats being used by them for management information system and monitoring of projects and programmes to the MNES for the purpose of standardization of such formats for creation of renewable energy database/databanks which can be accessed by all the agencies through the RENET-VSAT-NICNET-based communication links.

Home page/web site

The MNES has prepared and launched a Web-Page providing information on fiscal and financial incentives that are available for renewable energy projects and implementation details of various programmes of the Ministry. The MNES Web-site can be accessed through Internet on http://www.nic.in/mnes. Some of the State nodal agencies have also created their respective Web-Pages.

Training for officials

Training sessions in the use of computer hardware, software and E-mail have been organised with the help of NIC during the year. A number of officials of the Ministry participated in these training sessions. Training programme in the use of computer systems for officials of MNES Regional Offices have been organised during the year through NIC Regional Centres at respective locations.

The facilities, so far created, mark a very good

beginning towards large-scale computerisation in all the MNES offices. Efforts are under way for integration of the State nodal agencies, MNES Regional Offices, Solar Energy Centre, technology institutions and the industry with the MNES Headquarters through RENET for creating an Electronic Information Pathway in the area of renewable energy in the country.

Seminars and symposia

One of the most important ingredients of the renewable energy programmes of the MNES is creation of awareness and human resource development through information dissemination, training of manpower, organisation of seminars, symposia, workshops, conferences and study tours, besides participation of scientists and technologists in international events.

Organisation of seminars, symposia, workshops and conferences etc. helps in creating awareness about renewable energy besides providing necessary feedback on the implementation of the ongoing programme and inputs for their continuous refinement. These events also provide a platform to scientists, technologists, policy planners, managers, economists, financial institutions, industry representatives, consultants and entrepreneurs to interact with each other and share their views on various aspects of development of renewable energy sector.

To facilitate these, the MNES has been providing financial and technical support to the government and semi-government organisations, academic and R&D institutions and NGOs for organising seminars, symposia, workshops, conference, short-duration awareness campaigns etc.

During 1998-99, the following major events were supported by the Ministry:

i) International Workshop on Energy for Growth and Sustainability organised by Indian National Academy of Engineering.

ii) Energy Summit '98,- the 3rd International Exhibition and Conference on Energy Management organised by Confederation of Indian Industry.

iii) Sixth International Symposia on Renewable Energy Education organised by Tata Energy Research Institute, New Delhi.

iv) Seminar on "Use of Renewable Energy Sources" organised by Vivekanand Kendra, Kanyakumari.

v) Seminar on Battery Operated Vehicles organised by MEDA, Pune, Maharashtra.

vi) Seminar on "Effective use of Non-conventional Energy Sources in High Altitude Areas" organised by the College of Military Engineering, Pune.

vii) Seminar for opinion leaders on non-conventional energy sources organised by NEDA, Lucknow.

viii) Orientation programme for managers of science and technology at Hamdard Nagar, New Delhi.

ix) Workshop on Renewable Energy organised by Assam Science, Technology and Environment Council, Guwahati.

x) Business Meet on Renewable Energy organised by the Forum of Scientists, Engineer and Technologists (FOSET) at Calcutta.

In addition to the above, the Ministry supported eight training programmes.

Information dissemination and awareness generation

Dissemination of information and generation of pubic awareness play an important role in promoting any new device or technology. This is true all the more in promoting systems and devices based on new and renewable sources of energy (NRSE), particularly in the context of the general impression that the NRSE devices are costlier than those based on conventional fossil fuels. The task of removing this impression and convincing the prospective users about the benefits of using the NRSE devices calls for a well thought out strategy. The information dissemination and public awareness programme, initiated by the MNES, aims at popularisation of the non-conventional renewable energy devices and systems throughout the country by highlighting the advantages of using NRSE devices in the long term, though not initially, and bringing to the fore a number of other tangible and intangible benefits that accrue by using NRSE devices.

The programme seeks to disseminate information on technological developments and promotional activities, taking place in the NRSE sector, through a variety of media to reach the target groups in all sections of the society. This has also helped in creating an environment conducive for the manufacturers of these devices and the users to come together on a common platform, leading to market development and rapid commercialisation of NRSE technologies and devices. The message for adoption of NRSE devices is conveyed through the electronic media, print media and postal stationery, and exhibitions-both static and mobile.

Electronic media

A sponsored programme titled "Nai Rah Apnao" is broadcast on every Tuesday at 20:15 hrs. from 30 Commercial Broadcasting Stations (CBS) of the All India Radio in 12 languages (list given in Table- 1). This is a drama-based programme, wherein the drama sequences, technical information on NRSE devices and popular film songs are interwoven in a manner interesting to the listeners, providing in the process entertainment as well as valuable information about the renewable energy products and devices to them.

During 1998-99, the following modifications were incorporated in the programme to make it more appealing to the listeners:

— Introduction of 'Inami Yojana'. Under the Inami Yojana a cash prize of Rs. 200/- is given to a listener, on draw basis, for replying correctly to the question asked for in each episode of the programme.

— The subjects of renewable energy namely Biomass — Gassification/Briquetting, Solar Drying Systems, Integrated Rural Energy Programme, Energy Parks, Solar Passive Architecture, and Water Mills were included in the programme.

— The launch of the Inami Yojana was announced through a "Promo" of 30-seconds capsule from FM and CBS Stations.

— Since the launch of the Inami Yojana, questions and answers of listeners were dropped.

— The programme style has been changed to make it more pleasant to listen.

— The programme broadcast from the commercial broadcasting stations in Goa is now produced in Konkan language, instead of Hindi as in the past.

The programme has been in operation since July 20, 1993. Its continuation in the next financial year i.e. 1999-2000 is under consideration. The programme covers almost all the renewable energy technologies being propagated by the MNES. During 1998-99, as many as 44 episodes have been broadcast by the end of January, 1999. Another 8 episodes would be broadcast by 31.3.99.

Table 1

List of commercial broadcasting stations & languages covered

Stations	Languages
Mumbai	Marati
Nagpur	-do-
Pune	-do-
Chennai	Tamil
Tiruchirapalli	-do-
Hyderabad	Telugu
Vijaywada	-do-
Bangalore	Kannada
Dharwad	-do-
Thiruvananthapuram	Malayalam
Khozikode	-do-
Vadodara	Gujarati
Ahmedabad	-do-
Rajkot	-do-
Chandigarh	Punjab
Jalandhar	-do-
Calcutta	Bangla
Delhi	Hindi
Jaipur	-do-
Kanpur	-do-
Lucknow	-do-
Patna	-do-
Allahabad	-do-

Bhopal	-do-
Jodhpur	-do-
Indore	-do-
Ranchi	-do-
Panaji	Konkan
Srinagar	Urdu
Cuttak	Oriya

Besides the above programme through the AIR, production of films, fillers videospots radio spots and jingles/serials is undertaken based on the requirements of the Ministry. Video films and fillers were telecast through Regional Kendras of Doordarshan on biogas, improved chulha, solar cooker, solar water heating systems and solar photovoltaic devices.

Print media & postal stationery

Thematic advertisements and press releases on various renewable energy technologies, systems and devices are being issued for publication in English, Hindi and other regional language newspapers and magazines. The Ministry also brings out brochures, folders, booklets on different renewable energy programmes in English, Hindi and regional languages.

During 1998-99 the following advertisements were released :

— One full page advertisement in the issue dated August 15, 1998, on the occasion of Independence Day.

— One full page advertisement on "Power from Renewables" in the issue dated January 26, 1909 on the occasion of Republic Day.

Table 2

Radio sponsored programme 1998-99 Renewable energy technologies covered

Name of the Programmes	Number of Programmes	Date of Broadcast
Solar Passive Architecture	2	14.4.98 & 09.3.99
Solar Photovoltaics Systems (Solar Lantern, Home Lighting Systems)	3	26.5.98, 30.6.98 & 2 8.7.9 8
Solar Photovoltaic Pumping	3	19.5.98, 16.6.98 & 21.7.98
Solar Photovoltaic Power Plants (Decentralized)	3	12.5.98, 09.6.98 & 14.7.9 8
Solar Water Heating Systems (Domestic)	3	01.12.98, 12.1.99 & 09.2.99
Solar Cooker	3	22.9.98, 02.3.99 & 30.3.98
Solar Drying Systems	2	17.11.98 & 02.2.98
Solar Water Heating Systems (Industrial)	3	15.12.98, 26.1.99 & 23.2.99
Wind Electric Generators	3	21.4.98, 11.8.98 & 15.9.98

Wind Pumping	2	28.4.98 & 25.8.98
Cogeneration	3	05.5.98, 01.9.98 & 29.9.98
Biogas	3	07.4.98, 05.1.99 & 23.3.99
Improved Chulha	3	06.10.98, 27.10.98 & 29.12.98
Biomass Gassification/Briquetting	2	04.8.98 & 08.12.98
Urban & Industrial Waste	3	13.10.98, 24.11.98 & 16.2.99
Small Hydro	3	07.7.98, 18.8.98 &08.9.98
Solar Photovoltaic Power Plants (Grid-interfaced)	2	02.6.98 & 23.6.98
Battery Operated Vehicles	2	10. 11.98 & 19.1.99
Energy Parks	2	03.11.98 & 16.3.99
Integrated rural Energy Programme	2	20.10.98 & 2 2.12.98
Total	52 Nos.	

— Two quarter-page advertisements on Solar Energy Centre regarding "Competition on Renewable Energy" for school children and "Visits of Students at SEC".

Two booklets one on "Wind Power Development in India", and the other on "Energy Recovery from Urban, Municipal & Industrial Wastes" have been printed. Cne booklet on "Renewable Energy" in English, and special issues of Urja Bharati on "Women, Energy & Development" and "Small Hydro Power" are under print. Three booklets on Solar Water Heating Technology, Glimpse of Solar Energy Centre, Consultancy Services on Renewable Energy by Solar Energy Centre are also under print. Statutory publications like the Annual Report of the Ministry are also published in Hindi and English.

The renewable energy devices are also promoted through crisp messages printed on postal stationery like post cards, inland letters, aerogrammes, post office saving bank pass books etc. This activity is undertaken through the Department of Posts in an effective manner (the details are given in Table 3).

Table 3

List of postal stationary and the renewable energy technologies covered

Postal Stationery	Quantity to Be printed (in million)	Message/ Subject
Post cards	10	Improved Chulha
Inland Letters	08	Biogas
Aerogrammes	03	Wind Farm
Post office Saving Pass Books	02	Solar Lantern

Exhibitions

Exhibition is one of the most effective media at the grass roots through which any product can be popularised. Since "seeing is believing", the prospective users can see for themselves the working and the advantages of the devices exhibited. The Ministry has, therefore, been participating in exhibitions at international, national and State levels every year on the basis of proposals received from State nodal agencies, Indian Trade Promotion Organisation, the NGOs and other institutions, The Ministry tries to cover almost every State/UT with at least one exhibition by giving financial assistance to the State nodal agencies.

The exhibitions organised/supported by the Information & Public Awareness Division are in two parts. One is the indoor display consisting of attractive photographic panels of the systems and devices with informative write-ups, working models, LED models, charts, posters, etc., besides screening of video films on renewable energy in English, Hindi and regional languages. Publicity material such as brochures, handouts and folders are distributed free of cost to the visitors. The second part is the outdoor display consisting of live demonstration of renewable energy systems and devices like solar cooker, solar photovoltaic lantern solar photovoltaic street fighting system, solar photovoltaic pumping system and other devices for domestic applications like solar water heating systems, improved woodstove, etc.

The Ministry has taken the initiative to promote the participation of renewable energy industry in national and international trade fairs and exhibitions. Under this, the Ministry provided partial financial assistance to the industry to participate in exhibitions in India and abroad such as the Dakar International Trade Fair '98, and the Clean-Tech Environment Exhibition '99. New Delhi.

During 1998-99 the Ministry participated in two major exhibitions of international level namely India International Trade Fair '98 at Pragati Maidan, New Delhi, and International Trade Fair at Dakar in Senegal. So far, 13 State level exhibitions have also been organised in different States of the country through the State nodal agencies. As a result of the participation in the exhibition at Dakar there was all-round appreciation of the renewable energy industry and of India's achievements in the development and promotion of NRSE technologies.

Mobile Exhibition Vans (MEVs)

Besides participating in international, national and State level exhibitions, the Ministry, as a matter of deliberate policy, promotes renewable energy in rural and remote areas through mobile exhibition vans. There are two kinds of mobile exhibition van, one with a large chassis and the other with a small one. The large one costs around Rs. 13.00 lakh, whereas the small one costs around Rs. 11.00 lakh.

The Ministry provides 50% of the procurement cost of the MEV as financial assistance to the States, except those in the North East and Sikkim for whom 100% grant is provided. The MEVs are fitted with working systems and devices of renewable energy viz. biogas, improved chulha, SPV street lighting system, SPV home lighting system, SPV pumping system, wind mill, solar water heating system, solar cooker, etc. These MEVs also have provision for showing video films, photographic display and printed material to the viewers.

The recurring expenses i.e. cost of diesel, driver, maintenance and other incidental expenses, are to be borne by the concerned State/UT Government. The MEVs and the renewable energy devices are provided by the MNES according to the needs of the concerned State/UT. These MEVs are currently being designed and fabricated by the Punjab Energy Development Agency (PEDA), Chandigarh under the supervision of the MNES. The PEDA also provides training in the operation and maintenance of the MEV to the staff of the concerned State/UT Government in Chandigarh before handing over the MEV to them.

During the year, a mobile exhibition van was made available to Andaman & Nicobar. The mobile exhibition vans meant for Nagaland and Karnataka are under fabrication. During the year, 400 exhibitions through the MEVs were organised. The list of States/Uts, which are having MEVs, is given in Table 4.

Table 4

List of states having MEVs

Small size	Big size
1. Arunachal Pradesh	I. Assam
2. Mizoram	2. Delhi
3. Manipur	3. Bihar
4. Himachal Pradesh	4. Haryana
5. Jammu & Kashmir	5. Madhya Pradesh
6. Tripura	6. Punjab
	7. Pondicherry
	8. Orissa
	9. Kerala
	10. Rajasthan
	11. Tamilnadu
	12.Gujarat
	13. Uttar Pradesh
	14. Meghalaya
	15. Andaman & Nicobar

Exhibits like photographic blow-ups, write-ups have also been prepared during the year 1998-99. The Ministry is having a Photo Unit for the coverage of NRSE installations and providing photographs, transparencies and slides for use in the print media, exhibitions, seminars, conferences and to outside agencies. The photo unit also arranges for photographic and video coverage of important activities of the Ministry.

Other activities

Library

The Ministry has a library which caters mainly to the day-to-day requirements of the staff and for reference. The library, which also runs a reading room, is well stocked with literature and publications on technical, financial and administrative topics. The library has proposed to acquire more books and journals, besides starting a newsletter and an abstract service. It is also proposed to have exchange of literature with State nodal agencies, including translation in respective regional languages to facilitate wide publicity for NRSE devices. It continues to provide clipping services. During the year a number of books including books in Hindi were purchased for the Library

Annual awards

During the year it was decided to give awards to four State implementing agencies for their outstanding, and significant performance in the area of publicity. Gujarat and Punjab were awarded respectively for outstanding and significant performance under Category-I (large States) while Kerala and Meghalaya won these awards respectively under Category-II (small States).

Miscellaneous

The Ministry is a member of the National Science Centre, which has a permanent Energy Hall at the Pragati

Maidan, New Delhi. This is managed by the National Council of Science Museum. The National Science Centre has a permanent display of various NRSE systems and devices, photographic panels and models.

Energy parks

A new scheme for the setting up of Energy Parks in educational institutions and in public places to create awareness and give publicity amongst the students, teachers and the rural and urban masses, about the use and benefits of renewable energy systems and devices was approved by the Ministry in 1994-95.

The energy park projects are sanctioned to well known educational institutions, registered consumer fora and well established registered NGOs which have adequate facilities for science and environment education. The energy park projects set up in educational institutions help technical experimentation by, and practical knowledge of, the students and to provide opportunities for hands-on-experience in the various renewable energy technologies. Energy parks may also be set up by the State Governments and renewable energy agencies. Under this scheme, the MNES provides 100% funding towards procurement of systems and devices and their installation as one-time funding. A maximum of 10 Energy Parks are sanctioned in each State. The cost of Energy Parks ranges between Rs. 1.00 lakh and Rs. 10.00 lakh.

In order to strengthen the Energy Park scheme, an Expert Group was constituted by the Ministry in March, 1997. The Expert Group has given its recommendations on various aspects including provision for maintenance and service charges to the State Government nodal agencies which have been incorporated in the revised guidelines of the scheme. As per the recommendations of the Expert Group, 7% of the capital cost of the energy systems and devices may be provided as maintenance charges to the institutions to ensure proper upkeep and maintenance for a period of 4 years starting from the second year. The State Government nodal agencies will now be paid Rs. 5000/- per institution/park for monitoring the progress of implementation of the project. Under the scheme, the funds are routed through the State nodal agencies.

So far, 140 Renewable Energy Park projects have been sanctioned to various educational institutions including IITs, universities, colleges, schools etc. These projects have been sanctioned in 25 States/UTs namely Andhra Pradesh, Arunachal Pradesh, Assam, Bihar, Delhi, Goa, Gujarat, Haryana,, Himachal Pradesh, Karnataka, Kerala, Madhya Pradesh, Maharashtra, Manipur, Mizoram, Orissa, Punjab, Rajasthan, Tamil Nadu, Tripura, Uttar Pradesh, West Bengal, A&N Islands, Chandigarh and Pondicherry.

A typical Energy Park scheme includes improved chulhas (Fixed/Portable type), solar PV street lights system, solar PV domestic lights, solar PV lanterns, solar water heating system (100-500 lpd), solar cookers, solar still (2.5 to 3 lpd), biogas plant (cut model) and solar radio, with one of the energy systems such as solar PV colour TV, solar PV pump and wind pump (depending upon the availability of water well and wind speed) as optional. However, modifications in the package are done on case-to-case basis after assessment by the Committee on Energy Park of the Ministry.

During 1998-99, 27 Energy Park projects were completed. This is in addition to 33 projects completed during the previous financial years. Of the 27 Energy Park projects completed in 1998-99, 5 are in Andhra Pradesh, 8 in Kerala, 6 in Punjab, 3 in Rajasthan and 1 each in Karnataka, Orissa, Tamil Nadu, Tripura and Uttar

Pradesh. The response of the visitors and users to the completed Energy Parks has been enthusiastic. The State-wise number of Energy Park project was proposed to take up 36 new Energy Parks during 1998-99. An amount of Rs. 90.00 lakh was provided for 1998-99. Fourteen Energy Park projects have been cleared by the Committee on Energy Parks for sanction during 1998-99.

4

Rural Energy

Energy is a basic necessity of life and the main sources of energy for the rural people, who constitute the majority of the population of the country are biomass fuels like firewood, agricultural residues, and cattle dung. The rural people are not merely the consumers but also the producers and owners of these biomass fuels. However, the extraction of energy from biomass resources has, over the years, become unsustainable due to the ever increasing population pressure on the one hand and the low level of efficiency of traditional stoves like chulhas used for burning these fuels to extract energy. Moreover, the low efficiency of the traditional chulhas leads to higher smoke discharge in the kitchens, which leads to deterioration in the indoor air quality and adversely affects the health of women.

The time spent by rural women and girl children in gathering the biomass fuels also has a social impact in terms of opportunity cost of the lost time that could otherwise have been spent in child care, enhancing literacy levels and in other productive activities. The age-old practice of burning dried cattle dung cakes in the kitchen is depriving the soils of the much needed organic manure, thereby affecting the agricultural productivity. All these bring to the fore the urgent need to develop and promote technologies for efficient conversion and utilisation of biomass fuels, with a view to extracting more energy from the same quantity of materials, reducing household consumption of fuel wood and improving the general standard of living of the rural population. The Ministry of Non-Conventional Energy Sources (NINES) has been working in this direction ever since its inception through a number of programmes aimed at promoting the development and deployment of efficient technologies for biogas production, improved chulhas, biomass gasification and biomass briquetting.

Biogas production

The biogas system comprises collection and processing of cattle dung, production and delivery of biogas and handling and application of the digested slurry in agricultural fields. The production process consists of mixing wet cattle dung with equal quantity of water and allowing it to get into the biogas plant, where it is retained for a set period of time for digestion in the absence of air. The gas thus produced contains about 55 to 75 per cent methane which is inflammable. It is collected and piped to the kitchen. When this gas is burnt in silk mantles, it serves as a source of light. It can also be used in dual-fuel engines for motive power and generation of electricity.

Three basic designs of biogas plants have been developed. These are the Fixed Dome Deenbandhu Model, the Floating Gas Holder KVIC (Khadi and Village Industries Commission) Model and the Bag Type Digestor. These biogas plant models are promoted under two projects. One is the National Project on Biogas Development (NPBD), which seeks to promote biogas plants for household use and the other is the Community, Institutional and Night-Soil based Biogas Plants Programme, which aims at promoting biogas plants for use at the community and institutional levels.

These programmes help in recycling cattle dung to harness its fuel value without destroying its value as manure.

Improved chulhas

A variety of biomass-based, efficient, smokeless chulhas have been developed to meet the requirements of different types and mix of fuel materials, varied food habits and household sizes and communities. The thermal efficiency of the improved chulhas approved for promotion is about 20 to 35 per cent, as compared to 6 to 10 per cent in the traditional chulhas. The fixed type improved chulhas have one, two or three pot-holes and chimneys and are made of bricks/stones and clay, pottery liners, cement concrete, etc. Portable chulhas are made of metal, metal-clad ceramic and metal clad re-castable material. A model of a high altitude chulha has also been developed for cooking and space heating in colder areas. The National Programme on Improved Chulhas is being implemented since 1985-86.

Biomass gasification

The biomass gasifier converts fuelwood and agricultural residues into a 'producer gas' through a thermo-chemical process. The producer gas generally contains, by volume, about 13-15% hydrogen, 18-25% carbon monoxide, 5-10% carbon dioxide and 48-54% nitrogen. Its calorific value is about 5,500 kJ/Nm3. it can be used in burners and boilers. When it is used in dual-fuel engines, it is first cleaned to remove particulates and tar and then cooled. Biomass gasifies with capacity ranging from 500 to 750 kW have been developed indigenously and are promoted under the Biomass Gasifier Demonstration Programme.

Biomass briquetting

Loose biomass is either charred and compacted or directly compacted in the form of briquettes to serve as

'B grade" coal. Biomass briquettes made through manual process can be used as cooking fuel in the domestic sector, whereas briquettes produced through mechanical presses, which are hard and dense, can be used in boilers and furnaces. Die and punch type machines of capacities up to 1500 kg/hr are manufactured in the country for production of briquettes from agricultural residues and agro-industrial by-products. These are being promoted through an Interest Subsidy Scheme.

National project on biogas development

The National Project on Biogas Development (NPBD), which seeks to promote family type biogas plants, was started in 1981-82 with the objectives of providing fuel to rural households for cooking purpose and organic manure for application in agricultural fields thereby mitigating the drudgery of rural women; reducing the pressure on forests and recycling human waste by linking toilets with bio-as plants, thereby improving sanitation. Multi-model and multi-agency approaches are being adopted for promoting biogas plants in the country. Both the Fixed Dome and the Floating Gas Holder models are being popularised.

The nodal departments in the States, the State-sector corporate bodies and societies are implementing this project. Besides, the Khadi and Village Industries Commission (KVIC), the National Dairy Development Board (NDDB) and non-governmental organisations (NGOs), such as the All India Women's Conference (AIWC) in New Delhi and the Sustainable Development Agency (SDA) in Kanjirapally (Kerala) are actively associated in promoting biogas plants. The KVIC, the AIWC and the SDA are, in turn, involving a large number of grassroots level NGOs and trained masons and technicians. So far, over 27.10 lakh family type plants have been set up in the country. But this represents a coverage of only one-fifth of the total estimated potential of 12 million plants based on the assumption that one-third of the dung produced annually from 232 million cattle in the country would be available for biogas production and recycling in agriculture.

Target and achievement

A target of setting up 1.33 lakh family type biogas plants was set for 1998-99 with a Budget Estimate of Rs. 54.24 crore. Around 54,250 plants were setup during the period April - December 1998. The State-wise and agency-wise achievements vis-a-vis the targets are given in Table 3.2. The target set for the year is expected to be achieved in full.

Toilet-linked plants

Sanitary disposal of human waste can be ensured when the toilets are linked with biogas plants. Hence, under the NPBD, toilet-linked biogas plants are being promoted. A target of setting-up of 15,000 cattle dung-based biogas plants, linked with household toilets was fixed for 1998-99. Against this target, 3,000 plants have been set up during the period April - December 1998. This scheme has gained popularity in West Bengal, Maharashtra, Gujarat, Himachal Pradesh, and Uttar Pradesh.

Financial incentives

The NPBD provides for the following financial incentives:

i) Central Subsidy: A fixed amount is given as Central subsidy according to the category of the beneficiaries and area. The amount was enhanced for North-Eastern States and Sikkim during 199899. The details of Central subsidy are given in Table 3.3.

ii) Sanitary Toilet-linked Plants: An additional Central subsidy of Rs 500 per plant is given for linking plants with sanitary toilets wherever feasible.

iii) Turnkey Job Fee: A sum of Rs. 5001- per plant is given to approved entrepreneurs, trained masons and technicians, the State-sector corporate bodies and non-governmental organisations for installation of plants on a turnkey basis with free maintenance serving warranty for the first three years. However, the turnkey job fee is higher, i.e. Rs. 700/- per plant, in North-Eastern States (excluding the plains in Assam); Sikkim; Jammu and Kashmir; Himachal Pradesh; other notified hilly areas; Andaman and Nicobar Islands and Lakshwadeep.

iv) Incentive for Saving Diesel: Financial assistance is provided at the rate of Rs. 2,500/- per plant for purchase of a kit to modify a diesel engine to work as dual-fuel engine and for one or two plastic or rubber balloons.

Target ranges	Amount of service charges
100- 3000 plants	Rs. 0.50 lakh + Rs. 250 per plant in excess of 200 plants.
3001-7000 plants	Rs. 7.5 lakh + Rs. 100 per plant in excess of 3000 biogas plants.
Above 7001 plants	Rs. 11.50 lakh + Rs. 75 per plant in excess of 7,000 plants subject to a maximum of Rs. 22.00 lakh

v) Assistance for Demonstration Plants in Schools: A sum of Rs. 10,000 or 70 % of the total cost of a small capacity biogas plant, two toilets and a water storage tank is given to schools, especially girls schools in rural areas for demonstration purpose. A target of covering about 500 schools was planned for 1998-99.

vi) Service Charges and Staff Support: The rates of

service charges are linked with the target-ranges as indicated below. However, the North-Eastern States, Sikkim and Jammu and Kashmir are given full Central financial assistance for the sanctioned staff.

Table

National project on biogas development achievements vis-a-vis targets

Family-type Biogas Plants.

(In Nos.)

State/UT/Agency	Annual Target	Achievement (April-Dec., 98)
Andhra Pradesh	14000	9848
Arunachal Pradesh	100	-
Assam	500	61
Bihar	500	580
Goa	75	70
Gujarat	10200	948
Haryana	1500	955
Himachal Pradesh	750	442
Jammu & Kashmir	50	-
Karnataka	12500	796
Kerala	1000	280
Madhya Pradesh	13000	2297
Maharashtra	12000	3050
Manipur	200	130
Meghalaya	100	-
Mizoram	200	112
Nagaland	200	-
Orissa	6000	3054
Punjab	8000	3676

Rajasthan	1000	574
Sikkim	200	166
Tamilnadu	1500	907
Tripura	100	9
Uttar Pradesh	8500	4276

Table

Rates of central subsidy for family type biogas plants followed in 1998-99 under NPBD.

Category	Amount of Central Subsidy per plant.
North Eastern Region States and Sikkim, Himachal Pradesh, Jammu & Kashmir, 8 hilly districts of Uttar Pradesh (excluding Terai region of 2 hilly districts) Andaman & Nicobar Islands and Lakshwadweep, Nilgiris of Tamil Nadu; Sadar, Kursoong & Kalimpong Subdivisions of Darjeeling Distt. (West Bengal).	Rs. 6,000
SC, ST, desert distts., small and marginal farmers, Land-less labourers, Terai Region of two hilly Distts. Of UP, Western ghats and other notified hilly are as	Rs. 2,300
All others	Rs. 1,800

vii) Grant for Biogas Extension Centres: A nonrecurring grant of Rs. 10,000/- and a recurring grant of Rs. 20,0C0 per year is given to district level Biogas Extension Centres sanctioned for organisation of users' courses in villages.

viii) Training Courses: Financial assistance is given for organising different types of training courses as mentioned below:

Course	Duration	Central financial assistance per course
Users' training	One day	Rs. 1,250
Staff training	2-3 days	Rs. 5,000
Refresher/Construction cum Trainers training	16 days	Rs. 17,000 for BTCs and Rs. 19,000 for Nodal deptts and agencies
Turnkey workers training	25 days	Rs. 30,000

ix) Communication and Publicity: The Central financial assistance for communication and publicity work linked with target ranges is given to each State nodal department and agency as mentioned below:

Target Range	Amount
Up to 1,000 plants	Rs. 1.00 lakh
1,001 - 10,000 plants	Rs. 2.50 lakh
More than 10,000 plants	Rs. 5.00 lakh

Technical backup support

In order to provide training, technical and publicity support in a decentralised manner to the State nodal departments and agencies for effective and accelerated implementation of the NPBD, Biogas Training Centres (BTCs) have been established in all the major States. The BTCs are functioning at the University of Agricultural Sciences, Bangalore (Karnataka); Haryana Agricultural University, Hisar (Haryana); Andhra Pradesh Agricultural University, Hyderabad (Andhra Pradesh); Assam Agricultural University, Jorhat (Assam); Indian Institute of Technology, Kharagpur (West Bengal); Punjab

Agricultural University, Ludhiana (Punjab); H.P. Agricultural University, Palampur (Himachal Pradesh); Rajasthan Agricultural University, Udaipur (Rajasthan); and Tamil Nadu Agricultural University; Coimbatore (TN). These Centres are also carrying out applied research on area-specific problems. Full financial assistance is given for staff, contingencies, training, etc.

District-level Biogas Extension Centres (BECs) have been established in selected areas to create decentralised infrastructure for organising courses for the users. So far, a total of 15 BECs have been sanctioned, one each in Assam, Gujarat, Kerala, Orissa, Tripura, SDA, and AIWC; two each in Uttar Pradesh and Tamil Nadu and four in Maharashtra.

Training

The State Governments, the programme implementing agencies, the BTCs and the BECs have targeted organisation of 2,500 users' courses; 145 construction-cum-maintenance courses; 85 staff training courses and 30 turnkey workers courses during 199899. The details of the targets are given in Table.

Table

State/Agency-wise targets for construction-cum-maintenance and users' training courses planned during 1998-99

State/U.T.	Number of construction-cum-maintenance training course	Number ofus users training course
Andhra Pradesh	3	100
Arunachal Pradesh	1	2
Assam	1	5
Bihar2	10	
Goa	1	5
Gujarat	5	100

Haryana	-	5
Himachal Pradesh	1	5
Jammu & Kashmir	1	1
Karnataka	5	50
Kerala	3	30
Madhya Pradesh	5	100
Maharashtra	1	50
Manipur	1	4
Meghalaya	1	2
Mizoram	1	5
Nagaland	1	5
Orissa	5	too
Punjab	1	10
Rajasthan	1	10
Sikkim	1	4
Tamilnadu	2	20
Tripura	1	2
Uttar Pradesh	10	200
West Bengal	2	100
A & N Islands	I	I
Dadra & Nagar Haveli	I	I
Pondicherry	I	I
Others	38	347
Total	100	1275

Institutional financing

The Reserve Bank of India (RBI) and the National Bank for Agriculture and Rural Development (NABARD) have been supporting the biogas programme. There are detailed guidelines with both commercial and co-operative banks for financing biogas plants. The NABARD is providing automatic refinancing facility to the commercial banks for the loan amount disbursed for biogas plants.

Publicity and awareness generation

Publicity and awareness generation campaigns continue to form an important component of the NPBD. Advertisements about the benefits of biogas technology and the details of Central and State financial assistance available to the beneficiaries are released periodically in local newspapers. The State Governments and the programme implementing agencies, such as, Punjab Energy Development Agency, the Department of Rural Development, Government of Tamil Nadu; the KVIC, the NDDB, the AIWC and the SDA have widely distributed booklets, brochures, posters, leaflets etc. In Punjab, special efforts have been made to display panels both outside and inside 60 buses running in rural areas.

The Government of Kerala has included the subject of biogas technology in the district-level seminars. The Governments of Manipur and Orissa are publicising the biogas programme through the regional stations of All India Radio and Doordarshan. Besides, the Ministry has got a fifteen-minute programme on biogas broadcast on the commercial stations of All India Radio. A booklet entitled "Biogas Users Guide" published in English in 1997 has been translated into Hindi and Tamil and distributed widely in the States concerned.

Monitoring

A three- tier monitoring system is being followed. The first-tier is self-reporting by the State Governments and the agencies involving 100% physical verification at the block level on a quarterly basis and sample verification by the State headquarter staff. The second tier is field inspection of the plants on a random basis by the Regional Offices of the Ministry and Biogas Training

Centres. The third tier is the evaluation study to be conducted once in 3 or 4 years by an independent agency.

Awards

The State Governments and nodal agencies involved in the implementation of NPBD are given awards for their qualitative and quantitative performance. The details of the awardees selected for the year 1997-98 are indicated in Table.

Table 5

Awards given for 1997-98 under National Project on Biogas Development

Category	First Prize (Gold Plated Shield)
States having a target of 10,000 plants or more	Gujarat
States having small targets	Manipur
States which have set up highest number of sanitary toilet linked plants	Maharashtra
Best State under the aegis of KVIC	West Bengal
Best districts for overall performance	Belgaum (Karnataka) Warrangal (A.P.) Nadia (West Bengal)
Best grass roots level NGO under the aegis of AIWC and NDDB.	Unniyan Sansthan, Chunar, Mirzapur, U.P.

Socioeconomiccost benefit analysis

A socioeconomic cost-benefit analysis survey of the NPBD was conducted by the National Council of Applied Economic Research (NCAER). The survey covered a sample of 2,755 biogas plants set up in different years in

102 villages, distributed in 47 Blocks of 10 States, namely, Assam, Gujarat, Himachal Pradesh, Karnataka, Madhya Pradesh, Maharashtra, Orissa, Tamil Nadu, Uttar Pradesh and West Bengal. The Report of the survey was released in September 1998. According to the Report, on an average, 78.9 per cent of the plants surveyed, belonging to the pre-NPBD period and 1982-83 to 1996-97, were functioning. It was observed that the use of biogas helped in reducing the consumption of firewood and twigs by about 1,200 kg per household per year. Besides, a biogas plant produced digested slurry containing nitrogen equivalent to 299 kg of urea every year.

The pay-back period for the investment was found to be 7 years in the case of a 3 cubic metres capacity Fixed Dome model and 12 years for the Floating Gasholder model of the same capacity.

Community, institutional and night-soil biogas plants program

The Community and Institutional Biogas Plants (CBP/IBP) Programme was initiated in 1982-83 to provide fuel for cooking purpose and organic manure to rural households, including the poor families, through large-sized community and institutional biogas plants. Subsequently, in order to facilitate the sanitary treatment of human waste at the community and institutional level, the setting up of night- soil-based biogas plants (NBPs) was included in 1993-94.

The programme is implemented by State Governments, State nodal agencies and the KVIC. A non-governmental organisation, namely, Sulabh International, New Delhi has also been involved in the promotion of community toilet-linked large-sized biogas plants. So far, a total of 2402 plants, including 550 nightsoil-based have been installed. Of these, as many as 263 plants were set up in 1997-98 alone. The State-wise details of the number of community, institutional and night-soil based biogas plants set up are given in Table.

Target and achievement

A target of setting up of 350 plants was fixed for 1998-99 with a Budget Estimate of Rs. 7.80 crore. Particulars of the targets allocated to different States and agencies are given in Table. During the period April to December, 1998, a total of 40 plants were set up in Karnataka, Maharashtra, Punjab and Uttar Pradesh, while work is in progress in different States to achieve the remaining targets.

Table

CBP/IBP/NBP Programme : State/UT-wise plants set up Up to the year 1997-98

State/U.T.	Number of large sized plants set up under CBP/IBP/NBP
Andhra Pradesh	71
Assam	2
Bihar	15
Gujarat	124
Haryana	14
Himachal Pradesh	3
Jammu & Kashmir	4
Karnataka	18
Kerala	5
Madhya Pradesh	96
Maharashtra	295
Orissa	33
Punjab	341
Rajastan	48
Tamilnadu	112

Uttar Pradesh	439
West Bengal	32
Delhi	17
Pondicherry	1
Total	2,362

Financial incentives

A fixed amount is given as Central financial assistance (CFA) to the panchayats, local bodies, institutions, dairies, etc., for setting up community, institutional and night-soil based biogas plants as per the details indicated in Table-3.8. In addition, project contingency assistance is provided at the rate of 10 per cent of the CFA to State nodal departments and agencies for determining the feasibility and supervising the construction work for CBP, IBP and small-sized NBP. The amount of project contingency is 20 per cent of the CFA for 35, 45 and 60 cubic metres capacity NBP, with a provision for a minimum of 20 years' free operation and maintenance warranty.

Table

CBP/IBP/NBP Programme : State-wise/Agency-wise targets allocated for 1998-99

State	Target (No. of plants)
Andhra Pradesh	2
Assam	2
Bihar	1
Gujarat	5
Haryana	5
Karnataka	5
Kerala	2
Madhya Pradesh	3
Maharashtra	40

Nagaland	10
Orissa	5
Punjab	40
Rajasthan	10
Tamil Nadu	10
Uttar Pradesh	40
West Bengal	10
KVIC	150
Sulabh International	10
Total	350

Community toilet-linked biogas complexes

The concept of community toilet-linked biogas complex has become popular in Uttar Pradesh and Maharashtra. The Non-Conventional Energy Development Agency of Uttar Pradesh (NEDA) has installed about 150 community toilet linked biogas complexes, mostly in the slum areas of Agra, Faizabad, Ghaziabad, Kanpur, Lucknow, Varanasi cities. These complexes have been given on 30 years' lease to private entrepreneurs, who, in turn, have engaged workers for the day-to-day maintenance of these complexes. Each complex is serving a population of about 1000-2000 persons.

The beneficiary families pay Rs. 30/- per month for utilising the toilet facility. The casual users pay Rs. 1/- per use. Biogas is used for operating a dual-fuel engine to lift the underground water to an overhead tank. About five families, living close to the complex, are supplied with biogas for cooking purpose on a payment of Rs. 60 per month. Thus, these complexes are not only operated and maintained on a sustainable basis but also generating income to workers.

In Maharashtra, 15 community toilet-linked biogas plant complexes have been functioning. During 1998-99, the Maharashtra Energy Development Agency (MEDA) has taken up construction of such complexes with an additional financial support from the Local Area Development Fund of the Members of Parliament, Maharashtra Pollution Control Board and Municipal Councils concerned. The Maharashtra Jeevan Pradhikaran has also agreed to provide funds in the gram panchayat areas. During 1998-99, a large toilet complex with three biogas plants of 35 cubic metres capacity each has been commissioned at Sri Sai Baba Ashram in Shirdi. The toilet complex is facilitating daily about 6,000 persons. The biogas is utilised for generation of electricity for lighting the complex and heating of bath water.

Benefits

So far, cumulatively 27.65 lakh family type biogas plants and 2,360 CBP/IBP/NBPs have been put up in the country. These plants are estimated to save about 28 lakh tonnes of firewood per year, based on the finding of the NCAER survey earlier cited, that 79 per cent of the plants are functional and one biogas plant saves about 1,260 kg of fuel wood per year on an average. Besides, these plants are producing digested slurry containing nitrogen equivalent to 6.50 lakh tonnes of urea which is valued at Rs. 260 crore per year.

Apart from these economic benefits, biogas plants are providing many indirect social benefits, such as reduction in the drudgery of rural women and girl children involved in the collection of fuel materials from long distances and cooking in smoky kitchens; reduction in the incidence of lung and eye diseases among women and girl children and improvement in the standard of living. Construction of biogas plants is also generating large-scale employment opportunities for skilled and unskilled labourers. During 1997-98, the employment generation was estimated to be of the order of 5 million man-days from the construction of 1.75 lakh biogas plants. About 1.75 lakh families in rural areas and three lakh persons living in the slums in and around cities have been benefited with sanitation facility from the linking of biogas plants with toilets and community toilet complexes.

Research and development on biogas

Research and development play a vital role in promoting new devices and practices. The following thrust areas of research on biogas have been identified and are being pursued:

— Studies in the field of microbiology, biochemistry and engineering for increasing the biogas yield especially at low and high temperatures;

— Development of cost-effective designs of biogas plants;

— Development of designs and methodologies for — utilisation of biomass other than cattle dung, besides agro-residues for biogas production;

— Reducing the cost of biogas plants by the use of alternative building materials and construction methodology; and

— Diversified use of digested slurry for value-added products.

Production of fuel gas in biogas plants is highly dependent upon ambient temperature and the rate of production gets substantially reduced when the temperature touches less than 25°C. This necessitates the construction of higher capacity plants in the northern States and hilly areas, resulting in a relatively high capital investment. With a view to developing a cost-effective methodology for improving biogas production at low temperatures, four R&D projects sanctioned in

1996-97 and 1997-98 were continued. A brief summary of the work done under these projects is given below:

i) Under a project on Technology for Enhan-cement of Biogas Generation at Low Temperature via Chemical-Microbial Route" at the Indian Institute of Technology, Chennai, laboratory- scale biogas reactors have been stabilised at. 20-25° C. Enrichment studies on cellulose and hemi-cellulose degrading bacteria, acetogens and methanogens present in the samples taken from Nilgiris, have been started.

ii) The Tata Energy Research Institute, New Delhi has taken up a project on "Methanogenesis under Low Temperature Conditions for Optimum Production of Biogas from Agricultural Residues, and Cattle Dung." Digesters have been set up with samples collected from Nainital in Uttar Pradesh and Shimla and Palampur in Himachal Pradesh to function at 10°C. Studies on substitution of cattle dung by different wastes have indicated that lantana weeds, and sugarcane trash are not suitable, whereas apple waste is found to substitute 20 per cent with high gas production at 17+ 1° C.

iii) Studies for the development of an efficient heating system for biogas digesters have been carried out at the Department of Chemical Engineering, University of Roorkee, Roorkee. A heat exchanger unit has been designed for using a laboratory-scale digester for further studies.

iv) Under the project, "Optimization of Functional Biogas System in Hilly Areas" at Shri AMM Murugappa Chettiar Research Centre, Chennai, the effect of low temperature on the production of biogas is being studied by using experimental reactors buried below the ground level and insulated digesters.

With a view to developing efficient microbial culture for biogas production at high temperatures, i.e. 550 C., work is in progress under the project entitled "High Rate Anaerobic Digestion by Thermophilic Anaerobes" at the Tamil Nadu Agricultural University, Coimbatore. A consortium comprising of high temperature loving cellulose degraders isolated from rumen and biogas digestors and thermophilic methanogens has been developed and a small unit of up-flow reactor has been designed. The studies have shown that inoculation of specialised consortia enhanced the gas production and reduced the retention period.

With the objective of studying the survival of human pathogens and developing guidelines for safe disposal of effluent from night-soil based plants, a project for the development of a design suitable for processing of night-soil mixed with garbage, vegetables, etc., with special reference to pathogens' survival and sanitary disposal of the effluent has been taken up at the All India Institute of Hygiene and Public Health, Calcutta. Studies have been conducted on sludge collected from primary sedimentation tanks and vegetable wastes from market yards and experiments on composite waste feed-stocks, including water hyacinth are in progress.

The Indian Institute of Science, Bangalore, has developed a new plug-flow design of a digester based on leafy biomass under an R&D project sponsored earlier. A few plants have been set up in and around Bangalore for field trials. A biogas plant with capacity to produce 4-5 cubic metres of gas requires a daily feed of about 60 kg. of pressed herbacious and semi-fibrous biomass.

With a view to assessing the emission of methane from biogas plants, a project entitled "Greenhouse Gas Emission from the exposed areas of Biogas Plants" has been sanctioned to the Division of Environmental

Sciences at the Indian Agricultural Research Institute, New Delhi, in December 1998 for a period of one and a half years. The project will also develop a methodology for mitigating the emission of harmful gases.

National programme on improved chulhas

The National Programme on Improved Chulhas (NPIC) was started in 1985-86 with the objectives of conserving fuelwood, thereby checking deforestation; eliminating smoke from kitchens; reducing the drudgery of women and girl children and generating employment in rural areas. So far, over 28.50 million improved chulhas have been promoted in the country against an estimated potential of covering about 120 million rural and semi-urban households.

Models

During 1998-99, special efforts were made to promote only the fixed type efficient chulhas with chimneys to ensure pollution-free kitchens and improve health of women and children. Besides, the fixed chulhas with pottery liners were given importance with a view to increasing the life span of the chulhas and creating employment for potters in rural areas. Portable metallic chulhas with certification of Bureau of Indian Standards (BIS) have also been promoted in selected areas and for selected categories of beneficiaries, where the acceptance and utility of such chulhas will be high. High altitude chulhas were also promoted for cooking and space heating purposes in hilly areas.

Implementation

The NPIC is implemented with a multi-agency approach. In addition to the State Governments and the Union Territory Administrations and the State nodal agencies, the KVIC, the NDDB and the AIWC have been involved. At the village level, several NGOs, Mahila Mandals,

Anganwadis, etc., have been actively involved. In many States, such as Gujarat, Rajasthan, Maharashtra, Madhya Pradesh, Karnataka, Kerala, Haryana, Tamil Nadu, Uttar Pradesh, West Bengal and Tripura, the panchayats have been involved in the identification of beneficiaries. A large number of trained "Self Employed Workers" (SEWs), mainly women, are providing service for the proper construction and maintenance of the fixed type chulhas.

Central financial assistance

Financial assistance is provided by the Ministry for various purposes under the NPIC, which are listed below.

i) Central Subsidy: A fixed amount is given as Central subsidy which varies according to the type of chulhas, the category of beneficiaries and the areas The rates of Central subsidy are listed in Table 9

Table

Rates of central subsidy given during 1998-99 under NPIC

Type of Chulhas	Amount of Central subsidy per chulha
(a) Fixed chulha with chimney	
(i) N.E. Region States & Sikkim	Rs. 80/-
(ii) Other States	Rs. 40/-
(b) Portable Chulha	
(i) N.E. Region States, Sikkim, Andaman & Nicobar Islands, Lakshadweep and notified hilly and desert areas.	Rs. 75/-
(ii) SC/ST beneficiary in other States/Uts	
(c) High Attitude Chulha	Maximum Rs. 250/ limited to 50% of the cost

ii) Technical Support: Full financial assistance is given to Technical Back Up Units (TBUs) functioning in 9 States. Besides, five State Governments, which are supporting TBUs under their respective State Plan Sectors are entitled to receive a sum up to Rs. 5.00 lakh each as additional support specially for publicity and entrepreneurship development.

iii) Assistance for Self Employed Workers: Remuneration is given to trained self-employed workers at the rate of Rs. 20/- per fixed single pot chulha with chimney and Rs. 30/- per 2 or 3 pot fixed chulha with chimney and also for a community chulha. These self-employed workers provide services for construction of chulhas true to approved designs and free maintenance during the first year of installation.

iv) Organisational Infrastructure Support: A sum of Rs. 4/- per chulha is given as organisational support to State Governments and programme implementing agencies.

v) Publicity and Awareness: A minimum assistance of Rs. 30,000/- is given to the States and agencies having an annual target up to 15,000 improved chulhas. The other States and agencies which have an annual target of more than 15,000 chulhas are entitled to receive funds @ Rs. 2/- per chulha, with an upper ceiling of Rs. 2.50 lakh.

vi) Training Support: Full financial assistance is given for organisation of different types of training courses as mentioned below:

vii) Dealership Support: With a view to organising the distribution of portable metallic chulhas with ISI mark through private retailers, dealers, Fair Price Shops/Public Distribution System/village panchayats, Aditya Solar Shops, etc., an incentive is given at the rate of Rs. 51- per chulha promoted either with or without the Central subsidy.

User	Duration	Central financial assistance per course
Self Employed		
Workers Training Course	10 days	Rs. 16,000/-
Entrepreneurship		
Development Course	10 days	Rs. 27,000/-
Trainers' Training	3 days	Rs. 10,000/-
Users' Course	One day	Rs. 1,250/-

Target and achievement

A physical target of promotion of 16 lakh improved chulhas with a Budget Estimate of Rs. 16.65 crore was fixed for 1998-99 after taking into account the spill-over liabilities of the previous years. Against this, about 5 lakh improved chulhas have been installed during April-December, 1998. Details of State-wise and agency-wise annual targets and achievements during April-December, 1998 are given in Table.

Table

National programme on improved chulhas: state-wise and agency-wise targets and achievements made during April-December, 1998.

State/U.T./Agency	Annual Target	Achievement (April to Dec. '98)
Andhra Pradesh	1,00,000	49,198
Arunachal Pradesh	10,000	NIL
Assam	12,000	374
Bihar	20,000	1,185

Gujarat	60,000	33,747
Goa	5,000	754
Haryana	40,000	10,054
Himachal Pradesh	15,000	6,998
Jammu and Kashmir	43,000	NIL
Karnataka	40,000	4,760
Kerala	80,000	11,466
Madhya Pradesh	1,00,000	12,240
Maharashtra	1,00,000	865
Manipur	10,000	242
Meghalaya	8,500	NIL
Mizoram	10,000	1,300
Nagaland	8,500	115
Orissa	1,00,000	69,151
Punjab	75,000	NIL
Rajasthan	75,000	1,081
Sikkim	5,000	3,451
Tamil Nadu	60,000	54,436
Tripura	15,000	3,600
Uttar Pradesh	1,00,000	49,738
West Bengal	1,00,000	86,042
Andaman & Nicobar	1,500	1,015
Dadra and Nagar Haveli	1,200	736
Delhi	2,000	NIL
Lakshwadeep	300	64
Pondicherry	3,000	1.016
KVIC, Mumbai	3,70,000	84,523
NDDB, Anand	8,000	2,544
AIWC, New Delhi	22,000	5,250
Total	16,00,000	4,95,945

Technical support

Nine Technical Back Up Units (TBUs) supported by the Ministry are functioning; one each at Warrangal (Andhra Pradesh); Guwahati (Assam); Indore (Madhya Pradesh); Bhubaneswar (Orissa); Patiala (Punjab); Udaipur (Rajasthan); Coimbatore (Tamilnadu); Kalyani (West Bengal) and Pune (Maharashtra). Besides, five TBUs located at Vadodara, Chandigarh, Solan, Bangalore and Thiruvananthapuram are being supported by their respective State Governments.

The functions assigned to TBUs include applied research and development, training to various target groups, testing and evaluation of chulhas, publicity and awareness generation and monitoring. Four more new models of fixed type improved chulhas with chimneys were developed during April to December 1998. These are detailed given in Table. A target of organising 140 technical training and 598 users' courses was allocated to the TBUs.

Publicity and awareness

Publicity is organised through both print and electronic media for achieving rapid expansion of the programme. The benefits of improved chulhas are publicised in rural and semi-urban areas in regional languages. Three programmes on improved chulhas were sponsored for national broadcast on All India Radio.

Pamphlets, calendars, etc. were brought out in different languages such as Bengali, Marathi, Hindi, Punjabi, English, Tamil, etc. These materials were distributed widely during the training programmes' exhibitions, melas, etc. Several State Governments have arranged display of hoardings and wall paintings on improved chulhas in regional languages at prominent locations. The AIWC displayed the laminated photographs of various models of improved chulhas at the 'Tech Mart - 1998' held at Delhi.

Table

Training Programmes allocated to TBUs and achievements made during April - December, 98

TBU Course	SEW neurship course	Entrepre-Training Courses	Trainers Courses	Users				
T A	T	A	T	A	T	A		
Warrangal	8	5	2	1	3	2	90	17
Guwahati	10	9	2	1	6	1	100	-
Indore	10	7	2	3	3	-	77	46
Pune	4	4	2	-	2	2	25	25
Bhubane-shwar	14	3	3	-	4	-	50	5
Patiala	10	5	2	-	2	-	30	9
Udaipur	15	5	2	-	2	-	84	-
Coimbatore	12	7	2	-	2	-	92	34
Kalyani	13	7	2	-	I	-	50	20
Total	96	52	19	4	25	5		

T - Annual Target

A - Achievement April-December, 1998

The TBU at Kalyani (West Bengal) organised a television programme on 'Improved Chulha - Kalyani Vishwavidalaya' in Bengali language in May, June and November, 1998 through Calcutta Doordarshan Kendra. The TBU has also published a booklet entitled "Unnat Chulha - Nirman, Bhabhar Rakshna Bekshan", containing the details of installation, training and maintenance of improved chulhas. Similarly, the Coimbatore TBU organised a demonstration on different of improved chulhas for the benefit of the tribal people of Valparai in Tamil Nadu. The Pune TBU has prepared a video-film on fabrication and installation of improved chulhas in Marathi language for use in the users' courses.

Monitoring

Under the NPIC, a three-tier monitoring system is being followed. This includes self-monitoring by the State Government Departments/nodal agencies, field inspections by the Regional Offices of the MNES and the TBUs and conduct of an evaluation survey once in three or four years by an independent agency. The State Governments/agencies have reported that about 76 to 98 percent of improved chulhas promoted during 199798 are functional. The details are given in Table.

Table

Functionality of improved chulhas set up during 1997-98 as reported by State Governments/Nodal Agencies

State/UT/agency	Functionality of improved Chulha (%)
Andhra Pradesh	77
Gujarat	76
Goa	95
Haryana	89
Maharashtra	90
Orissa	82

Punjab	88
Sikkim	97
Tamil Nadu	80
Uttar Pradesh	97
West Bengal	93
Andaman & Nicobar Islands	88
Pondicherry	97
KVIC, Mumbai	85
NDDB, Anand	85
AIWC, New Delhi	90

Award Scheme

With a view to encouraging a healthy competition among the States and other implementing agencies, awards are given annually on the basis of qualitative and quantitative achievements.

Table

Awards given for the year 1997-98 under National Programme on Improved Chulhas

Category	States
Best two States	Andhra Pradesh & West Bengal
Promotion of NPIC in far flung areas.	Sikkim
Best State under the aegis of KVIC.	Kerala

Socioeconomic cost-benefit analysis survey

A socioeconomic cost-benefit analysis survey of the NPIC was completed in November 1998 by National Council of Applied Economic Research (NCAER), New Delhi. It covered a sample of 5345 households distributed over 96 villages of 10 States, namely Assam, Gujarat, Himachal

Pradesh, Karnataka, Madhya Pradesh, Maharashtra, Orissa, Tamilnadu, Uttar Pradesh and West Bengal. The study has shown that an improved chulha saved fuel material equivalent to 210 kg coal/soft coke, valued at Rs. 388/- per year. In terms of kerosene, the saving worked out to about 40 litres per chulha per year, valued at Rs. 343/- per household.

Based on the market prices of fuels saved, the study has found the pay-back period on the investment is 5.8 months for a fixed chutha and 7.3 months for a portable chulha on the life cycle costing. In addition, the study has pointed out that the improved chulha has brought about social benefits in terms of saving in time in cooking and cleaning of utensils, and significant reduction in smoke inside the kitchen, thereby resulting in a reduction in the incidences of eye and lung diseases among the family members, particularly women and children. It has also found that promotion of improved chulhas has helped in generating 57,000 mandays per annum, assuming that a self employed worker constructed three fixed chulhas per day.

Biomass programme

The Biomass Production, Conversion and Utilization Programme includes: (i) research and development (R&D) on biomass production, especially to optimize productivity of fuelwood tree species in waste lands and marginally degraded lands and to develop and commercialise biomass gasifier systems for using in domestic and industrial sectors.' (ii) biomass gasifiers demonstration and (iii) promotion of biomass briquetting units.

R&D in biomass production

The new thrust areas identified for applied R&D in biomass production during the Ninth Plan Period are as follows:

— Field surveys of fuel-wood tree species most commonly used in domestic and industrial sectors;
— Feasibility studies on availability and consumption of fuel-wood in domestic and industrial sectors;
— Development of a database on fast growing tree and shrub species suitable for energy usages;
— Establishment of seed banks and seed testing certification facilities;
— Development and standardisation of low-cost high-technology nurseries for supplying improved quality planting materials;
— Studies on eco-physiological behaviour of seedlings and their production pattern under varied environmental conditions;
— Standardisation of suitable methodologies for mass propagation of clones from genetically superior trees;
— Development of packages for the use of bio-fertilizers for hing fuelwood tree species in marginal and degraded lands;
— Provenance testing of exotic tree and shrub species;
— Studies on progeny testing, clonal propagation and seed production stand for best provenance;
— Establishment of seed orchards and clonal gardens for the germplasm of selected fuel-wood trees and shrubs;
— Studies on adaptability, productivity and silvicultural practices, including soil fertility;
— Studies on plant responses to stress and selection of stress tolerant species;
— Studies on water use efficiencies of fuelwood tree species;

— Pest and disease management in ecologically sensitive areas.

So far, one R&D project envisaging studies on selection, adaptability and biomass production of shrub species suitable for sodic soil sites and another on identification of markers for selection of fast growing fuelwood species in relation to improved biomass production have been sanctioned in July, 1998 and September, 1998 to the National Botanical Research Institute at Lucknow and the Vishwa bharati at Shanti Niketan in West Bengal respectively for a period of three years.

R&D on biomass gasifiers

Four Biomass Gasifier Action Research Centres (GARCs) have been functioning since 1992-93, one each at the Indian Institute of Technology (IIT) Delhi; the Indian Institute of Technology (IIT) Mumbai; the Indian Institute of Science (IISc) Bangalore; and the Madurai Kamaraj University (MKU) Madurai. The objectives and activities of these Centres were reviewed by an adhoc committee of experts in January and February, 1998 as well as by the R&D Advisory Committee. The objectives of each of these Centres have been revised in 1998-99. The revised objectives and the work done during the period April to December 1998 are mentioned below :

i) The revised objectives of ıhe Centre at IIT, Delhi are: paralysed biomass based gasifier including briquetting and densification for hilly areas; maintenance and upgradation of biomass characterisation facilities for users and industries; development of beehive briquettes and stove sevaluation and pilot field testing from the angle of cooking and space heating specially in cold hilly areas; and village electrification through biomass gasifiers in a village. The Centre has characterized about 30 biomass samples in terms of proximate analysis, calorific value and thermogravimetric analysis. A throatless downdraft gasifier has been designed for using loose biomass materials. Cracking of the tar present in the gas, which was obtained by pyrolysis of rice husk, has been achieved on hot solid surfaces of different materials. The Centre organised one training course on beehive briquettes for rural youths at village Sitla in Almora district of Uttar Pradesh.

ii) The objectives of the Centre at IIT, Mumbai are: technology assessment with regard to qualifying tests and upgradation of standards for laboratories and field testing for downdraft, updraft and natural flow gasifiers; training courses for manufacturers and nodal agencies and publication of training manuals; application packages for plywood industry; development of specifications for down draft gasifier system; upgradation of the state-of-the-art report on gasification of biomass and preparation of a detailed project report for electrification of a village. Work was carried out for maximisation of diesel replacement in dual-fuel engines. Fuel droplet size, size distribution and consistency of injection process were identified as the main problems at low fuel injection rates.

iii) The objectives of the Centre at the IISc. Bangalore are: formulation of a techno-economic report for power generation packages at 20, 50 and 100 kWe; development of gas engine conversion kits for power level up to 100 kWe; training courses for manufacturers and nodal agencies and publication of training manuals; preparation of a detailed project report for electrification of a village; study of environmental impact due to gaseous emissions and liquid effluents from gasifiers; and application packages for tea and flower drying industries. The

Centre has modified a 25 KVA three cylinder RB 33 diesel engine having a compression ratio of 17 from diesel mode to spark ignition mode by using the same head, but modifying the threaded connection for diesel injection to introduce the spark plug, a magneto for generating high voltage electricity and engine shaft operated distributor to direct the electric charge to the appropriate cylinder at the appropriate crank angle. The results showed that the system worked smoothly on producer gas. The Centre has also developed fine filters by using fabric materials, which are water repellent and have high porosity with very low particle size.

iv) The objectives of the Centre at the MKU, Madurai are: monitoring the performance of gasifiers installed in Andhra Pradesh, Karnataka, Kerala, Pondicherry and Tamil Nadu; testing the performance of newly developed gasifiers; training courses for manufacturers and nodal agencies and publication of training manuals; preparation of a detailed project report for electrification of a village; and application packages for an industry. The Centre has carried out a feasibility study on the adoption of thermal gasifier systems for drying cardamom. One gasifier of 1,25,000 Kcal/hr installed in a chemical factory at Rajapalayani (Tamil Nadu) was evaluated and 10 other systems set up in Andhra Pradesh and Tamil Nadu were monitored during April to December, 1998.

Under the project on development of biomass gasifiers with heat resistant ceramic/ceramic coated metallic components, sanctioned to the Central Glass and Ceramic Research Institute (CGCRI), Calcutta in 1996, a gasifier having reaction zone made of heat resistant cordierite and alternately ceramic coated stainless steel components has been developed and is being evaluated. The Central

Building Research Institute (CBRI), Roorkee, in another R&D project on ecofriendly brick/tile kilns utilising biomass gasifiers, which was sanctioned in 1996, installed a gasifier of 750 kW thermal capacity especially designed by IISc., Bangalore in a down draft brick kiln and monitored its performance.

A Technical Back Up Unit was sanctioned in September, 1998 to the Sardar Patel Renewable Energy Research Institute (SPRERI), Vallabh Vidya Nagar, Gujarat to provide technical support to the State nodal agencies, the gasifier manufacturers and the user industries in Gujarat, Rajasthan and Madhya Pradesh. It will organise training courses and will serve as a trouble shooter.

Demonstration programme

The Biomass Gasifier Demonstration Programme was modified in 1993-94 with its focus on the adoption of a market- oriented approach for the promotion of gasifiers for thermal, mechanical and electrical applications. During the period 1994-95 to 1997-98, a total of around 220 biomass gasifier systems with an aggregate capacity of 17.7 MW were set up in different States for thermal and electrical applications.

A target of setting up of biomass gasifiers of a total capacity of 2.5 MW has been fixed for 1998-99 with a Budget Estimate of Rs. 1.50 crore. The Programme provides for a fixed amount to be given as Central financial assistance varying according to the ratings of the gasifier systems and applications as given in Table-3.16. A scheme for providing higher rates of Central subsidy for cooking applications and for SC/ST hostels, besides paramilitary and police mess rooms, which was initiated in 1995-96, was continued during 1998-99.

Greater emphasis is being laid on the promotion of

biomass gasifiers for village electrification. A sum of Rs. 25,000 is given for the preparation of a detailed project report for a village requiring 40 kW or higher capacity gasifier system. Central financial assistance up to 75 per cent of the project cost, including transmission lines but excluding the cost on land, is given to State nodal agencies and up to 50 per cent of the project cost is given to private entrepreneurs with the condition that 50 per cent of the electricity generated should be made available for community use.

Table

Rates of central financial assistance foe installation biomass gasifier for cooking application

System Capacity (kcal/br)	Amount of CIA for different categories		
	SC/ST Hostels	Govt. Hostels, School Hostels, Mess-Room of Police Paramilitary Forces, Registered Trust, etc.	Other Institutes and Industries
12,000	Rs. 30,000	Rs. 20,000	Rs. 12,000
25,000	Rs. 45,000	Rs. 30,000	Rs. 18,000
50,000	Rs. 75,000	Rs. 50,000	Rs. 30,000

Achievements

The State-wise number and total capacity of gasifier systems installed during April-December 1998 are given in Table.

The Non-Conventional Energy Development Corporation of Andhra Pradesh Ltd. (NEDCAP) has installed 23 gasifiers of 100 kW capacity each based on rice husk in rice mills. It is estimated that each rice mill will save about 9000 litres of diesel oil by utilising 100 tonnes of rice husk and generating 0.5 lakh units of power per year by using a gasifier. The Orissa Renewable Energy Development Agency has installed a 10 kW biomass gasifier- based power generation system in Similiguda village in Rayagada district for providing electricity to all the 75 households and for street lighting in the village. The fuelwood collected from 40 hectares of energy plantation taken up in the area in 1991-92, will be used for operating the gasifier system.

Table

State-wise number and total capacity of biomass gasifier systems installed during April to December, 1998.

State	Number of systems	Capacity (kW)
Andhra Pradesh	23	2300
Orissa	1	10
Tamil Nadu	3	70
Gujarat	1	5
Maharashtra	1	100
Madhya Pradesh	1	100
Karnataka	1	500
Total	31	3085

A biomass-based power project, comprising of 5 units of 100 kW capacity gasifier system each, was commissioned in June, 1997 at Gosaba in Sunderbans (West Bengal). At present, about 300 consumers are getting electricity from this for about six and a half hours daily on payment of Rs. 3.50 per unit. The commercial tariff fixed is Rs. 3.75 per unit. A cooperative society of the consumers has been set up to manage the power plant. Steps are being taken to extend the distribution line to about 800 consumers. The project on "Bio-energy for Sustainable Transformation of Rural Areas (SuTRA)", sanctioned to the Department of Rural Development and Panchayati Raj, Government of Karnataka in December 1996 has the objective of providing electrical energy to the villagers from locally available biomass resources with enhanced green cover in the area.

The progress of the project was reviewed by the National SuTRA Monitoring Committee in March and July, 1998. The Indian Institute of Science, Bangalore, which is executing the project, has located 18 borewells in the area of operation of 15 villages in Tumkur district by using satellite remote sensing imaginary data. Besides supplying electricity to two villages, namely, Kagganahalli and Sugganahalli, production of electricity from biogas has been restored in two villages, namely Pura and Ungra.

Biogas plants are being installed in Doddakoppalu, Kankere, Pallorayanahalli villages for home electrification and drinking water supply purposes. A drier based on bioenergy for drying vegetables has been installed in village Sugganahalli. A village forum for sustainable development has been organised in all these seven villages and the members have been trained in the management of bioenergy-based home electrification and water supply utilities. A nursery with grafted tree saplings has also been established for undertaking energy plantations,

Six gasifier systems, each with 50,000 kcal/hr capacity, were sanctioned in December, 1998 to the Tamil Nadu Energy Development Agency (TEDA) for installation in prisons for cooking purpose. An electrification project with a 30 kW gasifier has been sanctioned to the West Bengal Renewable Energy Development Agency

(WBREDA) for installation in Lolegaon village in Darjeeling district.

Biomass briquetting

The scheme of providing interest subsidy to biomass briquetting units was continued during 199899. It provides for provision of interest subsidy up to a maximum of 10 per cent on the loan amounts disbursed towards the capital cost of die and punch machines. Besides, financial assistance at the rate of 2.5 per cent of the interest subsidy amount is given as fund management charges to financial institutions. So far, three biomass briquetting projects, sanctioned by the IREDA during April to December, 1998, have been supported under this scheme.

UNDP/GEF project document

The Centre for the Application of Science and Technology to Rural Areas (ASTRA) at the Indian Institute of Science, Bangalore, has prepared a detailed project report on "Carbon Emission Reduction through Biomass Energy for Rural India" in January, 1999 for posing to the United Nations Development Programme (UNDP)/Global Environmental Facility (GEF) for multilateral funding. The report is based on a detailed survey in two panchayats, namely, Kodavatti and Yedavani in Tumkur district and preliminary survey in one village each in Pondicherry and in Ranchi district of Bihar. A detailed analysis of the incremental costs and the carbon benefits of the use of biomass gasifiers and biogas plants for generation of electricity has been attempted.

Regional review meetings

Two regional review meetings on rural energy programmes were organised at Ahmedabad and Hyderabad in November 1998. The Ahmedabad meeting was inaugurated by Shri Nitin Bhai Patel, Hon'ble

Minister of Agriculture and Small and Medium Irrigation, Government of Gujarat and hosted by Gujarat Agro Industries Corporation. It was attended by representatives of the Governments of Gujarat, Haryana, Jammu & Kashmir, Madhya Pradesh, Punjab and Rajasthan, besides those of the KVIC, the NDDB, the AIWC, NGOs, manufacturers, entrepreneurs, the RBI, the NABARD, commercial banks, the TBUs, the BTCs etc. The Hyderabad meeting, which was hosted by NEDCAP, was inaugurated by the Secretary, NINES.

It was attended by the representatives of the Governments of Andhra Pradesh, Karnataka, Kerala, Maharashtra, Orissa, Tamil Nadu and West Bengal and U.T. of Lakshwadeep, besides representatives of the KVIC, the NDDB, the AIWC, the SDA, the BTCs. The TBUs., the RBI, the NABARD, banks, NGOs, manufacturers and entrepreneurs. Besides these meetings, the rural energy programmes were reviewed at the meeting of North Eastern States and Sikkim held at Guwahati on October 14, 1998. Emphasis was laid on greater financial participation of the State Governments and on transformation of these schemes into people's programme. A rapid expansion in the coverage of these programmes to achieve the estimated potential in the shortest possible time and organisation of decentralised repair and maintenance facilities at the block and district levels were discussed.

Integrated rural energy programme

Rural areas account for the vast majority of the country's population and as such the country's efforts in the direction of sustainable energy security cannot be expected to succeed unless the problems encountered in meeting the energy needs of the rural population are addressed in a planned and systematic manner. It was in this context that the Integrated Rural Energy Programme

(IREP) was launched during the Seventh Plan with the aim of developing the planning and institutional capabilities at the State, District and Block Levels to formulate and implement area-based micro-level plans to tap in an integrated manner all types of energy sources with an optimum mix to meet the rural energy needs both for subsistence and productive purposes.

The IREP was initially administered by the Planning Commission and on April 1, 1994 it was transferred to the NINES. The IREP, envisages large-scale participation of the people in the planning and implementation of the programme through the involvement of the Panchayats, the NGOs and other institutions. It also envisages the setting up and the strengthening of mechanisms for effectively linking micro-level planning for rural energy with national and the State-level planning for energy and economic development.

The IREP, which is a Centrally Sponsored Scheme (CSS), provides for grants-in-aid for the support staff in the IREP project cells at the State, the District and the Block levels and for their training as well as for extension. The State-sector outlay is utilised for the implementation of IREP plans and projects, including funding of demonstration activities, provision of financial incentives for various energy devices, funding of extension activities and other related activities. The funds and resources from other ongoing energy-related programmes are also utilised in IREP Blocks to the extent possible.

Objectives

The major objectives of the Integrated Rural Energy Programme (IREP) are:-

— Provision of the most cost-effective mix of various energy sources and options for meeting the requirements of sustainable agriculture and rural development to the extent possible;

— Provision of energy for meeting the basic needs of cooking, heating and lighting especially for the weaker sections of the society ;

— Ensuring large-scale peoples' participation in the planning and implementation of the programme through the involvement of panchayats, local bodies and other institutions, wherever feasible.

Achievements

The programme has so far been extended to 860 blocks including the 200 new blocks sanctioned during 1997-98. With this, about 16% of the total number of blocks in the country have been covered under IREP. The State-wise figures of the Blocks in which IREP has been sanctioned for implementation are given in the Table.

Table

State-wise break-up of IREP blocks sanctioned (as on 31.12.1998)

State/UTs	IREP Blocks
Andhra Pradesh	32
Arunachal Pradesh	10
Assam	21
Bihar	56
Goa	5
Gujarat	25
Haryana	38
Himachal Pradesh	45
Jammu & Kashmir	28
Karnataka	42
Kerala	44
Madhya Pradesh	85
Maharashtra	37

Manipur	19
Meghalaya	16
Mizoram	11
Nagaland	25
Orissa	45
Punjab	40
Rajasthan	36
Sikkim	4
Tamil Nadu	21
Tripura	6
Uttar Pradesh	115
West Bengal	34
A&N Islands	5
Chandigarh	1
Dadra & Nagar Haveli	I
Daman & Diu	1
Delhi	5
Lakshadeep	1
Pondicherry	2
Total	860

The programme provides for building the capabilities in the States/UTs through education and training of potential beneficiaries as well as imparting training to those involved in the planning and implementation of the IREP plans and projects.

In addition, the implementation of the programmes in the chosen Blocks is being strengthened and intensified through coordination with various rural energy programmes such as the national biogas development programme, the national programme on improved chulha, biomass, solar thermal, solar photovoltaics etc. implemented by the Ministry as well by other rural energy programmes at the State level taken up by other Ministries/Departments-of the Central Government.

As many as 19 State-level and 171 District-level Technical Back-up Units have been sanctioned under the IREP to provide technical support at the local level for effective implementation of the programme. The State and UT Governments have been requested to review the functioning of these Technical Back-up Units and weed out those which are not functioning satisfactorily. To ensure accelerated development of the IREP blocks, 22 National Pilot Projects (NPP) have been sanctioned. These are designed to serve as model IREP blocks for replication in other parts of the country.

Inter-ministerial coordination

New initiatives were taken for effective interministerial coordination for the promotion of rural and renewable energy technologies by the concerned Ministries/ Departments in the IREP blocks. The Ministries of Rural Areas and Employment, Agriculture, Food Processing Industries, Health and Family Welfare, Human Resource Development, Welfare, Petroleum and Natural Gas, Industries, Tourism and Coal were identified for this purpose. The areas for coordination were discussed at the annual convention on IREP held in 1997 with the State/ UT Governments.

The concerned Central Ministries have nominated senior level officers as Nodal Officers for co-ordinating with the NINES and for identifying areas and renewable energy technologies which are to be promoted by them under their ongoing or new programmes. Senior level officers of the rank of Adviser and Joint Secretary in the MNES have been given the responsibility to coordinate with their counterparts in the concerned Ministries to prepare a catalogue of schemes/projects for promotion of renewable energy technologies by them. A number of schemes/projects have already been identified for some of these Ministries and further necessary action in the implementation of these programmes is being taken up.

Review meetings

In order to review the progress of the programme and to discuss various issues and problems relating to its implementation, the annual review meeting was organised on October 29,1998 in the MNES with the State and UT Governments. After detailed discussions/ deliberations, among others, the meeting recommended that for intensive implementation of IREP programme, the State and UT Governments should provide for a minimum investment of Rs. 5 lakh per IREP block per year in their budget outlays. It was also suggested that State/UT Governments should make all possible efforts to mobilise financial resources from other on-going programmes of other concerned departments for implementation of IREP. For this purpose the State/UT Governments should constitute a high level Committee chaired by the State Chief Secretary with the Secretaries of the concerned departments as members.

The State/UT Governments further recommended that the IREP should remain as a Centrally Sponsored Scheme in the current and subsequent Five Year Plans till the programme gets fully operational and the capabilities in the States become well established and developed for preparation and implemention of micro-level IREP plans and projects.

Training-cum-R&D institutes

Five training-cum-R&D institutions have been sanctioned for being set up at Village Bakoli (Delhi), Lucknow (UP), Bangalore (Karnataka), Kheda Distt. (Gujarat) and Shillong (Meghalaya). These institutions are meant to conduct training courses for different target groups like State Government officials working in the field of rural energy at different levels, the beneficiaries, professionals and the panchayat representatives on various aspects of rural energy including planning, implementation, monitoring, extension and maintenance of systems and devices. In addition, these institutions would be responsible for the preparation of course material, dissemi-nation of information on rural energy, creation of data base, propagation of appropriate technology, conduct of applied research and promotion of developmental activities in the rural energy sector.

The institutes at Lucknow and Delhi are operational. The institute at Bangalore is likely to become operational shortly while those at Shillong and Kheda Distt are in advanced stages of completion. The institute at Lucknow had proposed 25 training programmes for different target groups during 1998-99. In addition, 4 awareness programmes were proposed to be organised during 1998-99. The institute is also taking up R&D activities and has developed a solar cooker with electrical back-up which has been commercialised by Non -Conventional Energy Development Agency (NEDA), Lucknow.

The Mahatma Gandhi Institute of Integrated Rural Energy Planning and Development (MGIIREPD) Bakoli Delhi conducted 6 national training programmes during 1998-99 (till December), in which 1137 officials/ beneficiaries participated.

5

Public Sector Undertakings

Nuclear power corporation of India Ltd.
There are ten reactor units under operation with a total installed capacity of 1840 MWe. During the calendar year 1998 the total gross power generation from all station was about 11,483 NWs, which included about 709 NWs from RAPS-1. For the period April 1, 1998 to January 31, 1999 the total gross generation was about 9900 MUs achieving capacity factor of about 73%. The gross generation from all the units since commencement of commercial operation till end of Jan. 1999 was about 131 billion units.

Tarapur atomic power station (2 × 160 MWe BWRs)
The station completed 29 years of successful commercial operation. The cumulative gross generation of the station since the beginning of commercial operation till the end of Jan. 1999 was 52828 MUs. The station generated 2258 MUs during the calendar year 1998 and during the period from April 1, 98 to Jan 31, 99 generated 1840 Ws in the financial year 1998-99. Unit- 1 of TAPS performed well during the calendar year 1998. The unit achieved 100% availability factor and capacity factor above 95% in the months of May and then continuously for six months period from August 1998 to January 1999. Unit-2 was shut down from August to October 1998 for refuelling

and regulatory inspection of core shroud. The refuelling outage was completed in 76 days of record period. This was the shorter refuelling outage where in major works like Rx-core shroud inspection, enhanced in-service inspection of primary coolant system and turbine overhauling were taken up along with routine works.

Rajasthan atomic power station (100 MWe, 200 MWe PHWRs)
The cumulative gross electric generation of the station since the beginning of commercial operation till the end of Jan. 1999 was 25,165 MU's. The station generated 1308 MUs during the calendar year 1998 and during the period from April 1, 98 to Jan 31, 99 generated 1396 MUs in the financial year 1998-99. The unit-1 of RAPS has been operating at a maximum power level of 150 MWe. Due to problems of high vibrations in the turbine, it was shut down during April-June, 1998 to attend to LP turbine blade failure and carry out modification of blades. This unit was again shut down for about 22 days during August-September, 1998 for various maintenance jobs.

Unit-2 of RAPS which was under capital maintenance outage since Aug 1,1994 was recommissioned and resynchronised to the grid on Jun 6, 1998 after completion of all jobs related with enmasse coolant channel replacement and systems upgradation. Before making an approach to criticality all regulatory requirements and stipulations like Emergency Core Cooling System and Reactor Building Leak Rate Test, etc. were completed successfully.

Madras atomic power station (2 × 170 MWe PHWRs)
The cumulative gross generation of the station since the beginning of commercial operation till the end of Jan. 1999 was 26962 MUs. The station generated 2061 MUs during the calendar year 1998 and during the period from April 1, 98 to Jan 31, 99 generated 1902 MUs in the financial year 1998-99. Unit-1 of MAPS was shutdown for

in-service inspection of coolant channels (ISI) from Nov 15,1997 which was prolonged and continued upto May 24, 1998 due to increase in number of channels planned for inspection. Also, additional job of scrape sampling of two channels was taken up for studies as per regulatory recommendations. Unit-2 of MAPS performed well and exceeded generation target in the financial year 1998-99 upto Jan. 31, 1999.

Narora atomic power station (2 × 220 MWe PHWRs)

The cumulative gross generation of the station since the beginning of commercial operation till the end of Jan. 1999 was 15,262 MUs. The station generated 3141 MUs during the calendar year 1998 and during the period from April 1, 98 to Jan 31, 99 generated 2450 MUs in the financial year 1998-99.

Kakrapar atomic power station (2 × 220 MWe PHWRs)

The cumulative gross generation of the station since the beginning of commercial operation till the end of Jan. 1999 was 10,519 MUs. The station generated 2715 MUs during the calendar year 1998 and during the period from April 1, 98 to Jan 31, 99 generated 2311s in the financial year 1998-99. Unit-1 of KAPS shutdown for 66 days from Mar 9 to May 14, 1998 due to leak in stator water systems inside the generator casing and annual maintenance shutdown jobs. The unit was started back after replacement of leaky generator stator conductors. The second unit of KAPS performed well during the financial year 1998-99.

Nuclear power projects under construction

Kaiga atomic power project -1 and 2

The project, located at Kaiga in district Uttar Kannada of Karnataka, will feed electrical power to southern grid. It comprises two Pressurised Heavy Water Reactors (PHVYIR), each of 220 MWe installed capacity.

Kaiga- 1 & 2 is expected to generate 2420 MUs annually at normative capacity utilisation factor of 62.8%. The physical progress by December 1998 was about 93% and an expenditure of Rs.2189 Cr. (75.6%) has been incurred on the project upto November 1998. The units are expected to achieve criticality in June 1999 (for Kaiga-2) and June 2000 (for Kaiga- 1).

The regulatory clearance for commencement of work for the inner containment dome of Kaiga- 1 was received in October 1998. The concreting of the IC dome has been planned to start in February 1999. Civil works of internals of R.B, IC/OC dome upto the ring beam have already been completed. All other civil works related to turbine building, reactor auxiliary building, diesel generator building, service building and upgrading plant building have been completed. The turbine has been put on barring gear and water fill test of condenser is in progress. 80% of nuclear piping, 85% of secondary system piping and 95% of conventional piping have been completed.

About 65% of process fuel, and fuel handling instrumentation works have been completed. All the common services such as domestic water, demineralised water, fire water, chilled water, compressed air systems etc. have been commissioned. The 220 KV switch yard, class 3 and class 4 switch gears have been energised. All the diesel generators have been non-load tested. 90% cabling work has been completed.

At Kaiga-2, concreting of inner containment dome and its pre-stressing have been completed. Concreting of outer containment dome has also been completed. 97% nuclear piping and 96% conventional piping have been completed. All major equipment have been erected and released for commissioning. The main primary heat transport circuit has been hydrotested and the main moderator system has been commissioned.

Primary work of light water commissioning on primary heat transport system (hot conditioning) is progressing and is expected to be completed by March 1999. The main air lock has been moved to its final position and final welding is in progress. The main steam-line piping is hydrotested and other: circuits are under testing.

The liner installation in spent fuel bay and spent fuel inspection bay has been completed. Fuel transport system equipment erection has been completed. Water fill test of condenser has been completed and 90% of turbo generator erection has been achieved. All diesel generators have been load tested and the cabling works have been completed.

Rajasthan atomic power project 3 and 4

At Unit-3 completed works include the following: Concreting of Inner Containment (IC) dome the installation of feeders, air hold test of main moderator and PHT circuits, hydrotest of End-Shield/Calandria Vault cooling systems; Erection of the main plant equipment; Erection of feeder/header insulation cabinets and permanent seal plugs on coolant channels; Condenser tubing works, hydrotest of condenser and trial box-up of LP and HP turbines, the work on installation of SUT, 6.6 KV and 415V Switchgear, MCCs and switchyard, and cable tray installation, and SUT-3 and 415V switchgear.

Pre-stressing of cables progressed and balance civil work of the IDCT are expected to be completed shortly. 97% Nuclear Piping has been prefabricated and 84% erected. Out door piping and secondary cycle piping works are nearing completion. At Unit-4, the completed works included Reinforcement work for IC ring beam; Erection of support structures and form work for IC dome. Laying of reinforcement steel bars for the dome have started. The balance civil work of the IDCT progressed.

The completion status of various Nuclear & Piping works are Nuclear piping prefabrication (78% and erection (55%); Erection of feeders (57% of);Work on installation of Secondary - Shutdown System components (50%) and F/M bridge & column (90%).

Prefabrication and erection of APW/APWC and fuel oil piping are completed. Erection of Outdoor, Indoor and Secondary Cycle piping works (85%). Erection of TG equipment has commenced. Erection of compressors and chillers are completed and the systems required for PHT hydrotest are commissioned. Filtration and Chlorination and DM Water plant including domestic water tank are commissioned.

The completion status of various electrical works are Works on SUT and 6.6KV Switchgear (100%) and Work on 415V switchgear (97%). Cable tray installation (65%), and Cable laying and terminations (23%). Diesel Generator sets for both the unit have been test run on 100% load successfully. 6.6 KV and 415 KV switchgear and MCCs have been energised. Recharging of Switch Yard and SUT#3 has been also completed. Plant water make up system has been commissioned and non-active process water system has been partially commissioned. Pre-commissioning checks of air compressors have been completed and compressors have been made operational. RB Exhaust Fans have been test operated.

Electrical fire water pump has been tested on re-circulation mode and one of the three diesel fire water pumps has been also tested on re-circulation mode. Pre-commissioning checks on various equipment is in progress. The PHT hydro test and hot conditioning of unit-3 is expected to be completed by March 1999.

Tarapur atomic power project—3 & 4 (2 × 500 MWe)

The project is located adjacent to existing two units of TAPS (2× 160 MWe) of BWR type at Tarapur, District-Thane Maharashtra state and it will feed electrical power to western grid. The project comprises twin unit station of Pressurised Heavy water Reactor (PHWR) type each of 500 MWe installed capacity. The schedule criticality date for Unit- 4 and Unit-3 are October 2005 and July 2006 respectively. The excavation for construction of Main Plant Civil Works at TAPP- 3&4 site was started on 10th October, 1998.

The top soil from the RB-3&4 area has been removed and rock excavation is in progress. In RB-4, excavation upto the top of the raft (85 M elevation) has been done and complete excavation of this building will be over by March 1999. Excavation work for other area of main plant buildings, heavy duty roads and site grading is also in progress. In parallel, work of geotechnical investigation and construction of bund wall have also been started.

Tendering works for construction of package-2 civil work i.e. for Main Plant Safety related buildings has been completed and the work order is expected to be issued by April 1999. The first pour of concrete is scheduled to take place during October 1999. The site infrastructure was already developed. An additional storage capacity was created by constructing three more warehouses for providing covered space for proper storage of cement and critical equipment being stored at site.

Procurement actions for machinery for establishment of Mechanical and Electrical workshops have been initiated. The first phase of housing comprising 156 houses have already been made available. The second phase of housing consisting of 148 houses are under construction. The awards against most of the land acquisition applications for the additional land needed for the exclusion zone have been declared by the State Govt. Possession of the land will be given once the rehabilitation plan is finalised by the State Government.

Procurement activities of machinery and equipment have been reactivated to suit the six and half year schedule requirement of the project. Critical components like calandria, PHT pump motors, moderator pumps, reactor headers, pressurisers and TG components had already been procured for the first unit. Manufacturing of Moderator heat exchangers, End-shields, steam generators etc. are in progress. The order for shielding plugs has been placed. Orders for R.B. main structural steel, fuelling machine bridge and column, condenser etc. are being finalised and purchase proposals for many other equipment are being initiated as per the schedule.

Kudankulam atomic power station project (2 × 1000 MWe)

The Kudankulam Project is an Indo-Russian joint venture for construction of a nuclear power station consisting of two units of pressurised water reactors (VVER-1000) of 1000 MWe capacity each, to be located at Kudankulam in Tamil Nadu. The project will be implemented on a technical cooperation basis between India and the Russian Federation under the Inter-Governmental Agreement (IGA) signed in 1988. A 'Supplement' to the IGA incorporating the revised terms and conditions has been signed between the Governments of India and the Russian, during June 1998.

As a first step towards the implementation of the Kudankulam Project, a contract for preparation of the Detailed Project Report (DPR) was executed between Nuclear Power Corporation of India Limited and Atomstroyexport, Moscow, during July 1998. The work on the DPR is expected to start after completion of the procedural formalities by the two sides. The mandatory site related clearances to start the construction work of the Kudankulam Project have been obtained and the site investigations have been completed. Land for the project has also been acquired. The implementation of the project at the site shall be commenced after completion of the DPR and approval of the same by the Government of India.

Quality assurance

Quality Assurance has always formed the corner stone of all activities in the different phases of development of the Nuclear Power Programme. Evaluation and improvement of systems and procedures and aligning them with international practices have been the constant endeavour of NPCIL. An important mile stone in this continuing journey towards excellence was reached when NPCIL received the ISO 9001 Certification in the area of Quality Assurance activities during this year. The benefit of the rich experience and expertise available in NPC with the QA groups continued to be made available to the Indian Industry and other Organisation through QA Consultancy Services.

Safety, health and environment

The safety performance of NPCIL power stations and projects continued to be excellent during the year. The release of radioactivity to the environment was maintained much below the prescribed limits and the occupational doses to the plant personnel were kept at "As Low As Reasonably Achievable" ALARA level.

The functions relating to Health & Safety were continued for ensuring nuclear and conventional safety in the operating stations as well as projects under construction through internal safety reviews and audits. Corporate Self Assessment was conducted at all sites to ensure operational safety in a pro-active manner. NPC Safety Review Committee (NPC-SRC), the apex in-house safety body continues to conduct appropriate interdisciplinary review of all safety related events and safety submissions. So far 79 of such review meetings have been conducted. The review ensures that all proposals are comprehensive, implementable, consistent and conforming to codal requirements, enabling early resolution of the issues. Safety Audit was carried out for Industrial Safety, Fire Safety and Safety Culture at RAPS, MAPS, NAPS, KAPS and RAPP-3 and 4 during the year. Kaiga Project won AERB's Industrial Safety Award and also the NPC Industrial Safety Award for the 3rd consecutive time. RAPP-3 and 4 won AERB's Fire Safety Award for the year 1997. To celebrate the 50th Anniversary of India's Independence and as part of the "Green Site" project, NPCIL has launched a 3 year programme. During this period, 50,000 trees will be planted at each site, nearly 3,00,000 trees in all.

Uranium Corporation of India Ltd.

During the year 1997-98 the overall performance of the company has improved over the last year. The processing of ore as well as the production of uranium concentrates were higher than the previous year. The performance of the two uranium recovery plants was better than the previous year, and the production of uranium concentrates was about 2% higher than the previous year. Production of magnetite also increased by 27%, but the production of copper and molybdenum concentrates were more or less at the same levels as in the previous year.

The third stage shaft lining and equipping work at Jaduguda was in progress. The shaft equipping work is likely to be completed during the year 1999. At the Narwapahar mines, the work on shaft head frame erection was completed. The trial runs of Cage and Skip winders commenced during December 1998. Further, mine development work and production through the Decline was in progress below 140 metre level.

The expansion work pertaining to the Jaduguda Mills was completed and commissioned during December 1998. This raised the capacity of the mill to process 2090 metric tonnes of ore per day. To sustain the ore production of Jaduguda mine with lesser number of working faces, energy efficient, environment friendly electrically operated mining equipment for drilling and mucking operations were successfully used, achieving an overall output of two tonnes per man shift. For the mobility of the trackless equipment the technology for layout of ramps etc. was developed in-house and the same was being extended to other areas where feasible.

Safety and environmental monitoring

Full fledged Environmental Survey Laboratories (ESL) are functional at the Jaduguda and Narwapahar mines. These laboratories of BARC carry out routine radiological monitoring and check for potential of conventional hazards in the mines and mills. They also maintain surveillance on the environment in and around Jaduguda. Vocational training and safety classes were conducted for workmen in the Vocational Training Centres of mine and mill.

Electronics Corporation of India Ltd,

The Electronics Corporation of India Ltd. (ECIL) produces a variety of sophisticated electronic systems, instruments and equipment to meet the requirements of Atomic Power Stations, Defence, Railways, Telecommunications, etc. The Company is also a leading producer of computers and consumer electronics.

Operating performance

During the year 1997-98, the production of the company was about Rs. 3 11 crore and the gross income was about Rs. 348 crore. The corresponding figures in the previous year were about Rs. 296 crore and Rs. 356 crore respectively. A total of Rs. 318 crore worth of orders were booked during the year.

New products

The important new products introduced during the year 1997-98 were: Wireless in Local Loop (WLL) system, SAJ and LPJ for Samyukta Project; Programmable Tracking Axis Symmetric VSAT Antenna; Solar Photovoltaic Refrigerators; Table Top X-ray Inspection System type ECR-319; VLSI design services; 1.8M dia Axis Symmetric VSAT Antenna in Ku band, and Dual Polarised (LP) Feeds for TVRO.

Sales Plan for 1998-99

The Corporation has drawn up Sales Plan of Rs. 43 crore for the year 1998-99. This includes supply of.

— Instruments and Components, worth about Rs.56 crore,

— Special Products such as Fuzes worth about Rs. 55 crore,

— Communication Equipment and Antenna Systems, worth Rs.90 crore,

— Telecom Products, worth Rs. 47 crore,

— Computer Systems for Business Applications valued at Rs. 42 crore,

— Control and Instrumentation, Simulators, valued at Rs. 87 crore, and

— Industrial Controls and others value at Rs. 6 crore.

R&D Programme

The R&D programme of ECIL the year 1998-99 includes:

— Development of Automatic Vehicle Counting and Classification System.

— Introduction of Double-beam UV-VIS Spectro-photometers;

— Testing the data links at an international airport and obtaining the necessary certification from Airport authorities.

— Augmenting VLSI design capacity in complimentary areas like physical design, place and route etc.

— Upgradation of Man-Machine In face S/W to include multimedia, features.

— Development of High Sensitive Front-end and existing ATC Receiver better reception from farthest aircraft.

— 6. 1M dia Mobile Earth State Antenna with Stretch formed panel,

— Microstrip Patch Antennas

— Helicopter Antennas, Slimline MW Antennas.

— Dual Polarised (circular) feeds for TVRO with 0.5 dB Axial Ratio Technical Collaborations

— ECIL expects to enter technology collaboration with:

— M/s. Clex Electronics, Hyderabad for development of technology for Digital Loop Carrier.

— C-DOT for Out Door Unit (ODU) for VSAT Terminal.

— ISTRAC for Programmable Tracking Antenna.

Exports

During 1998-99, the Company expects to export products worth Rs. 1.4 crore. These include X-ray Generators to USA; Rate Gyros and to Malaysia; Notch Indicators to Hungary and Software to France. ECIL plans to make investments on several new products/projects commencing from 1998-99.

6

Industrial Facilities

Heavy water board

The production capacity of Heavy Water in the country is sufficient to meet the domestic demand. In addition, 100 metric tonne of heavy water has been exported to the Republic of Korea in May 1998. The overall performance and the safety record of Heavy Water Plants were good. The production of heavy water during the year of report was close to the target. The plants at Tuticorin and Baroda completed more than 7.3 million and 8.43 million man-hours of continuous operation respectively.

Operation of the Heavy Water Plant at Talcher remained suspended due to unsatisfactory operation of the connected plant of the Fertilizer Corporation of India on which the Plant depends for feed stock and other inputs. HWB continued its efforts towards reduction in energy consumption and the cost of production. A scheme for saving power by recirculating the treated effluent from the guard pond instead of using fresh water from Godavari for cooling and diluting exchange unit effluent, prior to its processing in chlorination unit, is expected to be commissioned shortly. A Sour Oil Treatment plant was set up at HWP—Manuguru to recover seal oil from compressor seal oil contaminated by hydrogen sulphide. This is running satisfactorily.

As a part of the effort to diversify, a Pilot Plant is under construction at HWP—Talcher for production of solvent Di-2-ethyl, Hexyl Phosphoric Acid (DEHPA). The process is based on the technology developed in BARC. This plant is likely to be commissioned in May 1999 and will also be used for synthesis of other solvents like Tributyl Phosphate. Ammonia Injection System is used for reducing resistivity of fly ash and facilitates larger collection of fly ash (dust) by the Electrostatic Precipitators. The system which was indigenously developed and commissioned in December 1998, is placed at the inlet of chimney of Captive Power Plant at HWP —Manuguru. It has yielded excellent results.

Baroda Ammonia Expansion Project has been taken up to generate an alternative heavy water production technology and for sustaining operation of HWP - Baroda in the face of the closure of M/s. Gujarat State Fertilizer Corporation's old ammonia plant. Efforts for finding non-nuclear application of heavy water were also made. In this respect, research done for the preservation of oral polio vaccine in heavy water showed very encouraging results. A process for removal of tritium from heavy water in the operating nuclear power plant was tried out at MAPS. This makes use of the distillation facility available at plant sites.

With a view to improve the knowledge base and provide motivation, plant engineers were deputed to various training programmes. A one day seminar on Heavy water Programme in India' was conducted in Mumbai as a part of Golden Jubilee celebration of India's independance in which key personnel from all the plants and the representatives of employees associations participated.

The plants at Manuguru, Kota and Nangal performed well, with planned and a very few unplanned outages. The plant at Hariza saw an interruption due to floods in Tapti River. The plants at Thal had unplanned maintainance of one of the heat exchangers of cracker unit, partial replacement of catalyst of the cracker, excahngers tower stage pumps and because of nonavailability of feed also had outages due to nonavailability of feed gas from Southern Petrol-Chemical Industries Ltd. (SPIC).

Nuclear fuel complex

In addition to meeting the requirements of reload fuel for all operating power stations namely RAPS, MAPS, NAPS, KAPS and TAPS, supply of the first charge of fuel for commissioning KAIGA-2 project was commenced. This year, the Unit recorded highest production of PHWR fuel bundles and highest production of reactor grade zirconium sponge. For the first time, seamless zircaloy square channels for TAPS were fabricated by initially pilgering a seamless tube followed by forming to a square section and the tubes were supplied.

Similarly, prototype blanket, control and safety rod assemblies involving intricately designed special stainless steel components for the development of 500 MWe Prototype Fast Breeder Reactor and sub-assemblies for sodium void coefficient measurement for FBTR were fabricated for the first time and supplied to IGCAR.

Further, process flow sheets were optimised for the manufacture of special 9Cr- 1Mo seamless stainless steel tubes for steam generators and special low nitrogen D9 grade seamless stainless steel tubes for fuel cladding of PFBR. Trial lots were manufactured and supplied to IGCAR.

Technology upgradation

In the Uranium Oxide Plant, the scrubber of turbo dryer unit was modified for improving efficiency and performance. Similarly, a new hot vapour-condensing unit and a modified head for rotary furnace were also introduced. In the Enriched Uranium Oxide Plant attrition of UO_2 powder, increase in hydrolysis and precipitation capacity of UF_6 and improved feeding system in the solvent extraction section were incorporated.

As a process modification for copper cladding of zircaloy billets, a new electroplating method as well as machine spinning process were developed by the Tool Room and the Extrusion Plant respectively. At Natural Uranium Fuel Assembly Plant, an on-line automatic unit for helium leak testing of PHWR fuel bundles in Seamless Zircaloy-2 Square channel for TAPS conjunction with product handling systems have been put into operation.

Indigenous equipment development

A fully automated continuous tube degreasing system for zircaloy tubes has been designed and commissioned in NZFP. This system is based on high pressure, hot alkaline detergent degreasing with jets for OD cleaning and rotating lance for ID cleaning, rinsing and hot air drying.

Two other major and critical equipment namely, a pellet feeding system for centreless grinding machine and an improved version of automatic resistance welding machine for welding the bearing pads on PHWR fuel elements have also been built and put into operation. Work is in progress for fabrication of high vacuum heat treatment furnace required for Rare Materials Plant, Mysore as well as a 15-30 size cold pilger mill for seamless tubes manufacture.

New projects

The Chairman, AEC formally inaugurated the New Zircaloy Fabrication Plant on June 26, 1998. The Plant has taken up finishing operations of trial lot of seamless titanium condenser tubes.

In the New Uranium Oxide Fuel Project, erection, testing and commissioning trials of equipment and process sections were carried out. The Plant has since obtained AERB clearance for operation and trial production has commenced. In the Natural Uranium Fuel Assembly Plant, tube preparation section has achieved full capacity.

Further, the plant has fabricated and supplied the first consignment of thoria assemblies for restarting RAPS-2 reactor and for Kaiga-2 and carried out enclosure welding for cobalt absorber pencils. Now, the plant has commenced production of PHWR fuel for operating reactors. A proposal has been put up to the Govt. for setting up a 400 tpa Titanium Sponge Plant at Palayakayal, Tamilnadu. For the production of this strategic material, DRDO and Department of Space have consented to contribute towards the capital cost. A 500 tpa Zirconium Oxide Plant is also proposed for co-location at the same site.

Quality assurance

As a reflection of the constant upgradation of technology and stringent Quality Assurance programme followed in NFC, the fuel failure rate during the year, in the operating power stations has come down drastically and is now on par with international standards.

With a view to further improving the operational discipline and explore the export potential, action has been initiated for getting ISO 9000 Certificate for NFC. The Inspection, Quality Control and Quality Assurance activities were continued by the various sections stationed in the production plants.

For the first time in NFC, fracture toughness measurements were carried out in Zr-2.5%Nb pressure tubes supplied to RAPS-2 reactor and established that the tubes manufactured from quadruple melted ingots have much higher and improved fracture toughness than those made from the earlier double melted route. An ingenious equipment was developed in-house for measuring Delayed Hydrogen Cracking parameters on Zr-2.5%Nb pressure tube samples. Work has been initiated to switch over to direct ultrasonic testing of PHWR end cap welds, instead of the destructive metallographic testing practised earlier.

Towards the development of Intelligent Processing of material, work is in progress for using acoustic emission as an on-line technique for monitoring the quality of all resistance-welds in PHWR fuel pins. In the centralised Control Laboratory, analysis were carried out in 30,000 samples involving about 2,25,000 determinations.

Energy conservation

Capacitor banks for power supply systems were optimised, resulting in lower line losses and a higher average power factor. Simultaneous, processing of three batches instead two, during high temperature vacuum distillation in the Zirconium Sponge Plant resulted in about 10% less energy consumption. A tie-up with a gas based Power Company, enabled assured supply as well as considerable saving in power bill.

Spin -off products

As a nonnuclear spin off, NFC has fabricated and supplied zircaloy tube components to M/s Rashtriya Chemicals and Fertilisers. The Special Materials Plant has transferred know-how for production of semi conductor grade gallium to M/s. National Aluminium Company. The plant has also supplied high purity tantalum pentoxide to outside parties for special tool manufacture and fabrication of special shapes and components of tantalum metal for various chemical and gem manufacturing industries.

Health, safety and environment

The Occupational Health Centre carried out routine and periodic medical check up of all employees and organised intensive awareness programmes on occupation health aspects and associated medicare. The industrial safety record of NFC for the year 1998 in terms of number of accidents and man-days lost has been the best achieved in the past 25 years. Specifically, the Fuel Group plants recorded more than 4 million manhours and the Tubes Group plants more than 2.5 million manhours without a single accident.

Refresher training programmes were conducted to all employees in safety aspects, production and maintenance activities. Regular environmental monitoring and effective treatment of effluents were continued by the Health Physics Unit and Effluent and Environment Protection Section respectively. A huge plantation programme in NFC environs has been launched in coordination with the State Forest Department.

Board of radiation and isotope technology

Radiochemicals

About 58 TBq (1570 curies) of a number of reactor produced radioisotopes were processed in over 160 batches for supply to various users and for formulation of a variety of radio-pharmaceuticals. These include radioisotopes such as molybdenum-99 phosphorus-32, sulphur-35, iodine-131, chromium-5 1, mercury-203 etc. About 20 kgs of phosphorus-32, calcium-45, and sulphur-35 labelled agrochemicals were supplied for use in agricultural research. Nearly 1.2 kg of promethium147 self-luminous compound was supplied for illumination of instrument dials and other devices.

Radiation sources

A total of 18.3 PBq (500 kilocuries) of radiation sources

of low, medium and high intensity were fabricated and supplied for use in industry, medicine, agriculture and research. These include radiation sources of isotopes such as Cobalt-60, Iridium- 192, and Cesium-137. Over 900 consignments of Iridium- 192, totalling about 1. 1 PBq (30 kilocuries) were supplied in the form of seated sources for industrial radiography. Over 120 consignments of Iridium-192 in the form of 0.3 mm dia wire were supplied to radiotherapy centres for use in brachytherapy.

20 Cs-137 manual after-loading kits complete with accessories each containing approx. 30 GBq (800 mCi) of Cs-137 were supplied to radiotherapy centres for use in brachytherapy. 14 large output sources of Cobalt-60 were supplied for treatment of cancers to various teletherapy centres. Twelve adjuster rods containing over 63 PBq (1.7 megacuries) of Cobalt-60 were unloaded from NAPS-11. These rods are being transported to cobalt handling facility at RAPS site (RAPPCOF) for processing.

About 28 PBq (800 kilocuries) of Cobalt-60 were recovered and transported to BRIT laboratories at Trombay to fabricate radiation sources. 150 kilocuries of Cobalt-60 in the form of composition source rods were supplied to Shri Ram Institute for Industrial Research, New Delhi, for loading in their radiation sterilization plant.

2.3 PBq (61 kilocuries) of Cobalt, 60 in the form of six composite sources rods were fabricated and loaded in to radiation plant at Food Irradiation and Processing Laboratory, (FIPLY), BARC. 3.7 PBq (100 kilocuries) of Cobalt-60 in the form of 8 composite source rods were fabricated and loaded in the Demonstration Plant for Processing of Spices at BRIT's Vashi Complex Navi Mumbai.

35 Cobalt-60 sources with a to activity of 560 GBq (19 curies) and Cs-137 sources with a total activity. 148 GBq (4 curies) were supplied for use in various nucleonic gauges. One consignment of 370 GBq (10 curies) of Sc-46, in the form of scandium glass was processed and supplied to Isotope Division, BARC, for silt movement studies in Calcutta Harbour by BARC.

Radio-pharmaceuticals

Over 45,000 consignments of different radio-pharmaceuticals and radio-immunoassay kits were supplied for use in nuclear medicine during the year, enabling an estimated 8,00,000 patient investigations to be carried out in the country.

The regional centres at Bangalore and Delhi regularly processed ready-to-use Tc-99m radiopharmaceuticals for use in the host nuclear medicine centres in addition to supplying the product to other needy hospitals in the region. The Centres at Dibrugarh and Bangalore continued to offer radio-immunoassay service to local hospitals. A wide variety of raw materials, radioactive materials, additives, reagents etc. used in the production of radiopharmaceuticals were tested by the Quality Control Group of Radio-pharmaceuticals Programme in addition to carrying out regular analysis of various batches of the radio-pharmaceutical products as per mandatory requirements. A Gel generator system using indigenously available low specific activity Mo-99 was further improved. An industrial model amenable to mass production incorporating features like economy, radiological and pharmaceutical safety is in advanced stage of development in collaboration with Industrial Design Centre, Indian Institute of Technology, Mumbai.

Product development

A superior agent for palliative treatment of bone

metastasis Sm-153 EDTMP was prepared using indigenously produced Sm-153. Several batches of this product were evaluated in collaboration with Christian Medical College, Vellore, where BRIT is setting up a facility for testing of new products in higher animal models under a BRNS project.

The findings were satisfactory and it is now proposed to seek clearance from Nuclear Medicine Committee for evaluation on humans (cancer patients) for its efficacy for palliation of metastatic bone pain. BRIT has standardized the protocol for Tc-HIG suitable for use in hospital radiopharmacy. Studies in small animals were satisfactorily completed and it is ready for clinical evaluation on humans.

A modified RIA kit for progesterone using tracer developed by BARC and other agents optimized at BRIT were extensively field tested and is now ready for regular production. A newly designed external packaging for radiopharmaceuticals, especially for Mo-99 was introduced which has resulted in greater ease and safety in handling at both packing end and user's end apart from improving the aesthetics and has obviated the need for wood for packing.

Number of batches of MIBG 1311 for diagnostic purposes were produced and supplied for limited trial. Studies are underway to establish methods for stabilizing the product at room temperature, which will enable the product to be transported without being packed in dry ice as is now required to be done.

Work on the development of new radiopharmaceuticals such as 51 Cr EDTA injection for GFR measurement, 99m Tc-EC for renal tubular function imaging, 99m Tc-HMPAO for brain perfusion studies was undertaken. As a part of BRIT's participation in IAEA's CRP on "Development of CNS Receptor Based

Radiopharmaceutical", work on standardization of methods for preparation and evaluation of radio-labelled peptides was undertaken. Radio-labelling of serotonin with both 99m Tc and 125 1 was carried out. A RIA Protocol for evaluation of Serotonin 125 1 was standardized using antibodies raised in-house.

Regional Centre for Radiopharmaceuticals, Bangalore, is working on development of IRMA kit for Alfa-Feto-Protein under an IAEA sponsored coordinated Research Programme. Immuno-radiometric assay kits for assay of T4, serum prolactin, LH, FSH was standardized based on magnetisable cellulose and commercial monoclonal antibodies. These kits are now ready for regular production and supply after approval by the Radiopharmaceuticals Committee.

Labelled compounds

Over 300 consignments of carbon-14 and tritium labelled compounds and 1700 consignments of P-32, P-33 and S-35 labelled biomolecules were supplied during the year. The JONAKI laboratory at Hyderabad produced P-32 labelled nucleotides on a regular basis, covering almost all the indigenous requirements of P-32 labelled biomolecules for studies in molecular biology.

For the first time P-33 labelled nucleotides were indigenously developed, productionised and regular supplies were started from mid- 1998. 100 consignments of non-radioactive (cold) kits for use in recombinant DNA technology were supplied. Custom synthesis of some important products for use in biomedical research was undertaken. Oligonucleotides (DNA primers of varying sequences and concentrations, as per researchers requests, were custom synthesized and supplied.

Realizing the importance of nonradioactive kits for molecular biology research, JONAKI laboratory is taking up R & D work in the areas related to non-radioactive kits. In order to take up full scale production, JONAKI laboratory at Hyderabad is being expanded by adding an additional floor, the construction of which is nearing completion with the cooperation of Centre for Cellular and Molecular Biology, Hyderabad.

Radiation sterilization

ISOMED, the first radiation sterilization plant in the country, completed 25 years of its service to health-care sector on December 31, 1998. This plant has enabled acceptance of the "Radiation Processing " as a technique for sterilization of medical disposable products. The plant availability factor was maintained at more than 90% and the capacity factor was also above 95%.

Approx. 13,000 cu.mtrs (1,50,000 cartons) of medical products such as dressings, disposable infusion and transfusion sets, surgical sutures, gloves and a number of other medical devices were sterilized at the plant during the year. Some of these cartons were radiation sterilized on behalf of user industries for export. During the year, ISOMED sterilised a few million Dai kits (midwifery kits) and delivery packs for the benefit of women and child population in rural areas to help bring down infection of mothers and help minimize the infant mortality under a rural programme funded by WHO.

ISOMED also continued production and supply of items relevant to gamma radiation processing and health care programme such as ceric-cerous dosimeters, biological indicators, go-no-go irradiation indicator buttons, and disposable sterile drapes and trolley covers. Action is in hand to obtain ISO 9002 certification for ISOMED Services.

Radiation equipment

40 remotely operated radiography cameras Model ROLI- 1 were supplied to industrial users for use in non-destructive testing. Servicing of ROLI cameras prior

to source replacement and mandatory checks, as recommended by Radiological Physics & Advisory Division, BARC, were carried out on all cameras Preliminary design of a light weight, portable, depleted uranium shielded remotely operated camera was completed and a fabrication of a prototype is being taken up. The camera will have capacity to hold upto 2.8 TBq (75 curies) of iridium 192. This will go a long way to meet the long felt demand of the industry for an indigenous light weight camera.

Two Gamma Chamber 5000 Units each loaded with 12,000 curies of cobalt-60 were supplied to Scientific & Technical Consultation Office Cairo, Egypt, and Reactor Control Division, BARC. One Gamma Chamber 900 Unit belonging to Anna University, Chennai, was refurbished and replenished with fresh cobalt-60 source. Irradiation of blood and blood products by gamma rays is the best technique to reduce the risk of transfusion associated graft verses host disease (TA-GVHD).

Irradiated blood is required to be given to patients whose immunity is suppressed. Preliminary design of a blood irradiator (BI 2000) using Cobalt-60 source and lead as shielding material is complete. An earlier model was in use for nearly four years at CMC Hospital, Vellore, with very satisfactory performance.

An advanced prototype unit is under fabrication which will provide a dose rate of 11 Gray per minute inside a chamber (2 litre volume, with a rotating mechanism. The documents are under prep; ration for submission to AERB seeking type approval. The unit will be ideal suited for use in the blood banks all over the country. Specialized NDT services we offered to BMF for measurement coating thickness on beryllium substrate and for inspection of beryllium shaft assembly. A number of institutions cluding Madras Atomic Power Station

Rubber Research Institute, Kakrapur Atomic Power Station etc were covered.

Sales

During the calendar year 1998, over 60,000 consignments of radioisotopic products valued at Rs. 16.67 crore were supplied for use in industry, research, agriculture and health care. Radioisotope products and equipment valued about Rs. 40 lakhs were exported to countries such as United Kingdom, Sri Lanka, Syria, Egypt, Indonesia, and Nepal.

Capital projects and schemes

BRIT had initiated projects under VIII Plan for setting up a facility for production of radioisotope equipment, upgradation of radiopharmaceuticals laboratory at Vashi, setting up a demonstration plant for radiation processing of spices and extension of nuclear medicine facilities in the country. The first two projects viz. Radiation Equipment Production Facility, and Upgradation and Modernization of Radiopharmaceuticals Laboratory were completed and regular production activities are being pursued.

The Demonstration Plant for Radiation Processing of Spices, continued into the first year of IX Plan, is now complete and is awaiting clearance from AERB and from Maharashtra State Drug and Food Administration for regular operation for processing of spices.

Once regular operation commences, the plant will be able to process about 6000 tons of spices during the first year of its operation. Under the Project on Extension of Nuclear Medicine Facilities, grant-in-aid was disbursed to P.B. Deshmukh Krishi Vidyalaya, Akola, to set up an RIA Centre. Under this project a total of Rs. 6.25 crore were disbursed to set up, 16 nuclear medicine centres and 6 RIA centre. The major objectives of the Project were met to a large extent.

Under the IX Plan, BRIT has initiated a project for setting up a National Medical Cyclotron Facility for production of positron emitting isotopes which are not produced in the country. In order to be able to process larger quantities of Cobalt-60 which are now produced from various power reactors, the RAPPCOF facility at Kota is proposed to be augmented by building additional hot cells with a sanctioned financial outlay of Rs. 17.0 crore. The detailed drawings are under preparation and machinery is being procured.

BRIT has initiated 3 new additional projects to strengthen the technical infrastructure for increasing the production of radioisotopes and take up production of new products. Financial sanctions for these projects are awaited. The new projects are:

1. *Augmentation of radiochemical laboratories at Radiological Labs., BARC*: The project is intended to replace the existing production plants used for processing of major radiochemicals like Mo-99,1-131, P-32 and miscellaneous isotopes by plants capable of processing larger quantities with lower radiation exposure to the operators. The project outlay will be Rs. 4.6 crore.

2. *Column Type Tc-99m Generator Production Assembly*: Under this project, it is proposed to set up a facility for production of user friendly Tc-99m column generators. The project outlay will be Rs. 3.0 crore.

3. *Design and development of radiation equipment*: There is a great demand for improved versions of radiation equipment such as depleted uranium shielded light weight radiography camera, blood irradiator etc. In addition, with the availability of large quantity of cobalt-60 from power reactors, there is a need to fabricate transport containers. All these equipment and containers need to be tested to demonstrate their compliance with relevant IAEA/AERB regulations. Currently, neither

BRIT nor any DAE unit possess a testing facility for equipment/flasks. Hence it is proposed to set up design, fabrication and a testing facility under the project for various radiation equipment. The total financial outlay for the project is Rs. 8.5 crore.

International relations

Six scientists from Uganda, Algeria, Malaysia, Iran, Romania, and Indonesia were trained in the production of radiopharmceuticals, radiation sources and radiation sterilization of medical products in BRIT under IAEA sponsored programme. One scientist from BRIT provided expert assistance to IAEA in Iran on programme relating to development of RIA kits. 10 scientists of BRIT took part in IAEA sponsored workshop/courses/ meetings, in different countries. Three scientists from BRIT visited Egypt and Indonesia to install Gamma Chamber 5000 Unit supplied against purchase order received from International Atomic Energy Agency, Vienna.

Centre for compositional characterisation for materials (CCCM)

The Centre, continued to provide analytical services to different end users; in addition, R & D work related to the development of novel analytical strategies was carried out, for applications in semiconductor, environment, nuclear and in material sciences.

Analytical services towards industrial quality assurance

Analysis of naphtha samples for P,V,Ni, As, Pb and Hg at parts per billion level and lower levels of concentrations were carried out using the ICPMS as these elements besides acting as catalytic poisons can also cause environmental burden due to the large volumes of naphtha consumed in the petro-product industry. The depth profiling of hydrogen on the surface of Zr-2.5 Nb samples was carried out for NFC.

Analysis of Cs at ppb levels and mercury in Hepatitis-B vaccine samples has been carried out for a firm manufacturing this vaccine indigenously. Stoichiometric assays of Pt-Rh, Pt-Rh-Pd-Au and many alloy used as catalysts were carried out for Fertilizer Corporation of India Ltd., Mumbai.

A host of raw materials like litharge, feldspar, zircon sand, soda ash and potassium carbonate, used in the manufacture of colour TV tubes were analysed for major, minor and trace elements for finding out the suitability of indigenous raw materials, to meet the stringent quality demands especially with respect to chlorine and fluorine.

Raw and purified quartz powder samples, from an export firm, were analysed for many elements with a view to assess the efficacy, the purification steps adapted and also the pick-up impurities in the process. Tantalum powder and capacitors samples, were analysed to identify the likely cause of mechanical failure of tantalum wire used in capacitors.

R and D work related to specific areas Semiconductors

To cater to the analytical requirements of semiconductor industry, procedures for the analysis of VLSI grade water samples for trace impurities at parts per trillion levels were investigated and the ability of the UTAL to cater to such analysis was established. A set of samples of 7N pure tellurium samples was analysed for about 15 trace elements using ICP-MS and Zeeman GFAAS at ppb and sub-ppb levels of concentrations. In addition, using a combination of different analytical techniques, methodologies for the analysis of high purity Ga, In, As, Sb, Te and Cd were developed. A post column derivatisation scheme was studied for the determination of trace element impurities in arsenic after the volatilization of the matrix.

Materials science

The use of polyaniline, a conducting polymer, as a standard for hydrogen estimation using nuclear reactor analysis was established. Bilayered films of Nickel and aluminium were formed using thermal evaporation of nickel and aluminium. The composition of these layers was studied using He-RBS and found to be in atomic ratio 80:20. The formation of different phases of nickel aluminides using different heat treatments was being studied.

Compositional analyses of wear resistant VN and ZrN films formed on SS using DC magnetron sputtering were carried out using IBA (Resonance BS) to correlate the micro-hardness and the stoichiometry. Similar studies on corrosion resistant CrN films formed on SS using ion-beam mixing were done. A comparison of the depth profiles obtained using GDMS and IBA (He-RBS and resonance BS) on these films showed very good agreement with respect to the composition of Cr and N in the surface film and efforts were made to use IBA to calibrate the depth profiles obtained using GDMS and also to study the homogeneity of such films, formed by different methods.

Investigations on the chemical composition of light emitting silicon layer formed by anodisation of silicon in different media were carried out using a combination of IBA and FTIR. The FTIR study revealed that the layer mainly consists of SiH and SiH_2 while IBA was used to establish the atomic composition and thickness of these films.

The non-destructive determination of fluorine in many industrial samples using PIGE was standardized. This will enable rapid and sensitive determination of fluorine and other low Z elements in different solid samples including ceramics. GDMS studies for the determination of chlorine at sub-ppm (<500 ppb) in the Zr-2.5Nb samples progressed.

Environmental

The Centre participated in the IAEA-RCA study of biomonitoring i.e. the use of plants as monitors of heavy metal exposure in the environment. Two sets of plants were collected from different locations and analysed for trace metals. Further studies were planned to validate this approach to identify environmental exposure to toxic heavy metals and to relate the trace element concentrations on these samples to various polluting sources through source apportionment approaches. A rapid slurry atomization GFAAS method was investigated and its use in the analysis of biological and environmental samples, without recourse to chemical dissolution, was established.

7

Solar Energy

Solar energy manifested in the form of heat and light, can be used in a number of ways for many purposes. Two principal means are the thermal route using the heat for heating, cooling, drying, water purification and power generation and the photovoltic route converting the light into electricity which can be used for a variety of purposes such as lighting, pumping, communication and refrigeration.

Solar energy has many distinctive features which make it quite an attractive option vis-a-vis the conventional sources of energy. These include its widespread distribution, polution-free nature and virtually inexhaustible supply. India receives solar energy equivalent to over 5,000 trillion kWh/year, which is far more than the total energy consumption of the country. The daily average solar energy incidence varies from 4 to 7 kWh/sq.m depending upon the location. There are 250-300 sunny days in most parts of the country.

Energy in the form of heat is required for a variety of purposes ranging from cooking of food to generation of power. Heat from the sun is being used from time immemorial for a number of purposes like drying of clothes, agricultural produce etc. In recent years, technologies have been developed to harness the heat from the sun more efficiently and optimally to meet some of the thermal energy requirements and thus meet a portion of the increasing energy demand of the country.

Solar thermal energy

Water heating

One of the areas of application of solar thermal technology is heating of water for domestic, commercial and industrial uses. With abundant sunshine for most part of the year, India has been making and using solar water heaters for more than two decades. Around 4,50,000 sq.m. of solar water heating collectors, which could heat more than 22 million litres of water to a temperature of 60-70 degrees C every day, have been installed in the country.

The Ministry of Non-Conventional Energy Sources (MNES) has been promoting this technology through a set of measures which include technology development, demonstration, financial and fiscal incentives, publicity etc. As a result, the technology of solar water heating has now become fairly mature even as further improvements are being pursued.

The economics, reliability and performance are found to be steadily improving. The areas of application which have emerged from extensive field trials are given below:-

— Individual residential and apartment buildings; Restaurants and canteens;

— Guest houses, lodges, hotels and hostels; Hospitals and nursing homes

— Boiler feed water for commercial and industrial applications;

—Process feed water for paint industry, electroplating, galvanizing industry etc. involving direct feed to the various process baths at 70 to 80 C;

— Bottling plants and distilleries for syrup making, bottle cleaning etc.;

— Pharmaceutical, chemical and fertilizer industries; Textile industry;

— Food processing industry

When a solar water heater replaces an electric geyser, it not only saves electricity but also contributes to a reduction in peak load demand. The use of 1000 domestic solar water heaters of 100 litres capacity each can contribute to a peak load shaving of 1 MW. Large solar water heating systems can not only lead to a substantial reduction in the use of conventional, finite, fossil fuel resources like coal and furnace oil but also in the prevention of emission of carbon dioxide and other harmful gases into the atmosphere.

A domestic solar water heater of 100 litres capacity can prevent emission of 1.5 tonnes of carbon dioxide every year. The life of such a system is normally 15 to 20 years. Because of the immense energy and environmental benefits, the market for solar water heating collectors has been steadily expanding in Europe, USA, Japan and the countries in the Mediterranean. In India too, the scope for large-scale use of these systems is enormous.

The manufacturing base of solar water heating systems has expanded substantially during the last five years. There are 37 BIS approved manufacturers at present with a production capacity of more than 100000 sq.m. of collectors per year. The annual sale of solar collectors is now estimated to be around 50000 sq.m. Export of solar collectors and systems has also started. To promote large-scale utilization of this technology in the country financial incentive in the form of soft loans and fiscal incentive in the form of 100% depreciation allowance, besides exemption from Central excise duty, are being provided. The soft loan programme for solar water heaters under the Interest Subsidy Scheme of the NINES is currently being operated by the Indian Renewable Energy Development Agency (IREDA) and five commercial banks viz. Canara Bank, Union Bank of India, Andhra Bank, Bank of Maharashtra, and Punjab & Sind Bank.

The IREDA scheme envisages soft loans at an interest rate of 8.3% for industrial and commercial organisations and at 5% for non-profit organisations. The solar water heating system can be of any capacity. However, the minimum loan available from IREDA is Rs. 2,50,000. For smaller capacity systems including domestic systems, the IREDA loan is made available through its financial intermediaries at an interest rate of 5% per annum. As on December 31, 1998 there are 20 companies empanelled with IREDA as financial intermediaries. These intermediaries are given a line of credit by IREDA in order to finance solar water heating systems in both domestic and commercial categories through leasing and loan modes.

The loans by the commercial banks are provided for installation of solar water heaters up to a capacity of 500 litres. Any individual, institution, association or small business establishments is eligible for this loan up to 85% of the cost of the system at an interest rate of 5% per annum repayable in five years. The soft loan schemes, operated either by IREDA or by the banks, can only be availed only for systems using BIS approved solar water heating collectors.

At the end of 1997-98, MoUs were concluded with Punjab & Sind Bank, Andhra Bank and the Bank of Maharashtra for operating the soft loan scheme on solar water heaters. The scheme of Punjab & Sind Bank was formally launched in June 1998 in Chandigarh. The bank is operating the scheme through all its branches in Punjab & Haryana and the Union Territory of Chandigarh, besides 66 major cities of the country. The scheme of Andhra Bank, formally launched in August 1998, is operated through its branches in most towns of Andhra Pradesh, besides 16 other major cities in country.

The Bank of Maharashtra launched the scheme in September 1998 and is operating it through all its branches in Maharashtra. In order to help/generate more business, the NINES provides an additional amount of Rs. 300 to the banks as promotional incentive / business development charge for each loan disbursed irrespective of the size of the system. Till January, 1999, six training programmes for bank officers have been organized at Delhi, Cochin, Thiruvananthapuram, Chennai, Coimbatore and Lucknow to sensitize the bank officers regarding this new technology. More such programmes in other cities of the country have been planned.

M/s Godavari Fertilizers & Chemicals Ltd., a leading DAP manufacturer at Kakinada in Andhra Pradesh, is the first fertilizer company in the country to install a solar water heating system. The system has a capacity of 120000 litres of water at 80 degree C which is fed to a boiler for conversion into steam. The project costing Rs. 1.43 crores was financed by IREDA. The system was dedicated in July 1998. This is one of the largest systems installed in the country so far and is saving energy to the tune of 6 million kcal/day which represents an annual saving of Rs. 14 lakh. In addition the company is also availing of the income tax and other benefits.

M/s Shivamrut Dudh Utpadak Sahakari Sangh Ltd. at Akluj in Solapur district of Maharashtra has installed a solar water heating system of 30000 litres capacity at 80 degrees C to supply boiler pre-heat water in their dairy unit. The system uses 330 solar collectors and has costed Rs. 34.8 lakh. The main activity of this cooperative is to collect the raw milk from villages and process the same. The handling capacity of the unit is 400000 litters of milk per day. The solar water heating project in this unit was sanctioned by the IREDA under the Interest Subsidy Scheme of the MNES. This system is expected to save 81250 kgs. of furnace oil costing Rs. 7.72 lakh per annum. The system has been fully commissioned in 1998 and is working satisfactorily.

Under the Interest Subsidy Scheme of the MNES, IREDA has also sanctioned a term loan of Rs. 37.49 lakh to M/s D.S.Kulkarni Developers Ltd., Pune for the installation of 56400 litres (12x400 litres & 22x1800 litres) capacity solar water heating systems at 60 degrees C at their Raanwara housing complex in Bavdhan village consisting of 17 flats.

The solar water heating system will cater to the requirements of hot water for bathing and washing purposes to the flat owners in winter months i.e. November to March. Hot water will also be available to the kitchen in the summer months for cooking/cleaning purposes. The project has been partly installed. It serves as a model for the other builders. As the system replaces electric geysers, the pay-back period for the investment has been estimated to be only 2 years. During the year, IREDA has sanctioned loans for 18 such projects to be set up in hotels, educational institutions, hospitals etc. Many State Governments are also pursuing this programme by offering various incentives. It is estimated that till December, 1998, a business of around 25000 sq.m. solar collector area has taken place.

The Expert Group constituted by the Ministry of Urban Affairs & Employment for drafting a Model Code/ Building Bye-laws for making the use of solar water heaters mandatory has had a number of meetings and a draft is being formulated. In the meantime, the Governments of Haryana, Himachal Pradesh, Madhya Pradesh, Punjab, Rajasthan and the Union Territory of Dadra & Nagar Haveli have made installation of solar water heaters mandatory in the functional buildings of the State sector.

Solar cooking

The heat from the sun can also be used for cooking food, thereby saving the conventional fuels to a significant extent. Different types of solar cookers have been developed in the past in our country. These include box solar cooker, steam cooker, solar meal maker with heat storage and concentrating type community cooker.

The Ministry has, till now, been promoting only the box solar cooker, which is ideal for domestic cooking during most part of the year. The cooker is also available with an electrical back-up which has the advantage of cooking the food during non-sunshine hours or cloudy days with nominal consumption of electricity.

The MNES had been offering a subsidy to promote solar cookers which was withdrawn in 1994. After this the MNES has been providing financial support to the State nodal agencies for promotional activities such as publicity, cooking demonstrations and competitions, training, development of marketing network and repair/ servicing facilities at sales outlets etc. Support is also provided to manufacturers and non- governmental organizations (NGOs) through the State nodal agencies. In the case of manufacturers, this support is on 50% cost-sharing basis. During 1998-99, two new concepts were introduced. One provided for the establishment of "solar food restaurants" by the State nodal agencies

In addition to the above, the two loan schemes

launched by the NINES in 1997-98, which were being operated through IREDA and a few commercial banks, were continued during the year. Under this, interest-free loans are made available for purchase of solar cookers to those interested. The loan through IREDA is available for bulk users such as corporate bodies and cooperative societies for supplying solar cookers to their employees and for the IREDA intermediaries for onlending to individuals or for supplying solar cookers to them on hire purchase basis. The bank loan is available for individuals only. In both the schemes the loans are available for purchase of solar cookers with and without electrical back-up.

Some State Governments, including Punjab, have even introduced the concept of organizing solar mandis on a fixed date of every month in major cities where all the manufacturers display their models and conduct cooking demonstrations to attract the buyers. This has been found to be very useful in creating public awareness and increasing the sale of various NRSE devices.

In Lucknow, a solar food restaurant has been established in the State Government office-complex where solar- cooked items are served to the employees during lunch time. This concept has helped in promoting awareness of solar cooking.

Around 5,000 solar cookers were reported to have been sold during the year till December 31, 1998, making the total number of solar cookers sold in the country since the inception of the Ministry to 4,62,000. The cookers are being sold from more than 500 district offices of State agencies and private dealers in the country apart from Aditya Solar Shops, established by the Ministry in major cities. Around 25 active manufacturers are involved in manufacturing and supplying box solar cookers.

Apart from promoting the box solar cooker, the Ministry has taken the initiative to introduce solar cookers for community use. The Ministry had sponsored a project to a few technical institutions and its Regional Test Centres for installation and performance evaluation of the concentrating type community cooker developed by ULOG group of Switzerland. To review the progress of this, a meeting was organized at the Centre for Energy Studies, IIT Delhi on January 28, 1999. This cooker is already being promoted by an NGO in Gujarat for cooking food in community kitchens.

The unique feature of this cooker is that it is possible to cook food with solar energy within the kitchen itself with the help of a secondary reflector. It can be used in the kitchens of ashrams, dharamshalas, army barracks, dhabas, boarding schools etc. as it can cook food for about 50 people at a time.

The Ministry plans to promote this cooker on a large scale in the country after obtaining the performance reports from the Institutions engaged in the evaluation. In addition, a smaller version of this cooker capable of cooking food for around 15 people under the sun is also being tested. This would be useful to individuals and small establishments like road side dhabas and tea shops. The results of the evaluation project are expected by June 1999.

In order to encourage the State nodal agencies to take up large-scale promotion of solar cookers in their respective States and to recognize their efforts made in this direction, the Ministry has been giving a annual awards. The award for the best performance among the States with larger targets for 1997-98 was given to the Gujarat Energy Development Agency, while the award among States with smaller targets was given to the Meghalaya Renewable Energy Development Agency.

Solar air heating

Apart from water heating and cooking of food, drying of farm produce is another promising area for using solar energy. Drying of farm produce in the sun is a common practice in our villages. However, the technology of solar air heating for drying agricultural produce, that has been developed in recent years, would help in reducing post-harvest losses caused by uncontrolled open sun drying. The solar air heating system can be designed as a Full Energy Delivery (FED) or as a Partial Energy Delivery (PED) unit. The PED units having about 2500 sq.m. of collector area, installed under the MNES programme, are already in operation mainly in the southern parts of the country for pre heating the air for drying of tea, spices etc.

During the year, M/s Sakthi Masala Pvt Ltd. has installed a 572 sq.m solar air heating system for drying 15-20 tonnes of coriander at their factory in Mamarathupalayam near Erode in Tamil Nadu. The IREDA had sanctioned a loan of Rs. 21.19 lakh for this project under the Interest Subsidy Scheme of MNES. This project has been installed by M/s Planters Energy Network (PEN), Madurai. The factory had been using firewood for drying coriander prior to this project. The company is expected to save 220 tonnes of firewood, estimated to cost Rs. 2.98 lakh per year. Besides, the quantity of coriander handled to make powder will be increased. The company is installing one more solar air heating unit in its another factory at the same place. The estimated pay-back period for the investment is 7 years. Another company has installed a system for drying of flowers near Coimbatore.

Demonstration & pilot projects

The Ministry has a scheme to demonstrate various solar thermal technologies, including solar water heating systems, for the purpose of evaluating the performance of new technologies and innovative designs, besides establishing their techno-economic viability for specific applications. Under this scheme, a project on solar heating of the hydrotherapy pool at the Spastics Society of Eastern India in Calcutta has been sanctioned.

The Ministry has sponsored a special demonstration project on the development and performance evaluation of improved solar steam cooking system for 10,000 people at Taleti near Mount Abu by the Brahmakumari's organization with part funding from the Ministry for a period of two years. The system envisages the use of automatic tracking solar dish concentrators to convert water into high pressure steam. The steam thus generated will be used for cooking purposes. The system has been completed and is expected to be dedicated soon. A similar system is already in operation at Brahmakumari Ashram in Mount Abu for cooking food for 1,000 people.

A large number of government departments/ agencies are increasingly evincing interest in using various solar energy devices in their existing establishments and new constructions. A number of activities which include special workshops, technical meetings, visits, preparation of reports etc. have been taken up during the year.

Solar buildings

An important role of a building is to provide comfortable indoor conditions for the inhabitants. The energy required for lighting purposes and to keep the building cooler in summer and warmer in winter is quite significant. In India, the energy consumption in the building sector is progressively on the increase and has been taking a larger share of the total electricity generated. Solar-efficient building design, popularly known as 'Solar Architecture' is essentially a climate-responsive architectural concept. By incorporating various innovative features in the building designs, the impact of climate both in summer and in winter can be minimised and as a result, the use of electricity or other conventional fuels can be reduced.

The country has a large potential for energy conservation in buildings through appropriate use of solar energy. A programme to promote solar-efficient building designs in the country is presently being implemented by the MNES with the following components : training and education; publicity and demonstration. The programme which was earlier known as Solar Passive Architecture Programme has been renamed as Solar Buildings Programme from the current year.

Under this programme two buildings, the' HIMURJA Building and the Himachal Pradesh Cooperative Bank Building at Shimla, have been constructed deploying these concepts. A number of buildings in Himachal Pradesh and one building in West Bengal based on this concept, for which detailed project reports have been prepared, are under construction. From this year, the limit for financial assistance for construction of solar efficient buildings under the Demonstration Programme has been increased to Rs. 10 lakh.

A visit by an Expert Team to Himachal Pradesh was organized during the year to assess the effectiveness of these buildings and to examine the feasibility of setting up a Centre in the State for promoting the use of solar energy in the cold regions of the country. The report of the team is under preparation. Meanwhile, IREDA had a meeting with architects to promote solar energy applications in the building sector. The building bye-laws of a number of cities are being examined by one of the groups through a sponsored R&D programme of the

Ministry with the objective of bringing in the energy efficiency aspect in the building codes. Workshops/ seminars to promote the concept of solar efficient building designs were also organized.

Standardisation and quality control

With a view to ensuring a minimum quality and performance of the systems, the Indian National Standards on solar flat plate collectors and solar cookers have been brought out by the Bureau of Indian Standards (BIS). The former was brought out in 1990 (revised in 1992) as IS 12933 (parts 1-5), while the latter was brought out in 1992 as IS 13429 (parts 1-3). The Ministry continued to collaborate with BIS in this regard.

A meeting of the Solar Thermal Sub-Committee constituted by BIS was held in April 1998 to revise these standards. The work for revision of the standards on solar water heating collectors is in progress. A draft revised standard for solar cookers has already been prepared and circulated to various experts for comments and suggestions.

During 1997-98, the use of BIS approved collectors (ISI marked) was made compulsory for any solar water heating system or project seeking soft loan from the commercial banks or IREDA. As a result of various initiatives taken by the Ministry, the number of BIS approved solar collectors has increased from 26 to 37 up to January, 1999. An interaction meeting with BIS officials and manufacturers of solar collectors was organized at Ahmedabad in November, 1998 in order to expedite BIS approval for solar thermal collectors in the Gujarat region.

Apart from the Solar Energy Centre, six Regional Test Centres have been established by the Ministry in different parts of the country for testing solar collectors and cookers and to provide technical backup services. These Centres also act as Technical Backup Units under the solar thermal energy programme. During the year, apart from conducting testing of solar collectors, cookers and related components/products for BIS, State nodal agencies, manufacturers etc., the RTCs conducted a number of training programmes for repair and servicing of products, testing and quality control and for promotion and business generation. A meeting of the Coordinators of the RTCs was held on January 27, 1999 at which a detailed review of the test facilities in these Centres was undertaken. Steps to upgrade the test facilities were identified.

ADITYA solar shops

Solar shops named as "ADITYA" are being established in different parts of the country to promote spot sale of different renewable energy products, servicing and repair of the devices and dissemination of information. The setting up and the overall coordination of the activities of the solar shops are normally being done by the State nodal agencies. The Ministry provides a one-time grant for setting up these shops, besides a nominal recurring grant for initial two years to meet the operational costs. The solar shops are expected to function as customer-friendly outlets on normal business lines and are expected to earn revenues for their operation and maintenance in future.

Table

List of regional test centers

1. Regional Test Centre (Solar Thermal), School of Energy and Environmental Studies & Research, Devi Ahilya Vishwavidyalaya, Taksh Shila Campus, Khandwa Road, Indore - 452 001 (MP)	Phone 0731 460309 Fax 0731 543352 Fax 0731 470372

2. Regional Test Centre(Solar Thermal), Energy Research Centre, Punjab University, sks%erc@PUniv.chd.nic.in Chandigarh - 160 014.	Phone 0172 541944 Fax 0172 541944 e-mail
3. Regional Test Centre (Solar Thermal), School of Energy, Environment & Natural Resources, Madurai Kamraj University, Madurai - 625 021.	Phone 0452 858689 Fax 0452 859139
4. Regional Test Centre (Solar Thermal), Sardar Patel Renewable Energy Research Institute (SPRERI), Post Box No.2, Vallabh Vidhyanagar, Gujarat - 388 120.	Phone 02692 31332 02692 35011 Fax 02692 37982
5. Regional Test Centre (Solar Thermal), School of Energy Studies, Jadavpur University sebsju@gisclol.vsnl.net.in Jadavpur. Calcutta - 700 032.	Phone 033 4732853 Fax 033 4732853
6. Regional Test Centre (Solar Thermal), School of Energy Studies, Physics Department, University of Poona, Pune - 411007.	Phone 020 336061 Fax 020 353899

As a special initiative for the North-East region, sanctions were accorded at the end of 1997-98 for setting up solar shops at Agartala, Guwahati and Manipur. During 1998-99, "ADITYA" solar shops have started functioning in Guwahati and Siliguri. Shops in Bhubaneswar and Lucknow area also likely to start functioning before the end of 1998-99. The construction of the solar shop at Agartala is in the final stage. Two more shops, one in Ahmedabad and other in Gurgaon, have also been sanctioned during the year. A workshop for initiating Renewable Energy Service Centres under Prime Minister's Rozgar Yajana (PMRY) was organized in Calcutta in September, 1998.

Research & development

The research and development activities in the solar

thermal area are aimed at developing new technologies besides improving the design and reliability of the systems already developed. During the year, the following projects have been sanctioned: (1). Survey of Energy Conscious Buildings in India to Tata Energy Research Institute, New Delhi. (2) Feed back Survey-cum-Performance Evaluation of Solar Water Heating Systems and House Heating Systems in Hilly (high altitude) areas of North-Western region to Energy Research Centre, Punjab University, Chandigarh; (3). Autonomous Hybrid Solar Energy System for Thermal/ Electrical Use in Buildings to Central Building Research Institute, Roorkee.

The on-going research efforts in various institutions include analysis of weather data and formulation of design conditions, development of concentrating type solar cookers, solar dryers for agro-products and utilisation of solar energy for buildings. To ensure the quality of solar cookers with electrical back up, being supplied by various manufacturers, a project had been sponsored to Sardar Patel Renewable Energy Research Institute at Vallabh Vidyanagar for developing specifications and test procedures. This was completed during the year. Based on the report submitted, the specifications and test procedures are being finalised for circulation to the State nodal agencies and manufacturers.

A special session on Solar Detoxification, a technology for detoxifying polluted water with the help of solar energy, was organised during the National Solar Energy Convention, 1998 held in Roorkee. This was attended by a number of experts in the field. In this session, a review of two R&D projects on the subject currently being financed by the Ministry was undertaken. A critical assessment of the technology was also made and the thrust areas for further development of the technology were identified.

Solar photovoltaic programme

Solar photovoltaic technology enables the conversion of sunlight into electricity without any moving parts and without causing pollution. The photovoltaic systems have emerged not only as useful sources of power for lighting, water pumping and telecommunications, but also as sources of electricity to cater to the needs of villages, hospitals, lodges, etc. The Solar Photovoltaic (SPV) Programme has resulted in significant technological developments and widespread field demonstrations for various applications. A strong research base as well as indigenous production capabilities have been developed in the entire area of SPV technology starting from silicon material to solar cells, photovoltaic modules and complete systems for various uses.

Research & development

The research and development activities in the solar photovoltaic area are aimed at achieving higher efficiencies of solar cells, reduction in the cost of production of solar photovoltaic cells, modules and systems and improvement in the design and reliability of systems.

Research and development efforts in amorphous silicon solar cell technology were continued and the development of double junction amorphous solar cells of 11% efficiency was reported during the year. The performance tests and reliability tests under controlled conditions were continued on amorphous silicon modules. Efforts were initiated for pilot scale demonstration of the double junction amorphous silicon PV modules.

The research efforts in polycrystalline thin film technology are aimed at developing solar cells based on Cadmium Telluride and Copper Indium Diselenide. The polycrystalline thin film technologies are expected to bring down the cost of photovoltaic modules in due course. Six research projects based on Cadmium Telluride and Copper Indium Diselenide materials are in progress. Laboratory-scale Copper Indium Diselenide solar cells of 11% efficiency were developed. Another R&D project on the development of silicon thin films is also under implementation.

Development and performance testing of components for PV system were continued during 1998-99. The Ministry continued to work with the Bureau of Indian Standards in evolving standards for solar photovoltaic systems. The test facilities created a the Solar Energy Centre of the Ministry and other authorised Test Centres were utilised effectively for testing and standardisation of photovoltaic modules, components and complete PV systems.

The R&D project sanctioned to the Indian Institute of Technology, New Delhi for demonstrating the solar roof concept on a building in their campus progressed satisfactorily during the year.

Demonstration and utilisation programme

The Ministry has been implementing a programme for the demonstration and utilisation of solar photovoltaic systems for various applications. The most common among the systems being deployed under this programme are solar lanterns, home lighting systems/solar home systems, street lighting systems and small capacity village level power plants. These projects have been found to be very useful in unelectrified towns and villages.

During 1998-99 this programme was implemented through the State Renewable Energy Development Agencies and selected NGOs having MNES recognised 'ADITYA' solar shops. In order to facilitate a better interface between the users and the manufacturers, the programme implementing agencies in the States were permitted to allow direct marketing of SPV systems by the manufacturers under the subsidy programme. The Ministry also encouraged the State agencies and the NGOs to avail of the soft loan from the Indian Renewable Energy Development Agency (IREDA) for installation of SPV systems.

The financial support provided by the Ministry for the implementation of the programme in 1998-99 was retained at the previous year's level for the general category of beneficiaries. The pattern of Central financial assistance (CFA) and the eligible categories of beneficiaries in the 1998-99 are given in Tables. Commercial organisations are not covered under the subsidy scheme.

Table

Pattern of Central Financial Assistance

S. No.	SPV System	Central Subsidy	Service Charge
1.	Solar Lantern	Rs. 1500/- (fixed)	Rs. 100/
2.	Home Lighting System /Solar Home System	Rs. 6,000 or 50 % of ex-works cost, which ever is less	Rs. 200/
3.	Street Lighting System	Rs. 12,000 or 50 % of Ex-works cost, which ever is less	-
4.	Power Plants & Other systems	Rs. 2,00,000 / KWp of PV array Capacity or 50 % of Ex-works cost, which ever is less	Rs. 10,000

The Ministry reviewed and modified the existing specifications of the systems for deployment in 199899. The revised specifications were circulated to all the implementing organisations and the manufacturers of the systems. Among the major changes made in the specifications are the inclusion of 6 Volts models for solar lanterns using spill-proof lead acid batteries and increased ratings of the PV modules used in home lighting systems / solar home systems and street lighting systems.

Table

Eligible Categories of Beneficiaries for Central Financial Assistance

SPV System	Eligible Category of Beneficiaries
Solar Lanterns	All categories of individual beneficiaries & non-profit institutions/organisations No individual would be given more than one solar lantern
Home Lighting Systems/Solar Home systems	All categories of individual beneficiaries & non-profit institutions / organisations. No individual would be given more than one solar home lighting system.
Street Lighting Systems	All categories of non -commercial institutions organisations, State nodal agencies, Electricity Boards, Panchayats, Zilla Parishads and DRDAs.
SPV Power Other Systems	All categories of noncommercial Plants / institutions/ organisations, State nodal agencies, Electricity Boards, Panchayats, Zilla Parishads and DRDAs.

To ensure that the solar lanterns supplied under the Programme are reliable and of good quality conforming to the specifications laid down by MNES, the testing and certification of solar lanterns by the Solar Energy Centre (SEC), Gwalpahari or the Electronics Regional Test Laboratory (East), Calcutta or the Central Power Research Institute (CPRI), Thiruvananthapuram continued to be mandatory during 1998-99 as was the case during

1997-98. In addition to the above organisations, the Electronics Test and Development Centre (ETDC), Bangalore was designated during this year as an authorised Centre for testing and certification of SPV modules for the systems to be supplied under the MNES Programme.

The other SPV systems like home lighting systems/ solar home systems and street lighting systems were also required to conform to specifications laid down by the MNES but testing and certification was not mandatory. The SPV systems installed under the Programme were required to carry a warranty for a minimum period of one year for the complete system and ten years for the PV module.

However, for giving a reasonable time to the manufacturers to develop products and get them tested according to the new specifications, at the same time maintaining a continuity in the programme implementation, the enforcement of new specification was phased during the year. For street lighting systems

November 1, 1998 was fixed as the date for enforcement and for solar lanterns and home lighting systems/solar home systems March 1,1999 was fixed. As per the existing requirement, the programme implementing organisations were advised that while placing orders on the manufacturers for the supply of SPV systems, a provision should be made for an annual maintenance contract (AMC) for a period of four years after the one-year warranty period. This would ensure satisfactory operation of the systems installed under the Programme on a sustainable basis.

For giving a thrust and ensuring visibility to the Programme, the following regions in the country were designated as High Focus Areas (HFAs) for implementation in 1998-99 and part of 1999-2000 :

1. All the North-Eastern States (including Sikkim);
2. Andaman & Nicobar Islands;
3. Lakshadweep Islands;
4. Jammu & Kashmir;
5. Hill Districts of Uttar Pradesh;
6. Chhota Nagpur Region in Bihar;
7. Sundarban & Sagar Island in West Bengal;
8. KBK Region in Orissa;
9. Jaisalmer & Barmer Districts in Rajasthan;
10. Bastar District in Madhya Pradesh.

The Ministry has made a provision for financial support to the implementing organisations, manufacturers, associations, authorised test centres, educational institutions and professional bodies for organising training programmes for the users, technicians, designers and field personnel dealing with the SPV systems.

While distributing solar lanterns and solar home lighting systems, preference should be given to girls' hostels, adult education centres meant for women, the DWACRA Centres and to households having a girl child going to a senior / high school.

Targets

Initially, the targets fixed for the year were: 60,000 solar lanterns, 25,000 home lighting systems and PV plants of 100 kWp aggregate capacity. However, in view of the additional proposals received from the programme implementing organisations, the targets were revised to 76,400 solar lanterns, 31,500 home lighting systems, 4,200 street lighting systems and SPV Power Plants with aggregate capacity of 120 kWp. These targets included specific targets for some of the High Focus Areas.

Achievements

Against the above targets, the achievements, as per the reports received till December 31, 1998, were : 20,484 solar lanterns, 15,206 home lighting systems/ solar home systems, 437 street lighting systems and 57 kWp capacity SPV power plants. The implementing agencies have been allowed to achieve the set targets by June 30, 1998. Thus, the programme of the 199899 will spill over to 1999-2000.

For encouraging the NGOs to get involved in the implementation of the SPV programme, the Ministry allocated targets directly to two more NGOs under the 1998-99 Programme and its spill over in 1999-2000. These are the Catholic Hospitals' Association of India (CHAI), Kerala and the All India Womens' Conference (AIWC), New Delhi. This is in addition to the Ramakrishna Mission Ashram, Narendrapur which is associated with the implementation of the SPV programme in the Sundarban region of West Bengal for the last three years.

During 1998-99, a 10 kWp SPV power plant was installed and commissioned at the M. S. Swaminathan Research Foundation (MSSRF) in Chennai. The 26 kWp SPV power plant set up by WBREDA at Sagar Island, West Bengal in the first phase during 1995-96 with MNES support continued to be managed satisfactorily by the local co-operative. The second phase of the project envisaging addition of 26 kWp SPV capacity, sanctioned to WBREDA during 1996-97, was also commissioned during this year and is working satisfactorily. In addition, 10 SPV power plants with an aggregate capacity of 21 kWp were installed in the villages of Punjab by the Punjab Energy Development Agency (PEDA) for street lighting.

As a part of its efforts to "solarise" the Sagar Island in West Bengal, the Ministry sanctioned during 1997-98 a project for installation of three SPV Power Plants of 25 kWp each in Sagar Island by the West Bengal Renewable Energy Development Agency (WBREDA) with MNES subsidy and IREDA's soft loan, besides contributions from the State Government/WBREDA. These power plants are currently under installation and are scheduled to be commissioned before March 31, 1999. The Ministry has sanctioned three more SPV power plants of 25 kWp capacity each for installation in the Sagar Island by the WBREDA with MNES subsidy, soft loan from IREDA and State/WBREDA contribution. These plants are expected to come up during the year 1999-2000.

The 38.7 kWp SPV power plant sanctioned during 1997-98 for installation at Nyoma in Ladakh by the Ladakh Autonomous Hill Development Council (LAHDC), Leh is under implementation.

The Ministry sanctioned three power plants of 5 kWp capacity each, 50 street lights and 35 solar sign boards for installation in the Anandpur Sahib area in Punjab on the occasion of the Tricentenary Celebrations of the Birth of Khalsa in April 1999.

The implementation of the Indo-US Joint Project for the installation of SPV systems for lighting and community activities, taken up in seven villages in the Sunderban region in West Bengal during 1995-96 under the bilateral co-operation programme between India and USA, was continued during 1998-99. This project is being implemented through the WBREDA and Ramakrishna Mission Ashram, Narendrapur (West Bengal). On the US side, the project was supported by the Department of Energy and implemented by the National Renewable Energy Laboratory. The project envisages the installation of 300 home lighting systems, two battery charging stations, a water pumping system, 15 street lighting systems and a medical refrigerator. Almost all the systems have been installed.

The pilot demonstration project for installation of 100 SPV powered water desalination systems in Rajasthan taken up during 1996-97 through the Rajasthan Electronics and Instruments Limited, Jaipur made progress and so far 69 systems have been installed, whose performance is being monitored.

During the year, significant progress was recorded under the World Bank assisted SPV Market Development Programme, which is being implemented by the IREDA. Solar photovoltaic projects with an aggregate capacity of about 2,000 kWp have been sanctioned so far, out of which systems with a capacity about 384 kWp have already been installed and commissioned, as on December 31, 1998. These systems have been installed mainly in the business and corporate sectors.

During the past few years, many organisations have started using SPV systems for a variety of applications on commercial basis as they are found to be economically viable in comparison to other alternatives. These systems are being used to provide power for rural telephones, railway signalling, low power transmitters, cathodic protection, etc. Solar photovoltaic systems with an aggregate capacity of 35 MWp have been deployed all over the country for different applications. In addition, PV products with about 4 MWp capacity have been exported. The sector-wise deployment of PV systems in the country is shown below:

The implementing agencies are responsible for implementing the projects as per the provisions of the respective schemes and are required to submit monthly progress reports during the implementation phase and periodic reports in the post- implementation phase on the performance of the systems. In addition, the field installations are inspected by officials from the MNES regional offices. It is also proposed to have independent evaluation of the SPV systems through professional institutions/organisations.

Awards to programme implementing organizations

Awards for 1997-98 were given during this year to the SPV programme implementing agencies for their performance. For the purpose of awards the programme implementing agencies are divided into two categories based on the size of the programme being implemented by them. Category - I comprises States/Organizations who were allocated targets of 20 kWp and above, while Category - 2 consists of States/Organizations with targets less than 20 kWp. The criterion for evaluation include the physical achievement i.e., the total capacity (kilowattage) of the systems installed as a percentage of the target, as well as the quality of implementation which takes into account factors like submission of progress reports on a regular basis, field performance of the systems, expeditious settlement of accounts, new initiatives and innovations, etc. The States and the agencies which were given awards for 1997-98 are indicated below:

Category - 1

First Prize:	Ramakrishna Mission (RKM) Narendrapur, West Bengal

Category - 2

First Prize:	Power & Electricity Department, Government of Mizoram, Aizawl
Special Prize:	West Bengal Renewable Energy Development Agency (WBREDA), for pioneering work in the implementation of 'ADITYA' Solar Shops & installations of SPV Power Plants.

SPV water pumping programme

The Ministry has been implementing a programme for

promoting SPV water pumping systems for agriculture and related uses and this continued in 199899. The objectives of the programme include gradual introduction of SPV water pumping systems, development of marketing infrastructure for SPV water pumping systems and obtaining direct feedback on the performance and utilisation of SPV water pumping systems for meeting the specific needs of the users in different agro-climatic conditions for different categories of users and various end-uses. The Indian Renewable Energy Development Agency (IREDA) has been entrusted with the implementation of the programme since its inception during 1993-94. During 1998-99 the Rural Electrification Corporation (REC) has been encouraged to participate in the programme. The programme is being implemented through State nodal agencies.

The SPV water pumping programme envisages a combination of subsidy and soft loan to the users. The programme covers water pumping systems in the range of 200 Watts to 2250 Watts of PV array capacity. The programme is open to all categories of users. A cumulative total of 2787 SPV water pumping systems have been installed by December 31, 1998.

During 1998-99, the subsidy on water pumping systems was Rs. 125 per peak Watt of PV array used with pumping system, subject to a maximum of Rs. 2.0 lakh per system. The users of PV water pumping systems continued to be eligible for soft loan @ 5% for the unsubsidised part of the price of pumping system, subject to a maximum of Rs. 2.5 lakh, depending on the size of the PV array used with water pumping system. The maximum amount of loan for SPV water pumping systems up to 700 Watts capacity was limited to Rs. 50,000. For SPV water pumping systems up to I 100 watts and 1600 Watts this limit was Rs. 1,20,000 and Rs. 1 80,000 respectively. For higher capacity systems up to

2250 Watts the maximum loan limit was Rs. 2,50,000. This loan is to be repaid in instalments, beginning at the end of the first year after the sanction of the loan.

A study was undertaken through the Administrative Staff College of India (ASCI), Hyderabad to find out alternative financing schemes for marketing SPV water pumping systems. The interim report submitted by ASCI has brought out the usefulness of SPV water pumping systems for agriculture and has come out with preliminary suggestions on a financing model.

Publicity & awareness generation

Publicity and awareness campaigns through electronic and print media and exhibitions were continued during the year. Through radio programmes in Hindi and other regional languages awareness was created about the SPV water pumping systems. To encourage publicity by the manufacturers a scheme for reimbursement of 50% of the cost of publicity on specific items, subject to a limit of Rs.1,00,000/- per supplier, introduced in 1997-98, was continued. IREDA has brought out brochures in Hindi, English and regional languages, The SPV water pumping systems were displayed in exhibitions and Kisan Melas.

Training

Training programmes on the operation, maintenance and water management aspects of the PV water pumping systems for actual users, local technicians and mechanics were continued during the year.

Performance evaluation

In order to study the field performance of the PV water pumping systems installed for agricultural use in different agro-climatic conditions, the Ministry continued to support an evaluation study by agriculture universities and ICAR institutions having expertise on water management. The initial findings of the evaluation of the water pumping system in terms of its performance and optimal utilisation of water for different crops and cropping pattern were quite useful from the users' viewpoint.

Industrial activity

The MNES functions as the administrative Ministry for all matters relating to industrial licences, foreign investments, imports and exports in the area of solar photovoltaics. During the year, nine companies were engaged in the regular manufacture of solar cells and 21 companies were involved in the manufacture of PV modules.

In addition, about 50 companies were actively engaged in the manufacture of a variety of PV systems. The overall production in the country during 1997-98 was 8.2 MW of solar cells and 11 MW of PV modules. The production during 1998-99 (till December 1998) is estimated to be about 4 MW of solar cells and about 5 MW of PV modules.

Water pumping windmills, small aerogenerators and hybrid systems

Water pumping windmills, small aerogenerators and wind-solar photovoltaic systems are capable of harnessing the vast wind energy potential in the country for meeting mechanical and electrical energy requirement in stand-alone mode especially in rural and remote areas.

Research & development

A cost-effective direct-drive windmill with rotor diameter of 4.5 metres and suitable for operation i wind speed range of 3-5 m/s is being developed by the Centre for Scientific Research (CSR), Auroville under a R&D project sponsored by the Ministry. With certain changes in the design of the windmill, the prototype expected to deliver more water at lower wind speed

Performance evaluation

The National Aerospace Laboratory (NAL) Bangalore was commissioned to carry out an evaluation of the performance of small aerogenerators installed under the programme of the Ministry from 1993-94 onwards. This evaluation continued during 1998-99 and the NAL, which has already inspected small aerogenerators installed in Assam, Rajasthan and Tamilnadu, has submitted its initial reports on these installations.

Demonstration programme

During the year, the Ministry continued with the demonstration programme on water pumping windmills, small aerogenerators and wind-solar PV hybrid systems. Small aerogenerators/ wind-solar PV hybrid systems up to 10 kW capacity can be installed under the programme. The programme is implemented through the State nodal agencies. The manufacturers of windmills are also eligible to market windmills directly to users. The State nodal agencies and the manufacturers identify the sites for installation of windmills as per the guidelines of the Ministry.

In the case of small aerogenerators and wind-solar PV hybrid systems, NINES also directly supports the user agencies. The Ministry provides a cost-sharing contribution of Rs. 20,000/- for a direct-drive windmill, Rs. 30,000/- for a geared type windmill and Rs. 45,000/- for a AV 55 Auroville type direct-drive windmill. A total of 515 windmills have been installed till December 31, 1998, of which 63 installations were reported during the year. A majority of the windmills installed under the programme are of geared type design, which are capable of lifting water from depths up to 60 metres. These water pumping windmills are being used for supply of water for drinking purpose, horticulture, aqua-culture, agriculture etc.

The NINES supports installation of small aerogenerators and hybrid systems not only by various Central/State Government organisations and communities but also by individuals and industrial units. The grant for community applications and direct use by the Central/ State Government, defence and paramilitary, is to the extent of 80% of the ex-works cost of the system subject to a maximum of Rs. 2.0 lakh per kW. For R&D organisations, academic institutions, individuals and industrial users the grant provided under the programme was kept at 50% of the ex-works cost subject to a maximum of Rs. 1.25 lakh per kW.

Small aerogenerator systems with aggregate capacity of 35 kW have been installed under the programme. In addition, small aerogenerators and wind-solar PV hybrid system demonstration projects of an aggregate capacity of 28 kW are under different stages of installation.

Publicity

Publicity and awareness generation campaigns through electronic, print media and exhibitions were continued during the year. Through radio programmes in Hindi and other regional languages awareness is being created about water pumping windmills.

8

Power from Renewables

Electricity is the key to economic development and though the per capita electricity consumption in our country has risen from 15 units to 350 units over the past five decades it is still way behind the levels achieved in developed countries. It is not that there is no demand for more electricity. In fact, the continuing power shortage has been often cited as the main factor for the slowdown in industrial growth. The installed capacity is projected to reach 240,000 MW by 2012 which would entail an annual addition to power generation capacity 10,000 MW. The conventional fossil fuel resources for power generation are getting depleted fast and there is a growing concern over the environmental degradation caused by conventional power plants. Against this backdrop, power generation from non-conventional resources has assumed significance.

Wind power

Recognising this, the Government of India has been making conscious efforts to tap renewable sources for power generation. As a result, grid quality power generation from renewables, such as wind, small hydro and biomass has now attained maturity and 1378 MW, or around 1.5% of the total grid capacity in the country, is now based on renewable energy sources. With the wind power generation capacity reaching 992 MW, India now ranks fourth in the world in wind power generation. Most of this capacity has come through private investments. Over 3.7 billion units of electricity have been fed to various State grids from these projects. New initiatives have been taken towards reassessment and expansion of the wind resource base; establishment of a Centre for Wind Energy Technology; and motivating large private sector corporations, public sector units and power utilities to set up wind power projects.

Biomass power

Power generation based on biomass holds considerable promise in our country which produces over 400 million tonnes of crop resides besides large quantities of bagasse in the sugar mills. The potential of power generation from biomass materials and cogeneration based on bagasse is estimated at 19500 MW. To exploit this potential the Ministry of Non-conventional Energy Sources (MNES) has launched a well-planned programme to promote power generation from crop resides and other biomass products available besides cogeneration in sugar mills.

The Indian programme of cogeneration in sugar mills has been acclaimed as the world's largest. As many as 28 projects based on biomass and bagasse with aggregate capacity of 141 MW have so far been commissioned and another 27 with a total capacity of 180 MW are under installation. The recent installations include a 12 MW project in Tamil Nadu based on varied biomass material and a 6 MW project in Madhya Pradesh based on rice husk. The notable initiatives taken in this area include a Programme Partnership Initiative to accelerate financial closure of cogeneration projects; finalisation of several demonstration projects in cooperative sugar factories; and formulation of a new "joint venture" model for implementation of these projects.

Small hydel projects

Small hydropower generation, which is particularly suitable for remote, hilly regions, is being expanded. A capacity of 173 MW has so far been installed and a capacity of 188 MW is under installation. It has been decided to transfer the work relating to small hydro power projects with capacity ranging between 3 MW and 25 MW from the Ministry of Power to the MNES. A Plan of Action is being prepared by the NINES to cope with the enlarged scope of work. Surveys and investigations are now proposed to be undertaken on an area-based, cluster approach rather than the current site-based approach. It is planned to keep a shelf of projects ready, along with necessary clearances, which could be offered by the States to investors and developers.

Solar power

Yet another renewable source being tapped is solar energy which is available in abundance in our country. Besides promoting decentralised applications of solar energy, grid quality power generation programmes based on solar thermal and solar photovoltaic technologies are being supported. A 140 MW Integrated Solar Combined Cycle (ISCC) Power Project at Mathania near Jodhpur in Rajasthan is being given a final shape.

Techno-economic clearance from the Central Electricity Authority (CEA) is being obtained. This will be the first of its kind, and the largest such project in the world. The Ministry is also providing support to grid interactive solar photovoltaic projects for voltage support at the tail-ends of rural grids and for peak shaving/ demand side management in urban centres. Grid interactive solar photovoltaic power projects with an aggregate capacity of 815 kW have so far been installed and projects with total capacity of 750 kW are under installation.

Waste to energy

Urban, municipal and industrial wastes too are capable of being used for power generation. According to conservative estimates, at least 1000 MW can be generated from urban and municipal wastes and another 700 MW from industrial wastes. To exploit this potential fully, the NINES is providing attractive financial and fiscal incentives under the National Programme on Energy Recovery from Urban, Municipal and Industrial Wastes for promotion and development of projects based on appropriate conversion technologies such as biomethanation, gasification, pelletisation and land filling. While projects with an aggregate capacity of about 7 MW have been completed and projects with a capacity of 4 MW are under execution, a number of proposals for the installation of 'waste-to-energy' projects have been received from the State Governments, private promoters, urban local bodies and industries.

Policy initiatives

The MNES had issued guidelines to all the States on policies for power generation from renewables with a view to encouraging commercial developments in this sector. A dozen States have announced policies but there are several deviations from the guidelines issued by the Ministry in the policies announced by some States. The matter is being followed up with those States to bring about a near-uniform policy regime all over the country.

The Maharashtra Government has announced a very attractive policy, which includes third party sale, sales tax incentive, and protection against foreign exchange variations and 'pass through' for conventional fuels. Meetings have been held at the level of Chief Secretary in most of the potential States in regard to the policies and other institutional and infrastructural measures to accelerate commercial projects. A proposal has been made for earmarking a portion of the 'cess' on conventional electricity generation for development of small hydropower and other renewable energy power projects. A proposal has also been mooted for deregulating power distribution from stand-alone projects based on non- conventional energy sources, which are connected to the grid.

Wind power programme

India has a wind power potential of 20,000 MW according to initial estimates which have been scaled up recently to 35,000 MW at 30m hub height and 45,000 MW at 50m hub height. Considering such a huge potential, a national programme was initiated towards the end of the Sixth Plan in 1983-84 to tap this potential by adopting a market-oriented strategy and this has resulted in a successful commercial development of wind power technology and substantial additions to power generation capacity in the country.

The installed capacity of wind power generation has touched 992 MW by December 1998, of which commercial projects account for 941 MW and demonstration projects 51 MW. At the beginning of the Eighth Plan the installed capacity of wind power was about 40 MW and by the end of the Plan period the figure rose to 900 MW. Thus the Eighth Plan witnessed a substantial addition of 860 MW to total power generation capacity from wind energy. This represents a significant over- achievement of the initial target of 100 MW and the revised target of 500 MW. In the first two years of the Ninth Plan another 100 MW has been added—70 MW in 1997-98 and 30 MW in 1998-99 up to December 1998. The wind power projects have generated so far over 3.7 billion units.

The significant progress made in this sphere, which has earned for the country the distinction of being recognised as a " Wind Super Power" by the Worldwatch

Institute in 1998, was the result of a range of policy support measures and incentives announced by the Ministry of Non-Conventional Energy Sources (NINES) to promote research and development for inducting state-of-the-art wind energy technology on the one hand and to encourage private entrepreneurs to take up commercial projects.

The key elements of the strategy adopted were: comprehensive assessment of wind resource in different parts of the country, induction and demonstration of the state-of-the-art wind turbine equipment, association of the State Electricity Boards and the industry in the programme from the inception, development of infrastructure, building up of the capacity for manufacture, installation, operation and maintenance of wind electric generators. In short the programme is aimed at catalysing commercialisation of wind power generation in the country

Wind resource potential

The most prominent feature of the wind climatology in India is the monsoon circulation. The wind speed and power density are influenced by the strong southwest summer monsoon, starting in May-June, when cool, humid air moves towards the land and by the weaker northeast winter monsoon, starting in October, when cool, dry air moves towards the ocean. From March to August, the winds are uniformly strong over the entire Indian Peninsula, except the eastern peninsular coast. The wind speeds during the period November to March are relatively weak, though winds of higher speed blow during a part of this period along the Tamil Nadu coastline.

A Wind Energy Data Handbook was published in 1983, based on an analysis of the information and data on wind made available by the vast network of meteorological observatories. This served as a preliminary data source for the early initiatives taken during the Seventh Plan (1985-90). In 1985, an extensive Wind Resource Assessment Programme was taken up comprising wind monitoring, wind mapping and complex terrain projects. This programme which now covers 24 States, is today the world's largest wind resource assessment effort covering over 600 stations and is being implemented in co-ordination with the Field Research Unit of the Indian Institute of Tropical Meteorology at Bangalore and the State nodal agencies. As many as 101 wind monitoring stations are in operation at present. So far, five volumes of the Handbook on Wind Energy Resource Survey for India have been published covering the wind data from 152 wind monitoring stations.

The potential windy locations have been identified in the flat coastal terrains of southern Tamil Nadu, Kerala, Gujarat, Lakshadweep, Andaman & Nicobar Islands, Orissa and Maharashtra. Favourable sites have also been identified in some inland areas of Karnataka, Andhra Pradesh, Madhya Pradesh, West Bengal, Uttar Pradesh and Rajasthan. The norms for the selection of sites have been revised and according to these the annual mean wind power density will be used as a norm, instead of the annual mean wind speed, to identify the favourable sites. According to the revised guidelines, the locations having an annual mean wind power density which is greater than 150 watts per sq. metre at 30 metre height are considered suitable for wind power projects. On this basis, 160 locations with an aggregate potential of about 5000 MW have so far been identified in 13 States.

The wind resource assessment efforts have so far been concentrated mainly in the relatively simple, flat or coastal terrains. The zone of influence of a windy station identified in such terrains spans over several sq. km. where wind farm projects can be planned with a higher degree of confidence. However, it is expected that similar or even better wind conditions would exist for wind farm projects in areas yet to be explored particularly in the mountainous and hilly regions of north and northeastern India. In fact, some of the best locations identified so far in the country, such as Muppandal in Tamil Nadu, Jogimatti in Karnataka and Rammakkelmedu in Kerala, are in complex terrains. Different methods for wind resource assessment, such as Geographic Information System (GIS), Wind Atlas, etc. are proposed to be employed for complex terrains in view of the extreme variations over relatively small areas on account of local factors.

According to initial estimates, India has a wind power potential of around 20,000 MW. The exploitable wind power capacity is being reassessed considering the new generation of wind electric generators, higher unit sizes and increased hub-heights.

Several new initiatives have been taken to reassess the gross potential, estimate the potential on the basis of existing upper wind data and the revised guidelines for identification of favourable sites. According to a recent study, the gross wind power potential is estimated to be larger at higher hub heights. The technical potential presently estimated at about 9000 MW will also go up with the augmentation of grid capacity in the potential States.

The other initiatives include preparation of Master Plans for 80 potential sites taking into account the zone of influence around each mast. Efforts have also been intensified to identify windy locations, particularly in the Northern & North-Eastern Regions, based on local factors. Wind monitoring masts of 50 metre height are being installed at some of the locations to confirm the power law index for extrapolation of wind data.

Demonstration programme

The programme for demonstration wind farms was initiated in 1985 and the experience has been favourable with the technology generally performing up to expectations and the wind resource assessment programme continuing to reveal even more promising sites. The demonstration projects have been established at 23 locations in 8 States. Different types and designs of wind turbines have been demonstrated and new potential areas have been opened up. The wind machine availability in these projects has been of the order of 90-95 per cent and maximum annual capacity factors of up to 30 per cent have been reached. Generation of 2 to 2.5 million units per year per MW has been achieved.

The demonstration projects have helped to create awareness about the new technologies and provide information on operating and economic factors useful for taking investment decisions relating to development of large-scale wind farms on commercial basis. The basic capacity for planning, siting, layout and configuration design; execution of foundations and other civil and electrical site works, and grid interface has been developed in industry, technical institutions, electricity boards, nodal agencies and consulting organizations. Indigenous expertise and capability on handling, transportation, storage as well as local erection (with and without large cranes), commissioning, start-up, testing, maintenance and repair has also grown, obviating the need to seek foreign expertise for undertaking this work.

The demonstration projects are implemented through the State Governments, State Nodal Agencies or State Electricity Boards. Sixty per cent of the full cost of the WEG, including spares and erection/commissioning, is met by the MNES, while the balance cost and other local civil/electrical costs are required to be met by the concerned State. A benchmark of Rs 3.2 crore/MW has been fixed for the determination of the MNES support for Demonstration Projects. The concerned State/Agency meets all the expenses towards the cost of the project over and above the eligible cost including escalations, if any. For the wind-diesel projects, the full cost of the wind-turbine and control equipment is provided by the MNES, with the cost of the DG set or its upgradation and local works being met by the State Government.

The Ministry also supports projects in the developing and the neighbouring countries, wherein the full cost of wind turbine equipment, including spares and erection/ commissioning, is provided by MNES, with local works being undertaken by the recipient country. Inquiries have been received from Indonesia and Argentina for setting up demonstration projects.

The demonstration projects are under implementation at Gude Panchgani (1.84 MW) in Maharashtra and at Fraserganj (IMW) in West Bengal. A 500 kW wind-diesel project has been planned for Sagar Island in West Bengal. A wind-diesel project is also being finalised for Kavaratti & Agatti Islands in Lakshadweep. Proposals for demonstration projects at Jaisalmer (2MW) in Rajasthan and at Hanumanhatti (2 MW) in Karnataka are being finalised. Proposals have also been received for demonstration projects at Ramakalmedu (2 MW) in Kerala and at Sogi (2 MW) in Karnataka. The other States having wind power potential have been requested to finalise proposals for demonstration projects.

Commercial development

A notable feature of the Indian programme has been the interest evinced by the private investors/developers in setting up commercial wind power projects. Commercial projects with an aggregate capacity of 941 MW have so far been established, mainly in Tamil Nadu, Gujarat and Andhra Pradesh. The largest installation of wind turbines in the country so far is in the Muppandal-Perungudi area near Kanyakumari in Tamil Nadu, with an aggregate capacity of about 400 MW. This represents one of the largest concentrations of wind farm capacity at a single location.

The Indian Renewable Energy Development Agency (IREDA) Ltd., a public sector enterprise under the MNES, has been operating a revolving fund for development, promotion and commercialisation of renewable energy technologies by providing soft loans. It has received considerable international assistance. It has received a World Bank and Global Environment Facility (GEF) line of credit amounting to US $ 78 million, co-financed by DANIDA, to promote commercial wind power generation. An ADB line of credit for commercial wind power development has also become available to IREDA which is negotiating lines of credit from the KfW (Germany) and the OECF (Japan). Apart from IREDA, a number of major financial institutions, such as IDBI, ICICI and IFCI, besides the Rural Electricity Corporation and the Power Finance Corporation have been financing wind power projects. The financing and leasing companies in the private sector have also extended support to the wind sector.

The interest rates of IREDA has been brought down to 14%, with a repayment period of 10 years, and the financing provided for up to 75% of the project cost. The IREDA's fast track equipment financing facility has been extended to projects up to 2 MW. In fact, taking into account the concessions available as per IREDA's lending norms, the interest rate could now be as low as 8% for certain categories of commercial projects.

To give further impetus to the wind sector in the country, large private sector corporations have been invited to avail of the fiscal and promotional incentives for setting up wind farm projects not only to meet their captive requirements but also as a business proposition. In addition, the public sector power generating entities such as NTPC, NHPC or State Power Development Corporations are being asked to earmark a certain share of all new capacity addition to the renewable sources. The large public sector undertakings in the category of Navratnas and Government departments like Railways and Telecommunications that are big consumers of electricity, are being motivated to go in for wind power generation. The NTPC and the NHPC are planning large wind power projects and have already initiated action in this regard.

An "Interaction Meet" was organised with large private industrial houses for promoting the establishment of wind power projects. The meeting evoked encouraging response. A Business Meet on investments in wind power was organised by the Indian

Merchants Chamber (IMC) at Mumbai in association with the IREDA, the State Nodal Agency and the MNES. A large number of manufactures of wind energy equipment, developers, investors, and Government agencies participated in the Business Meets and had detailed interaction with the representative from the MNES and the State nodal agencies, including the State Electricity Boards

Promotional policies

A package of incentives is available for promotion of wind farms. This includes tax concessions such as accelerated depreciation, tax holiday, soft loans, customs and excise duty reliefs, liberalised foreign investment procedures, etc. The income tax, import and excise duty regimes are constantly being reviewed to allow induction, development and deployment of the latest technologies and to provide for healthy competition. Guidelines were issued by the Ministry to all the States on the general policies and the facilities to be offered for wheeling/banking/purchase of power from such projects. It was proposed that the State Governments might consider purchasing such power at least @ Rs.2.25/kWh (base year 1994-95). Supplementary guidelines were also circulated, which provide for annual escalation @ 5 per cent and suggestions for security of payments for the power sold. Nine potential States have already come forward and announced attractive policies for private sector wind power projects. A few States, such as Gujarat, Madhya Pradesh and Maharashtra, have also announced attractive sales tax exemption/ deferment policies for investment in wind power projects.

The Maharashtra Government has come out with an attractive policy during the current year and this has initiated a large-scale development of wind power in the State. A commendable initiative of linking sales tax incentive to generation of energy has been announced. The Governments of Tamil Nadu and Andhra Pradesh were addressed separately by the Ministry on the deviation from the MNES guidelines. Specific suggestions have been made to the Tamil Nadu Government to restore the third party sale facilities, uniform buy-back rate and allow the period of banking to one year instead of three months. Similarly, the Government of Gujarat was advised to announce a policy for power projects based on non-conventional energy sources as per the Ministry's guidelines.

Manufacture of WEGs

The wind turbines installed so far in the country are predominantly of the fixed pitch 'stall' regulated design. However, the recent trend is towards better aerodynamic design, use of lighter and larger blades, higher towers, direct drive and variable speed gearless operation using advanced power electronics. Electronically operated wind turbines do not consume reactive power, which is a favourable factor for maintaining a good power factor in the typically weak local grid networks. The unit size of machines has gone up from 55-100 kW in the first few projects to 400-600 kW in the recent projects. The productivity of the larger machines is higher than that of the earlier smaller machines.

A large number of companies have tied up with foreign wind turbine companies for joint venture/ licensed production of wind electric generators in India.

As many as 15 manufacturers are engaged in the production of wind turbine equipment. The annual production capacity of the domestic wind turbine industry is about 500 MW at present. The progress in phased indigenisation has been satisfactory. Joint ventures have also come up in blade production. The annual turnover of the wind industry had reached about Rs. 1500 crore during the Eighth Plan. Five wind turbines of 600 kW capacity were exported to Srilanka for a pilot wind power project being implemented by the Ceylon Electricity Board during December, 1998. Export orders are also being negotiated with other neighbouring countries by the Indian wind turbine companies.

Research & development

Research and development activities are undertaken through research institutions, national laboratories, universities and industry for the development of cost-effective technologies and systems to improve the quality of power generation from wind power projects. The development of an Intelligent Power Controller has been taken up by the Electronic Research & Development Centre (ER&DC) in Thiruvananthapuram with the objective of maximising power generation from wind electric equipment. The first prototype has been developed and is being tested in the field. A project for improvement in the quality of power and integration of wind farms in the weak grids has also been taken up in coordination with RISO and DEFU of Denmark. The project aims at preparation of guidelines for integration of wind turbines in weak grids.

A project entitled "In-situ Power Curve Measurements on Grid Connected Wind Electric Generators" has been taken up by National Aerospace Laboratories (NAL), Bangalore. This project aims at the determination of on-site performance vis-a-vis the claimed performance. It envisages in-situ power curve measurements on about ten wind turbines of different makes and models. The Report is being finalised.

At an interactive meeting with the Ministry the manufacturers of wind electric generators agreed to take up technology development and progressive indigenisation of wind electric generators so as to produce efficient machines suited to Indian conditions related to grid, wind resource, and other infrastructure. The industry also agreed to create in-house R&D facilities for technology development. The MNES would support the R&D proposals from the industry on a cost-sharing basis, as per its new R&D policy for new designs/technology upgradation.

Centre for wind energy technology (C-WET)

A Centre for Wind Energy Technology (C-WET) is being established, as an autonomous registered society, at Chennai in Tamil Nadu which will cover R&D, technology upgradation, testing, certification, standardisation, training and information dissemination. The Centre will serve as the technical focal point for wind power development in India This is expected to improve further the price-performance ratio through technology development in association with the industry and to increase the competitiveness of indigenous wind turbine equipment, which, in turn, will minimise the need for fiscal incentives. A Wind Turbine Test Station is also planned to be set up as part of CWET, with assistance from DANIDA, for testing certification and standardisation activities. The testing of the first wind turbine is likely to be taken up during 1999.

Guidelines for setting up projects

The Ministry had issued comprehensive guidelines in July 1995 to bring about healthy and orderly growth of the wind energy sector and to achieve optimum generation of power in the most efficient and cost-effective manner. The guidelines were revised in June 1996, making them more comprehensive. They were again updated in early 1997. These guidelines relate to preparation of Detailed Project Reports (DPR), micrositing, selection of wind turbine equipment, operation & maintenance, performance evaluation, etc. These guidelines have created awareness in the State Electricity Boards, State nodal agencies, manufacturers, developers and investors about planned development and implementation of wind power projects. The guidelines have been widely welcomed and have helped in improving the performance of the sector. The list of manufactures is updated periodically during the year on the basis of testing/certification from international test centres and certification agencies.

Wind energy estates

In order to encourage small private investments in one or two machines, the concept of 'Wind Energy Estates' in the joint sector, with the participation of the private sector, State Governments and the MNES/ IREDA, was mooted by the Ministry. These "Estates" are to be set up in windy areas, where fully developed plots would be provided for installation of WEGs by individual investors. The joint sector company would undertake land acquisition/leasing, development of infrastructure and grid facilities, secure necessary clearances and undertake installation and operation/ maintenance of wind turbines on behalf of the investors. Such an approach would help to reduce the gestation period, provide infrastructural facilities and reduce costs for small investors. The first such company has become functional in Madhya Pradesh, and has set up a capacity of about 14 MW in its Wind Energy Estate near Indore. This company has performed well and declared a dividend of 20% in all the three years of its operations, namely 1995-96, 1996-97 and 1997-98. A capacity of 2.3 MW was added during 1998-99. The Governments of Andhra Pradesh, Maharashtra and Karnataka have, in particular, been requested to promote the concept of Wind Energy Estates in order to benefit the small investors.

Monitoring and evaluation

The performance of all the wind power projects is monitored on a regular basis. Monthly progress reports of the demonstration as well as commercial projects are prepared and their performance evaluated. Officers of the Ministry regularly visit various projects for an on-the-spot assessment and inspection. Wind farm coordination meetings are organised by the Ministry at regular intervals to monitor the progress of various projects. The Regional Offices of the Ministry also provide the feedback on the programme. A project on 'Performance Evaluation of Wind Farms has been taken up to provide monthly quarterly and annual reviews of performance.

Biomass power programme

Biomass constitutes 14% of the world energy resource and 38% of the energy consumed in the developing countries, predominantly in the rural and traditional sectors of the economy. In view of the rapid increase in the use of fossil fuel and the steady decline in the share of biomass in total energy consumption, there has of late been a renewed interest in promoting biomass as a source of power generation on a commercial scale which holds considerable promise. Moreover, the power projects based on biomass offer new avenues for employment through collection, storage, handling and efficient utilisation of biomass materials. It is estimated that a 5 MW biomass-based power project will generate at least 1 lakh mandays of employment per year, particularly in the rural area.

In this context, all the possible routes for conversion of biomass into electricity, viz. combustion, cogeneration, gasification route etc., have to be exploited. In our country more than 405 million tonnes of crop resides are produced every year, a large portion of which is either wasted or used inefficiently.

According to conservative estimates, even on the basis of the present pattern of utilisation of these resides and the use of only the surplus biomass materials, more than 16,000 MW of power can be generated. Bagasse-based cogeneration for surplus power generation is of particular significance. It has been estimated that around 3,500 MW of additional power can be produced if all of the 430 sugar mills in our country switched over to modern techniques of cogeneration. The power so produced will benefit not only the sugar mills but also the cane growers, as the mills would be in a position to pay more for the cane.

Biomass power potential

From Surpluss Biomass	16,000 MW
From Bagasse (Cogeneration) in the existing sugar mills	3,500 MW
Total	19,500 MW

Exploitation of the abundant biomass energy resources available in our country is therefore being accorded a high priority by the Ministry. Development of cost-effective and reliable technologies as well as field projects for tapping these resources assume special significance. The implementation of these projects is being facilitated through comprehensive programmes

Table

State-wise potential for bagasse-based cogeneration

State	Potential
Maharashtra	1000
Uttar Pradesh	1000
Tamil Nadu	350
Karnataka	300
Andhra Pradesh	200
Bihar	200
Gujarat	200
Punjab	150
Others	100
Total	3500

launched by the Ministry, which seek to create a favourable policy environment, encourage technology upgradation, ensure market for the power generated, promote greater public awareness and provide for training and manpower development. The market forces are being catalysed through various fiscal and promotional incentives. The Ministry also provides financial support to specific categories of projects through demonstration and interest subsidy schemes.

The demonstration projects are oriented towards promoting state-of-the-art technologies while the interest subsidy schemes seek to promote commercial projects. The use of contemporary technology is all the more important in the energy sector which is a key determinant of sustainable socioeconomic development. The strategy for the promotion of power generation form biomass is being periodically fine-tuned based on the experience and the feedback. As a result, a broad and competitive manufacturing base, a relatively large and sophisticated infrastructure for manpower development and R&D, besides a growing market for biomass- based power have been created.

As continuous technological innovation is both possible and necessary, the Ministry is keen to support research and development efforts. About a dozen areas in bagasse cogeneration have been identified initially for focused attention. These include bagasse drying, baling and storage, gasification of bagasse, energy audits of pumps and motors, and condensate recoveries. Use of alternative biomass sources, to improve the commercial viability of cogeneration during the off-season, is also being promoted.

The Ministry has recently broadened the coverage of the subsidy schemes with reference to the biomass resource and technology base. Several new features have been included in the schemes to enable the adoption of these options. The financing of commercial projects under the Interest Subsidy schemes has been widened to include State Financial Corporations, State Industrial Development/Investment Corporations, nationalised banks as well as other State public sector/leasing and financial corporations. Use of second hand equipment has also been permitted for these projects subject to certain provisions.

As a result of these measures, 28 biomass based power projects, including cogeneration plants, with a total capacity of 141 MW have been commissioned during the last two years and another 27 projects with total capacity of 180 MW are under construction as on December 31, 1998.

National programme

The national programme has the following components namely biomass-based power generation; biomass/bagasse-based power generation; taluka level biomass-based project and taluka level biomass assessment studies. The objective of the national programme is to establish the techno-commercial feasibility and viability of power generation from biomass materials which are either wasted or suboptimally utilised.

The biomass materials which are sought to be utilised for power generation include straw, stalks, stems and fines, agro-industrial processing residues such as shells, husks, deoiled cakes, forestry residues and woody biomass grown in specially dedicated energy plantation.

The conversion technologies include combustion, gasification, incineration, pyrolysis etc. deploying gas/steam turbine, dual fuel engine/gas engine, or combination thereof, either in "power alone" or in cogeneration (of more than one energy forms -steam and power) mode. Each plant will have a minimum capacity of 1 MW and will be grid interfaced.

The combustion technology is similar to that of coal-based thermal power generation wherein the biomass is burnt in a boiler to generate steam which is used to drive a turbine to generate electricity. The gasification technology involves conversion of solid biomass into a combustible gas through thermo-chemical combustion which is used in duel-fuel or gas engine/turbine to generate electricity.

Power from biomass: eligibility & support structure

Resource Base	Biomass (Stalk, Straw, Husk, Fines of biomass origin, Agro-processing residues etc.) Bagasse;
Technology Base	Any technology route, appropriate & efficient for conversion to power; gas steam turbine, dual fuel engine/gas engine route, involving pyrolysis, gasification incineration with/without intermediate pellestisation/briquetting; or a combination thereof;
Application Base	Cogeneration (Steam & Power) or Power
Capacity Base	Min 1 MW surplus; grid interfaced.
Financing Base	All FIs Industrial Development/Investment Corporations; All nationalised banks & State/Public Sector leasing & financial corporations severally or in consortia;
Implementing Arrangements	Through State Govt./State nodal agencies and FIs
Eligible Promoters	Promoters, individuals or in consortia with other promoter; Public Sector institutions, Voluntary agencies; registered industry associations-, registered companies and State nodal agencies;
	BOOT, BOT, BOLT, BOOM, BOO basis or IPP Mode

Cogeneration, i.e. multiple and sequential use of a fuel for production of steam and power in a process industry, aims at surplus power generation in industries such as sugar mills, paper mills, rice mills, etc., where biomass resources are either generated or consumed in their main processing/production process.

Incentives

The national programme provides for incentives to achieve the ultimate objective of increasing power generation from biomass materials. The cogeneration projects are of two types viz demonstration and commercial. The former seeks to help develop model projects in sugar mills using the state-of-the-art technology while the latter aims at encouraging commercialisation of surplus power generation.

Progress and status

At the beginning of the Eighth Plan biomass-based power generation through combustion and cogeneration routes was one of the activities under the Ministry's Bio-Energy Development Programme. A target of 25MW capacity was set and an outlay of Rs. 15 crore was provided in the Plan for this. From 1994-95, a major thrust was given to the creation of a conducive atmosphere involving State Government/State nodal agencies including SEBs for the utilisation of the surplus power generated in the sugar mills as well as other biomass-based power projects.

The Ministry has taken a number of steps to create widespread awareness and promote optimum cogeneration. A number of seminars, workshops, business meets and training courses on biomass/bagasse co-generation projects have been organised. The industry has been contacted through direct mail, advertisements and personal discussions. Interaction meetings were held with sugar mills, State Governments, financial institutions, State Electricity Boards, manufacturers and consultants to stimulate interest in, and generate support for, biomass power projects. Interaction meetings were held at Lonavala and Kalka in June and August 1998 respectively at which the prospective fast track sugar mills were identified. A Programme Partnership Initiative (PPI) involving M/s. MITCON, Pune and M/s. ITCOT, Chennai to step up generation of power from bagasse in prospective sugar mills was launched in April 1998. The Government of Tamil Nadu has accorded approval in principle for the formulation of a joint venture model, in association with M/s IL&FS for cooperative/public sector sugar mills.

A meeting to discuss the Joint Venture Model associating the State nodal agencies, M/s IL&FS, the Sugar Commissioners of Andhra Pradesh, Gujarat, Haryana, Maharashtra, Punjab & UP was held in the MNES. A meeting was also held in the MNES to short-list the fast track demonstration projects. As a result, four demonstration projects in Karnataka, Gujarat, and Maharashtra aggregating to a surplus capacity of around 30 MW have achieved financial closure.

Under the Interest Subsidy Scheme, cogeneration projects with an aggregate generation capacity of 50 MW of surplus power each in Karnataka and Tamil Nadu have been initiated. These projects are likely to be commissioned by the next year. The Governments of Maharashtra, Tamil Nadu, Karnataka, UP, MP, Punjab, AP and Haryana have already announced conducive and convergent policies for wheeling, banking, third party sale and buy-back of power by SEBs

Four cogeneration projects in Tamil Nadu and Uttar Pradesh using steam pressure of more than 60 bar have been successfully commissioned and no serious problem has been encountered on account of higher pressure, as was feared by many in the sugar industry. Six more cogeneration projects which have achieved financial closure and supported by the MNES under Interest Subsidy Scheme in Karnataka, Tamil Nadu and Punjab using steam pressure of 62 bar are likely to be commissioned during the next year. As a result of the momentum generated by these schemes, cogeneration projects with aggregate capacity of 106 MW of surplus power have already been commissioned and projects with total capacity of 170 MW are under construction.

A 5 MW indigenously developed power project based on rice husk was commissioned in August, 1998 in Madhya Pradesh. This project was initiated as a demonstration project under the erstwhile pilot programme of biomass combustion-based power generation and was provided capital subsidy. The project is, for the first time, using atmospheric fluidised bed boiler operating at 65 ata 485° C with rice husk as fuel. The project is expected to generate 30 million units of electricity per annum. Another private sector project of 6 MW capacity, based on *prosopis juliflora* in Andhra Pradesh is likely to be commissioned by June, 1999. A 0.5 MW grid-connected biomass gasification R&D-cum-demonstration power project based on energy plantations grown in the Kutch region of Gujarat was commissioned during the year.

Business meets were held in Tamil Nadu, MP and AP during the year. More business meets are planned in Karnataka, Orissa and Tamil Nadu. New projects with capacity of about 10 MW have achieved financial closure during the year and are likely to be provided interest subsidy by the Ministry. So far, power generation capacity of 35 MW has been created based on a variety of biomass materials. Another 7.5 MW capacity is under construction through three projects. Interest has been evinced in taluka level demonstation projects by AP, MP, Tamil Nadu and Orissa Governments. Formulation of two projects has been initiated, one each in AP and Orissa.

Sixty three biomass assessment studies were sanctioned in 12 States, as per the new guidelines finalised by an expert committee. Meetings of the expert committee to finalise the modalities of biomass assessment studies were held during May, 1998 in the NINES and a review meeting was held on August 1998 in Vadodara, followed by a midterm review meeting in January 1999. The final reports of these studies are expected by March, 1999.

During the last two years, a capacity of 140 MW surplus power has been commissioned. Projects aggregating to 180 MW capacity are under construction These are scheduled for commissioning by the end of next year.

A Programme Partnership Initiative (PPI) in bagasse-based cogeneration programme was launched in April 1998. This aimed at enthusing, motivating and assisting the participant sugar mills and others by providing them technical consultancy and other developmental services, besides ensuring sustained coordination and follow-up with all the concerned agencies viz. MNES, financial institutions, State nodal agencies, SEBs and other experts on the one hand, and the project promoter/client sugar mills on the other.

The action taken under the PPI to bridge information gaps, render assistance for 'pre-feasibility report' for the sugar mills and facilitate achievement of financial closure with the concerned financial institutions, has greatly helped in creating conducive conditions and in the generation of cogeneration project proposals. The PPI is fully backed up by State-level follow-up meetings, interaction/Business Meets etc. organised by the Ministry. Around 67 sugar mills with capacity of more than 3500 tonnes of crushing a day in the major sugar producing States are considered highly potential for surplus power generation through enhanced/advanced configuration for cogeneration. As a result, about 50 bagasse-based cogeneration project proposals, with a total generation capacity of 500 MW, spread over nine major sugar producing States have already been identified. Follow-up action by PPI Partners to help achieve financial closure has already commenced.

Presently, there are two PPI Partners and they are: (1) Maharashtra Industrial & Technical Consultancy Organisation. Ltd. (MITCON), Kubera Chambers, Dr. Rajendra Prasad Path, (J.M. Road Extension), Shivaji Nagar, Pune 411 005; and Industrial Technical Consultancy Organisation of Tamil Nadu Ltd. (ITCOT) 50-A, Greams Road, Chennai - 600 006. Encouraged by the response, the scope of PPI is proposed to be expanded to cover other potential areas in biomass power generation viz. paper industry; rice milling units; cotton, coconut and tea processing units and other such industries. All industrial/agro processing industries generating and/or using biomass resources for their heat and power needs are now eligible. The Ministry has already expanded the biomass resources base for cogeneration of surplus power in this context.

Joint venture model

M/s Infrastructure Leasing & Financial Services Ltd. (IL&FS) have come out with an innovative model to tap the cogeneration potential available in the cooperative/ public sector sugar mills. The Government of Tamil Nadu has accorded approval, in principle, to the formation of a joint venture company with M/s IL&FS, cooperative/ public sector sugar mills in Tamil Nadu and a joint venture partner. The Government of Tamil Nadu has engaged M/s IL&FS as advisers for preparation of "request for proposals" and DPR etc. towards formation of joint venture company. The Governments of Andhra Pradesh, Gujarat, Haryana,

Maharashtra, Punjab and Uttar Pradesh, have also shown interest in this model to promote cogeneration in their cooperative / public sector sugar mills. The salient features of this approach are as follows:

(a) The joint venture company shall establish 10 cogeneration projects with an aggregate power generation capacity of 200 MW (10 x 20 MW).

(b) The total investment required for the project will be of the order of about Rs. 560 crore. The total equity funds for the project will be approximately Rs. 168 crore to be met by private sector, TNEB, Sugar Cooperative Federation and financial institutions including IL&FS. The balance amount of Rs. 392 crore is proposed to be raised by debt funds.

(c) The Tamil Nadu Sugar Corporation Ltd. shall identify the participating sugar mills. The details on the royalty to be paid by the joint venture partner to the sugar mills will be finalised.

(d) M/s IL&FS shall act as a catalyst from the concept to commissioning stages, for the development of the said projects in Tamil Nadu.

State level review meetings

State-level review meetings were held with the Chief Secretaries of Tamil Nadu, UP, Gujarat, Punjab, Haryana and Maharashtra to discuss variations in the policies announced by these State Governments for purchase/ wheeling/banking of power from non-conventional energy sources. A positive outcome is expected from these.

Apex Bodies to Coordinate Assessment Studies

Apex regional institutions were assigned tasks during the first quarter of the current financial year to provide necessary and adequate guidance to State nodal agencies for carrying out biomass assessment studies. These institutions will provide guidance/supervision for appraisal, monitoring, coordination of the biomass assessment study reports in their respective regions. They will serve as an interface between the NINES, the SNAs and the Consultants. They will provide technical counselling besides reviewing and submitting the final reports to the MNES. The apex institutions will organise orientation/interaction course meetings periodically with the consultants and SNAs to familiarise them with the need-based aspects, the expected outcome and the methodology as well as the scope and content of the assessment studies for specific taluka/sub-regions. The apex institutions will periodically monitor the progress of studies, interact with consultants of their respective zones and provide guidance for preparation of final reports. Following is the list of five apex regional institutions at present functioning:

i Centre for University -Industry Collaboration, Anna University, Chennai-600 025 (Southern Region).

ii Administrative Staff College of India (Energy, Environment & Technology Area), Bellavista, Hyderabad-500 049 (Central Region).

iii Society for Rural Industrialisation, Bariatu, Ranchi-834009 (Eastern Region).

iv Tata Energy Research Institute, Darbari Seth Block, Habitat Place, New Delhi-110 003 (Northern Region).

v Operations Research Group, Rameshwar Estate, Subhanpura, Vadodara-390 007 (Western Region).

Technology development thrust areas

The Technology Development Committee, constituted by the Ministry earlier to identify the thrust areas for technology development in the area of biomass power generation and bagasse-based cogeneration, has identified the following thrust areas for R&D/ DDE:

modifications in the boiler to suit various mixes of biomass material for optimum efficiency of combustion; reduction in the steam consumption on cane; bio-technological route for drying of bagasse; and introduction of circulating fluidised bed and atmospheric fluidised bed boilers to reduce excess air requirements, etc. The draft report of the Committee for stepping up/ intensifying research & development activities in these areas by associating the in-house R&D centres, recognised by DSIR/DST, the industry and the technical institutions.

Advanced biomass gasification task force

The Ministry has constituted a Task Force to formulate the approach and the strategy to promote advanced biomass gasification which has been identified as one of thrust areas during the Ninth plan. Two meetings of the Task Force were held during the year. The Task Force also interacted with the R&D institutions, the industry, the consultants, State Nodal Agencies and prospective promoters with a view to ascertaining the scientific, technological and industrial experience in related fields in our country and abroad. The Report of the Task Force is under finalisation.

USAID/GEP project

The USAID/GEP Project (Green House Gas Pollution Prevention Project) for the promotion of "Alternative Biomass Cogeneration" (ABC) projects during the off-season has been approved with a total assistance of US $ 12.0 million for a period of 5 years from 1995. The primary objective of the ABC component of the project is to demonstrate and promote the commercialisation of bagasse-based cogeneration plants that use efficient high pressure multifuel boilers and rely in the off-season on supplemental biomass fuels rather than fossil fuels.

The ABC component provides for (a) US$ 3 million as technical assistance to catalyse the private sector investment in sugar mills using alternative bagasse/ biomass cogeneration technologies and (b) US$ 9 million as investment sub-component to lower the capital cost for 9 bagasse-based cogeneration projects in private sector sugar mills entailing use of alternative biomass fuels during off-season.

UNDP-GEF PA mission

A preparatory assistance mission for developing a full project document for "India Biomass Power Generation Project" for GEF funding commenced its work during October 1998. A series of meetings with national and international consultants were held in the MNES. Detailed discussions with the concerned officers in the MNES, the MOEF, the DEA, the UNDP followed by consultations with all other stakeholders including NGO's, public and private sector entrepreneurs were held. A draft project brief detailing the objectives, the output, the activities, the budget and the duration as per the GEF project document format is under finalisation.

EC-ASEAN programme

Discussions were held with EC-Asean Cogeneration Programme with a view to developing a component for biomass power projects in India, especially aimed at small-sized (IMW) biomass-based power generation units. The investment-cum-technical assistance component is likely to be about 6 million Euro Currency. The discussions are likely to continue to finalise the scope and contents of the sub-programme which would supplement the national effort to promote biomass power generation.

Policies and fiscal incentives

A package of fiscal incentives such as concessional custom duties, exemptions from excise duty and central sales tax, tax holidays, accelerated depreciation, etc. is offered under the national programme. The promotion of biomass-based power generation in the country is being encouraged through favourable policy regimes at the State and the Central levels. The Ministry continued its efforts during the year to persuade the State Governments/State Electricity Boards to announce remunerative polices for purchase/wheeling/banking of power generated from biomass projects. A series of State level review meetings were held to discuss the variations from the guidelines in the policy announced by the State Government for purchase/wheeling/banking of power generated from the non-conventional energy sources. The meetings were held with the Chief Secretaries of the Governments of Gujarat, UP, AP, Punjab, Haryana, Maharashtra and Tamil Nadu.

During the year, the UP Government has revised its policy and now provides escalation of 5% per year with 1994-95 as base year for purchase of power besides providing for wheeling charges for third-party sale within 5 km at 2 % instead of 12.5% of energy wheeled. The Government of Maharashtra has announced an innovative policy providing for protection against foreign exchange fluctuation risk. The policy provides for pass through of conventional fuel cost and bearing the cost of evacuation arrangement from project switch yard to MSEB substations.

During the year, the Punjab Government has decided to follow the MNES guidelines for purchase of energy from cogeneration plants including sugar mills. A standard power purchase agreement (PPA) has also been developed. Payment against energy purchase shall be insured by the PSEB within 30 days. Interest rate at 15 % per annum shall be allowed for delayed payment for the actual period of delay. The Karnataka Government has also developed a model PPA for cogeneration power plant.

Among the various renewable sources of energy, small hydro is significant from the point view of decentralised power generation and that too in hilly regions where the terrain is difficult for the promotion of other energy sources Recognising this and the fact that small hydel projects are economically viable and environmentally benign, the Ministry has been taking a number of initiatives to promote small hydel projects up to 3 MW station capacity and is giving a major thrust to this programme in the Ninth Plan in order to exploit to the maximum extent possible the estimated potential of 10,000 MW of power from this source. The initiatives taken by the Ministry include financial assistance for survey & investigation and preparation of detailed project report, capital subsidy for government owned demonstration projects, interest subsidy for commercial projects, support for renovation and modernisation of old small hydel project and development/upgradation of Water Mills.

While announcing the "Policy on Hydro Power Development", the Ministry of Power in August 1998 recognised the need for improving the share of hydro power projects in the overall power generation capacity created in the country, having regard to its potential of providing an environmentally benign solution for the energy problems specifically along the canal systems having sufficient drops and in the remote/hilly areas, where extension of grid system is comparatively uneconomical, and proposed the transfer of promotion of SHP projects between 3 and 25 MW capacity to the NINES. Modification in the Allocation of Business Rules and the issue of formal notification are under process in the Cabinet Secretariat.

Assessment of potential and identification of sites

An initial data base of over 2600 potential sites for SHP

projects up to 3 MW capacity, aggregating to a capacity of about 2000 MW, was created. This is being continuously updated in consultation with the State Governments. As part of UNDP-GEF Hilly Hydro Project, a detailed exercise was undertaken to prepare zonal plans in the 13 participating States in the Himalayan and Sub-Himalayan Region. Models have been developed taking into consideration the regional flow duration curves, geological and seismological data, vegetation cover etc. The data base now includes 3349 potential sites with an aggregate capacity of 2852 MW for projects up to 3 MW capacity and 662 identified sites with an aggregate capacity of 5519 MW for projects of 3-15 MW capacity. The State-wise details of the identified sites are given at Table - 5.10.

In order to facilitate speedy development of SHP projects, the Ministry is implementing a composite scheme covering, detailed survey and investigation (S&I) and preparation of detailed project report (DPR). Under this scheme, the Ministry provides financial support of up to Rs. 1.5 lakh for survey and investigation work and up to Rs. 1 lakh for DPR preparation. This has helped in the preparation of a shelf of small hydro projects for implementation in various States, or for offering them as commercial projects. The scheme has attracted a large number of private sector and government agencies to undertake S&I and DPR preparation for potential SHP sites. So far, 219 sites have been supported by the Ministry under the scheme.

Progress of implementation

At the start of the 8th Plan, the installed capacity of SHP projects was 93 MW. As per reports received by the Ministry from the State Departments of Power/SEBs/State nodal agencies, up to September 1998, 225 projects in 24 States aggregating to 172.8 MW have been completed and

185 projects in 25 States aggregating to 188.41 MW are under implementation. During April-December, 1998, SHP projects aggregating to 17.5 MW were commissioned.

Under its now discontinued scheme on capital subsidy, the Ministry is supporting 82 demonstration SHP projects aggregating to 96.87 MW capacity in 19 States and UTs. The Ministry's support to these projects is in the form of capital subsidy of up to 50% of the cost of project subject to a maximum of Rs. 2.50 crore per MW. So far, 27 projects aggregating to a capacity of 15.75 MW have been commissioned. The other projects are at various stages of execution. These include projects in Arunachal Pradesh, Mizoram, Madhya Pradesh, Uttar Pradesh, Punjab, Himachal Pradesh, Maharashtra and Orissa which are likely to be completed during 1999. The Ministry took up a demonstration project of free supply of 50 portable micro hydel sets of 5-15 kW in 7 States for studying their performance in the field conditions. These sets have been provided to local bodies/ communities through State agencies. Thirty two sets have been installed and the response from the local communities has been very good. Five sets in Meghalaya are ready for commissioning.

The commissioning of all the 50 sets is expected to be completed by March, 1999. The annual meeting with the State Governments to review the progress of small hydro power programme and the projects supported by the NINES was held on August 6, 1998, in New Delhi. The State Governments were requested at this meeting to expedite the completion of the on-going projects and identify new sites to take up economically viable projects. The State Governments were also requested to take up renovation and modernisation of old SHP projects. The Sub-Committee on Non-Conventional Energy Sources of the Standing Committee of Parliament on Energy visited small hydro power projects in Sikkim and West Bengal in October, 1998.

Special incentives for the northeastern region

The Ministry has announced a special incentive package for the promotion of SHP programme in the region. The package provides for capital subsidy of a maximum of Rs. 3 crore per MW or 50% of the project cost in respect of small hydro power projects up to 3 MW station capacity executed by State agencies/Power Departments/SEBs in the North-Eastern States. As many as 55 small hydro projects with a total capacity of 37.5 MW are operational and 42 projects with a total capacity of 38.8 MW are under construction in the North-Eastern States. Out of this, the Ministry has so far supported 18 projects with an aggregate capacity of 29.3 MW. In addition, the Ministry has supported 34 sites in the region for feasibility studies.

Development of commercial projects

In order to accelerate the pace of setting up commercial small hydro projects the Ministry has introduced an interest subsidy scheme through financial institutions. The scheme provides for a maximum capitalised interest subsidy of Rs. 1.12 crore/MW for SHP projects in the hilly areas, North-Eastern States, and the Andaman & Nicobar islands and up to Rs. 38.3 1akh/MW for projects in other regions. A capital subsidy of Rs. 15,0001- per kW' is being given to projects up to 100 kW capacity undertaken by Government Departments/ SNAs/NGOs/local bodies in the N-E Region, hilly regions and the A&N islands.

As a result of the policy initiatives taken by the Ministry, including the issue of guidelines to the State Governments for adopting a uniform policy in relation to non- conventional energy power projects, eleven States, which have large potential for small hydro, have announced policies on wheeling, banking, and buyback of energy generation to attract private sector entrepreneurs, Sites with a total potential of over 1000 MW have been offered so far by the State Governments for commercial projects. During the year, the Governments of Punjab, Himachal Pradesh and Haryana offered additional sites to the private sector. The allotment of sites has been finalised in Punjab and is in the process of finalisation in other States. Feasibility studies were completed by the developers in Himachal Pradesh and power purchase agreements (PPAs) are under finalisation.

IREDA's soft loan scheme

The Indian Renewable Energy Development Agency (IREDA) has so far sanctioned loan for 56 SHP projects with an aggregate capacity of 234.43 MW under the World Bank Line of Credit of US $ 70 million launched in 1993- 94 and from its own resources. As many as 17 projects with an aggregate capacity of 39.33 MW, funded by IREDA, have been commissioned so far. A business meet with SHP developers, consultants and financial institutions was organised by the IREDA and the MNES on August 12, 1998.

Renovation, modernisation and capacity uprating

The Ministry had announced a scheme on June 17, 1997 for financial support for renovation, modernisation and capacity uprating of SHP Stations. Under this scheme, financial assistance is provided up to 75% of the R&M cost or Rs. 2 crore per MW, whichever is lower to the utilities in Government sector/public sector. The main aim of the scheme is to renovate the plants and extend their life with improved performance and reliability. The Ministry has so far received proposals from Sikkim, West Bengal, Himachal Pradesh, Meghalaya, Assam and Uttar Pradesh. 'In principle' approvals have been given to 7 projects so far. During the year, the Ministry has approved grants for the renovation of Jali and Rongnichu II(5 x 500kW) SHP projects in Sikkim

Development/upgradation of water mills

Water mills have been used traditionally in the Himalayan Region for mechanical applications such as rice hulling and milling of grain etc. It is estimated that there are more than 1.5 lakh water mill sites in our country. However, the use of water mills is continuously decreasing. It has been realised that the efficiencies of water mills can be improved and such locations can also be used for small electricity generation. Keeping this in view, new designs of water mills for mechanical applications as well as electricity generation were developed by AHEC, Roorkee under the UNDP-GEF Hilly Hydro project.

Twenty five water mills, including two for electricity generation, have been installed and their performance is being monitored. The firs electricity generating water mill of 5 kW was installed at Neergarh, U.P. during the year. This unit, which was inaugurated in April, 1998, is operating in mechanical as well as electricity generating mode.

The Ministry has also announced a Promotional Incentive Scheme for development and upgradation of water mills. As per the scheme the Ministry is providing financial support up to Rs. 30,000 or 75% of the actual cost in mechanical mode and Rs. 60,000 or 75% of actual cost in electrical and mechanical mode. The scheme, is being operated through the local organisations such as the water mill associations, cooperative societies, registered NGOs, local bodies, and State nodal agencies. During the year, interactions were held with various concerned agencies and preliminary proposals have been received from Uttar Pradesh, Arunachal Pradesh, Jammu & Kashmir and Manipur.

UNDP/GEF technical assistance project

The Ministry is implementing a UNDP/GEF technical assistance project on Optimising Development of Small Hydro Resources in Himalayan and Sub-Himalayan regions' of the country. The project is being implemented in Arunachal Pradesh, Assam, Bihar, Himachal Pradesh, Jammu & Kashmir, Manipur, Mizoram, Nagaland, Sikkim, Meghalaya, Tripura, Uttar Pradesh and West Bengal. Under the project, Zonal Plans and a Master Plan for these regions are being prepared and 20 demonstration projects based on commercially viable and environmentally sound technologies will be set up. It is also proposed to upgrade 100 existing water mills. The project is scheduled for completion by December 1999.

The zonal plans have been prepared for all the 13 States and as a result 2162 potential sites with an aggregate of 3827 MW have been identified. These sites have been categorised under different ranges of capacity and head. The demonstration project sites have been

State-wise List of Sites & total Capacity offered to Private Sector

S. NO.	Name of state	No. of sites	Capacity in MW
1.	Himachal Pradesh	404	579
2.	Uttar Pradesh	57	
3.	Punjab	48	
4.	Madhya Pradesh	74	
5.	Maharashtra	6	
6.	Andhra Pradesh	30	
7.	Karnataka	36	
8.	Kerala	29	
9.	West Bengal	63	
	Total	747	1033.95

selected in consultation with national and international consultants. The selection of appropriate technology for each project and preparation of tender documents for both civil and electromechanical works have been completed. The execution of four projects has already started. The prototype models of multi purpose power unit (MPPU) for water mills have been developed and 25 water mills based on the modified designs have been installed in Uttar Pradesh, Himachal Pradesh and Jammu & Kashmir.

Research & development

While there is a good manufacturing base for small hydropower sets in the country, industrial R&D is required to further improve the efficiencies and reduce the costs of equipment. The main objectives of the R&D efforts are (a) to simplify the systems, equipment designs and engineering practices and at the same time optimise their efficiency; (b) to reduce the costs of all the elements of SHP projects; (c) to improve the reliability of the equipment; and (d) to find techniques for speeding up the construction work. Various new concepts are being tried out in the demonstration projects undertaken as part of UNDPGEF Hilly Hydro project. These include the use of rubber dams, COANDA system, SCADA system for computerised project monitoring etc. The industry is being encouraged to take up R&D activities in collaboration with research and academic Institutions to commercialise the various new concepts.

Training and manpower development

Human resource development is an important component of the SHP programme to meet the demand for trained manpower in the design, planning, operation and maintenance of SHP stations. Training courses at various levels, workshops and business meets are a regular feature of the programme implementation. The

Alternate Hydro Energy Centre, University of Roorkee has started a post-graduate course in the field of small hydro power. The NINES has sanctioned 10 fellowships in each academic course to attract talented students to the small hydro area. A training programme was also organised on water mills for the NGOs and the actual users of water mills.

Progress monitoring

The monitoring of the SHP programme is carried out through monthly progress reports received from various States and implementing agencies. In addition, regular State coordination meetings are held in the Ministry, wherein the status of implementation is reviewed. The State-wise review meetings were held in the Ministry in August, 1998. Officials from the Ministry visited the project sites in various States for assessment of physical progress. The States visited during the year were, Punjab, Himachal Pradesh, Uttar Pradesh, West Bengal, Assam, Arunachal Pradesh, Sikkim, Bihar. Besides this, the regional officers of the Ministry sent monitoring reports on the small hydro projects supported by the Ministry.

Publicity and awareness creation

Business meets were organised by the Ministry in different parts of the country so as to create awareness about the Ministry's policies and programmes and have greater interaction with the prospective developers, State agencies, consultants etc. In collaboration with the Ministry IREDA also organised, regular business meets in various regions of the country. Publicity is being provided through advertisements in national dailies as well as in regional newspapers, apart from business magazines. A publicity campaign through radio programmes in Hindi and other regional languages was also undertaken.

9

Aided Institutions

Tata institute of fundamental research

The Institute has a School of Mathematics, a School of Natural Sciences and a School of Technology and Computer Science. The academic programmes are backed by state of art common research facilities.

School of mathematics

Even as work in areas like Algebra, Algebraic Geometry and Ergodic Theory continued to be pursued with vigour, the Mathematics Faculty decided to make special efforts during the academic year 1998-99 to promote the area known as Automorphic Forms, as this is a central and important subject and there has been intense activity in this field. As apart of this activity, the school has organized an International Conference on Automorphic Forms towards the end of December, 1998. A National Conference on Commutative Algebra

School of Natural Sciences Theoretical Physics and High Energy Physics

Models of neutrino mass and their relations with neutrino oscillation data were worked out. Higgs signatures were studied for large tan B hadroproduced bbtt final states. A demonstrated dimensional reduction of high temperature QCD (Quantum Colour Dynamics.) disallowed magnetic masses blit showed disoriented chiral condensate formation with power low exponents.

Deconfinement phase transitions in the mixed SU(2) and the SO(3) gauge theories, with suppression of monopoles and vortices, were shown to lead to similar self-dual critical behaviour. Polarized and unpolarised structure functions and parton densities for the nucleon were correlated.

String theory and mathematical physics

Gravity-gauge theory correspondence was used to study local properties in gravitational fields around blackholes and to make precise the brane calculation of Hawking radiation for minimal fixed scalars. A duality anomaly in type IIB string theory was obtained from T-duality and related to modular invariance of its 2-D compactifications.

An N = 1 super-symmetric field theory living on branes at a conical singularity was derived from branes and studied in terms of an M theory description. String islands, without any adjustable modular parameters other than the coupling constant and disconnected from known string theories, were constructed.

Condensed matter and statistical physics

Drift to no-drift transition was demonstrated for strong fields in biased diffusion on percolation networks and the logarithm of the relaxation time found to strongly diverge there. Local conservation laws were found to exclude local thermal equilibrium in two simple models of heat conduction.

Persistent exponents in smooth non-equilibrium as well as in non-smooth Gaussian processes could be treated in new analytical ways. A new nonequilibrium phase transition was discovered in a class of aggregation models. Nonmagnetic impurities in an S-wave superconductor were studied and the reduction of superfluid density, the break-up into superconducting islands and the eventual drive into a non-superconducting state established.

Foundations of quantum theory
A maximally realistic causal Hamiltonian quantum mechanics was constructed in 2n-dimensional phase space.

Astronomy and astrophysics
The highlights of the current year includes study of transient cosmic x-ray sources with the Indian X-ray Astronomy Experiment, plan of spectroscopic studies of Molecular clouds using Fabry-Perot spectrometer with 1 m TIFR telescope and the strudy of solar interiors from helioseismic observations with GONG project.

High energy physics
The participation in the international collaborations in experimental high energy physics like L3, Dzero and CMS continued. For the study of p-p collisions using the CMS detector at LHC, members of the group participated in test beam studies at CERN. The fabrication of the 2nd set of 16 Pre-production prototype trays was completed. Involvement in CMS software and Physics Studies and the data analysis of DZERO Expt and LEP continued.

In the area of Experimental Gravitation, (i) design and fabrication of the low temperature insert, and (ii) construction of preliminary version of servo system for drip transfer of liquid helium was carried out. Datataking for the GRAPES (Gamma Ray Astronomy at PeV Energies) experiments has started in early 1998 with 217 electron detectors of the air shower array and the fully operational muon detector.

Nuclear and atomic physics
The heavy ion beams from the Pelletron accelerator have been used in a variety of experiments in nuclear, atomic and condensed matter physics. Studies of hexa decapole

moments have been initiated for a detailed investigation of nuclear shape in the rare earth nuclei. GDR-? rays are also used as a probe to investigate shape of nuclei at high excitation energies.

A prototype resonator for superconducting LINAC booster has been tested successfully. Subshell resolved L-K electron transfer cross sections and saturation effect in single electron excitation in ion atom collisions have been studied at intermediate velocities. The laser based research activities focuses mainly on the following aspects: (a) the study of formation of negative ions in intense laser field excited gases (b) Studies on dissociative electron attachment of laser excited molecules (c) Nonlinear optical characteristics of organic and inorganic molecules and (d) New methods for estimating x-ray yields from laser produced solid plasmas.

Condensed matter physics and materials science

Work has progressed in magnetism and superconductivity, semiconductors and nano-materials and thin films. Investigations on Quaternary Borocarbide Superconductors, interplay of superconductivity and long-range magnetic order in magnetic borocarbides and search for new superconducting quaternary phases were carried out.

The investigations on vortex state of superconductors have revealed two new results, namely, the first observation of Fishtail Effect and Peak Effect in an isothermal scan and the step increase in equilibrium magnetization across the peak effect (PE) in a weakly pinned crystal 2H-NbSe2. The spin glass properties of high temperature superconductors have been investigated and based on that a new model for high temperature superconductivity proposed.

Detailed investigations on several Gd based alloys suggest that the issues of magnetic precursor effects and associated magneto-resistance anomalies are conceptually puzzling even in such relatively simple systems. In the: area of semiconductors, Optoelectronic materials and devices several compositions of InGaAsP lattice matched to GaAs and InP have been synthesised. Pulsed laser ablation (PLD) technique has been extensively used for the realization of high quality multi component films of oxides such as high Tc superconductors, ferroelectrics and colossal magnetoresistive manganites.

Chemical sciences

Research in the Department of Chemical Sciences is focused on the areas of Chemical Dynamics, Molecular Biophysics and Bio-inorganic Chemistry. In the area of Chemical Dynamics Intramolecular and Intermolecular dynamics of organic molecules in gaseous and condensed phases was investigated using a variety of laser spectroscopic techniques in picosecond to microsecond time scale.

In the area of Molecular Biophysics, high resolution structures of biological macromolecules such as multistrand DNAs, proteins binding to specific DNAs, calcium binding proteins, halophillic proteins were investigated by NMR spectroscopy. In the area of Bio-inorganic Chemistry, structural and functional aspects of several metalloproteins, especially those with important roles in bioenergetics and biological redox processes were studied.

Biological sciences

The main focus of the research activity at Department of Biological Sciences is in the fields of Neurobiology and Molecular and Cellular biology. In plants, phytohormone abscisic acid (ABA) mediates the responses to abiotic stresses. How the transduction mechanisms to various stresses crosstalk is not known? The studies in moss protonema suggest that the cells integrate the response at level of heterotrimeric G-proteins and each abiotic stress induces only a subset of the ABA induced G-proteins.

Biochemical and genetic approaches are being employed to understand the transport and utilization of sugar in yeast. A gene involved in sugar transport in S.pombe (fission yeast) has been cloned. The malaria group is investigating the host-parasite interactions. Several novel putative protective malaria proteins have been identified and are being further characterized.

National Centre for Radio Astrophysics, Pune

The GMRT, consisting of 30 fully steerable parabolic dishes of 45-m diameter each, is being set up as a national facility for frontline research in radio astronomy in the frequency range 38 MHz to 1420 MHz. Most of the subsystems of the GMRT are in an advanced stage of completion.

A major progress was in installing the 30 antenna correlator system, a crucial component importantly to materials being brought for making high resolution radio maps with GMRT. Preliminary observations with the telescope to test and debug the instrument are currently underway. The research interests of the academic staff at NCRA cover a wide range, addressing some of the fundamental questions in the frontiers of several fields in Astronomy and Astrophysics.

These include understanding the Sun, its activity and the solar wind, physics of pulsars, the interstellar medium (ISM) in our galaxy and external galaxies, energy generation and transport in nearby galaxies and in radio galaxies and quasars, formation and evolution of galaxies, generation of magnetic fields, and structure formation in the universe. NCRA also run a large radio telescope located at Ootacamund in the Niligiri Hills, the Ooty Radio Telescope.

Homi Bhabha Centre for Science Education, Mumbai

An important achievement of the year was the inauguration of the physics olympiad programme in the country. The first Indian National Physics Olympiad (INPhO) (Theory and Experiment) was held in May 1998 at 10 centres in the country. HBCSE organized a month long training camp in May June 1998 for the INPhO awardees.

A team of 5 students selected at the end of the camp represented India at the 29th International Physics Olympiad held at Reyjavik, Iceland in July 1998. HBCSE has initiated through the support of DST and DAE, similar olympiad activity in chemistry and biology also. With its involvement in the mathematics olympiad programme of NBHM (DAE), HBCSE has now emerged as the country's premier centre for olympiads in basic sciences.

An Activity-based Foundation Curriculum in Science, Technology and Society for post school students was completed and a series of books have been brought out in this novel curriculum. HBCSE members contributed out by IGNOU and the revised primary science books of the State of Maharashtra.

Orientation programmes were carried out for teachers, teacher educators and science popularisers. HBCSEs mobile low-cost laboratory and history of science exhibition displayed at various sites evoked much popular response. HBCSE is organizing an International Workshop on History of Science and its implication for Science Education in February 22-26, 1999.

National Centre for Biological Sciences, Bangalore

The NCBS has made significant progress in Structural Biology, of Disease, Neuroscience and Developmental Biology. The research activities are now being carried out in the newly built campus. It is spread over an attractive

20-acre plot surrounded by forests and green fields. In the first phase of construction a laboratory of about 80,000 square feet and a housing cluster of 50,000 sq. ft. have been built. Built up area includes a research block with twenty well equipped laboratories; lecture halls of varying capacities; seminar halls; auditorium; library; housing for students, post-doctoral fellows, visiting scientists and faculty: a dining and recreation block; central stores and a maintenance building. Most buildings, including some housing, are networked.

School of Technology and Computer Science

A new laboratory for Computational Mathematics has been set up at Pune with the active support of several members of BARC. One of the main objectives of the laboratory is to develop a new paradigm that synthesizes symbolic and numerical computation. Work was also carried out in the areas of theoretical computer science embedded systems, networks and architectures and speech recognition.

Saha Institute of nuclear physics

The Institute made impressive strides in respect of the projects envisaged in the IXth Five Year Plan period. It published about 150 papers in international Journals and edited volumes with some more to add to the list. Several national and international collaborative efforts were launched with the Institute at the nodal centre. With the addition of state-of-the-art equipments, informatics and ultrafast computer networks, a substantial improvement has obtained in the central facilities.

In nuclear science, a significant progress has been made towards setting up of (a) an X-ray fluorescence system for materials analysis, (b) a Rolling machine and e-evaporation systems for the preparation of targets for nuclear and atomic physics experiments, and (c) two Detector Doppler Broadening setups in the Positronium

Laboratory. In addition, design and fabrication of the following equipments have been initiated: (a) a multi-gamma detector array to be used in experiments with heavy ion beams at VECC, (b) a multi-detector setup with small CsI (t1) scintillators to be employed in the study of LCP emissions in heavy ion collision at various accelerator centres, and (c) various types of gas detectors.

Penetration effects on the internal conversion processes of the 134 KeV Gamma-transitions in 13 1 Cs has been found unambiguously for the first time. carbon-and silicon-induced L and M X-ray production cross-sections of Au and Pb, and the anisotropic parameters of the carbon ion-induced M X-rays of Au were measured in the 4 to 12 MeV energy-range using the 3 MV Pelletron at IOP, Bhubaneswar.

Fusion enhancement and reaction dynamics, back-angle quasi-elastic scattering and excitation functions have been studied for 12C, 160 + 142Nd systems around the Coulomb barrier. Studies on quasi-fission were continued with pulsed 160 beams on 18 1 Ta with the fission fragments detected by the TOF method.

Data analysis for assessing angular distribution and anisotropies in different mass bins is in progress. Target and projectile breakup reaction studies were carried out using the TIFR-BARC Pelletron as also in collaboration with the RCNP group in Japan. A formalism was developed to evaluate the pre-equilibrium cluster-emission spectra and angular distributions in heavy ion using a closed form expression free from empirical parameters.

Spectroscopic study of 79Br has been carried out at NSC, Delhi, with significant new results for lifetimes of high-spin states and band deformation substantiating the Cranked-Shell-and Particle-Rotor Model calculations. A new 3-quasi-particle band was identified in 1251. Traces of heavy elements in industrial wastes were quantified by the PIXE method. Role of substitutional alloying elements in the recovery processes pertaining to the proton-induced defect, in ziro (a new zirconium-based alloy) was studied.

Positron annihilation with high-momentum inner-shell electrons of Ag nanoparticles, grown in a polymer medium, was studied by a 2-detecto coincidence spectroscopic method. Thi Bubble Model, with the sharp boundaries giving way to diffusiveness, was applied to the study of positroniur in liquids, making rooms for high surface tension and study of chemical complex formation with an electron acceptor in liquids. In Nuclear and Radiochemistry production and separation of seven carrier-free rare-earth radionuclides (biomedical importance was effected using the heavy ion beams at BAR) TIFR Pelletron.

A laboratory is being developed for hybrid optical information processing like, photoelastic and birefringence analysis, using some novel technique The electronic workshop facility is fa coming up to stand by the research requirements in various laboratories. The Condensed Matter Physics Group has started building up facilities for materials preparation and characterisation as envisaged in the IXth Plan. A Float Zone Crystal Growth facility has been set up and has become operational.

Structural studies of several organic molecules have been carried out microwave rotational spectroscopy microwave double resonance techniques. Studies of the acoustic properties of beta-brass and KSCN n their order-disorder transition are progress. NMR measurements on several metal hydrides to study different features of proton-pairing have been carried out. In addition, NMR and susceptibility measurements have been made in low-dimensional topologically frustrated systems, as also Hg-based High-Tc compounds.

Experimental and theoretical research on several aspects of superconductivity continues to be a thrust area. Extensive and precise measurements of transport properties of High-Tc compounds are being carried out. Investigations on the effect of grains, magneto-crystalline anisotropy and microstructures on the physical properties of mechanically milled alloys Co-Ge, spinel ferrites is continuing.

Studies on several aspects of correlated electron systems with special reference to organic superconductors, High-Tc systems, Quantum Hall Effect and Hubbard-like models are in progress. The atomic distribution in some bimetallic nanostructures have been studied under different adsorption conditions to investigate the effectiveness of nanoparticles in oxidation of CO, an important pollutant. In Surface Physics, X-Ray and diffuse scattering measurements have demonstrated that nanometer—thick US layers can reside at the metal-organic interfaces of Langmuir-Blodgett films. Parallelly, a theoretical scheme based on the inversion method—within the framework of the Born approximation has been developed to extract roughness and inter-diffusion profile as a function of depth in multi-layered thin films.

The behaviour of chiral conformal was studied. In the case of quantum Hall systems interacting at one point a twisted representation of the KacMoody current algebra was obtained and novel oscillations of Hall currents were redicted. A bound on heavy baryon form factors was obtained using dispersion relations and analyticity. It was shown that near-extremal four dimensional dyonic black holes can be described by a model consisting of a one-dimensional gas of massless particles.

It was demonstrated that unlike the extremal Reissner-Nordstrom black hole in ordinary space-time, the one in anti-de Sitter space-time is a minimum of action and has zero entropy if quantisation is carried out after extremalisation. However, if extremalisation is carried out after quantisation, then the entropy is still a quarter of the area.

String theory in the long wavelength limit admits certain kind of states whose mass, charge etc are protected from any perturbative corrections by large super-symmetry. The non-perturbative symmetry of string theory as well as properties of these states which include black holes, p-branes, D-branes etc were studied. Further consequences of a new sum rule derived here recently for twist-four longitudinal structure function in QCD were explored. A detailed investigation of the orbital angular momentum operator in light-front QCD was carried out in the context of deep inelastic scattering.

A new mechanism for proton decay was discovered in super-symmetric models. In the linearised quantum theory of gravity, it was shown that gravitational interactions in a medium are in general non-universal. The effect of vacuum neutrino oscillations on all types of supernova neutrinos and antineutrinos was explored and neutrino events detected at Superkamioka and Sudbury observatories were explained.

Phenomenological implications of R-parity investigated in the context of proton decay and in the context if recent neutrino data. Production of photon, dilepton, open-charm etc are being studied with inclusion of medium effects to use as signatures for QGP formation in high energy heavy ion collisions.

Nuclear level densities were calculated including thermal and quantal fluctuations. The reliability of isotope thermometry in multi-fragmentation and nuclear liquid gas phase transition was investigated.The production of pions and several strange particles in energetic pp collisions was studied within an effective Lagrangian model which compares well with experimental data.

The astrophysical s-factor for the solar reaction 7Be(p,) 8Be was evaluated in the DWBA formalism. The enhancement of neutrino emissivities in presence of a strong magnetic field resulting in rapid cooling of neutron stars was studied in a Dirac-Hartree approach.

In Plasma Physics significant progress has been made in completion of Slow Bank System for increasing the plasma pulse duration, and 2 mm microwave interferometer for density measurement. Time-of-flight system for neutral particle analysis is in an advanced state of completion. Electron Cyclotron Emission (ECE) radiometer has been tested and is ready for shipment from FOM Institute in Netherlands. Vertical array of Soft Xray detectors has been installed and tested. The feedback control system for plasma position is under development.

Several interesting experiments in the SINP-Tokarnak, like anomalous ion heating, runaway electron studies, anomalous current penetration, estimation of electron temperature have been carried Out. Theoretical studies have been made in the area of MHD relaxation & wave propagation in plasma.

The ECE radiometer is likely to be installed and put to regular use by February 99. Hard X-ray analyser would also be ready for use around March 99. The RF power source for driving lower hybrid current in plasma is to be procured by March 99. In Bioscience Group, the previously determined 3D structure of the protein WCI at 2.3 resolution revealed a directional change in the polypeptide chain near its C-terminus and helped predict for the first time the location of the second reactive site. The protein and its two mutants have been cloned and expressed in E. Coli and suitable crystals for diffraction studies have been obtained.

Crystal structures of several other biologically and pharmacologically important systems have been determined. Study of conformational response of an important eye lens protein to various stimulations revealed a change at pH below 4.6. Base sequence dependent structure and flexibility of DNA double-helix were investigated by MD simulations and crystal-based data-analysis.

Thermodynamic studies of interactions between anticancer drugs and other macromolecules e.g. DNA, a cytoskeletal protein, spectrin and phospholipid membranes were made to understand the molecular mechanism of drug action. Studies on the process of transcription initiation by T7 RNA polymerase and membrane and miceller interaction of cytoskeletal proteins are under way.

Relative importance of the different inisitol phosphate second messengers in Entamoebia histolytica was worked out and the role of phytase on signal transduction pathways in mung bean seed studied. Conditional changes in cellular signalling networks were studied for easy diagnosis of Huntington disease and myotonic dystrophy.

Fluorophore microenvironments of biologically important flavonoids in membrane mimetic systems and interaction of chemical denaturants with different proteins were spectroscopically investigated. Genotoxic studies on the effects of pesticides, toxic metals and radiations on different plant, animal and bacterial systems were made. Studies are under way to design a gene based vehicle for cancer therapy.

The Post-M. Sc teaching programme, in its forty-fifth year, continues in its efforts imparting adequate training to the freshers selected for the Ph. D work both in physical and biological sciences. Like in the past years, the Institute held regular seminars, weekly colloquial and workshops on current issues. Collaboration programmes include, for example,

1) SINP-VECC projects with (i) Radioactive Ion Beams and (ii) Superconducting Cyclotron.
2) CERN-India collaboration on the Photon Multiplicity Detector Programmes.
3) The continuing Crystallography, Molecular Biology and Structural Biology programmes financed by the Dept. of Bio-Technology.

Tata memorial centre

The Tata Memorial Centre (TMC), comparing of Tata Memorial Hospital (TMH) and Cancer Research Institute (CRI), is engaged in research, education and treatment of cancer. Following were the activities of the Centre during the period of this report:

Tata memorial hospital

Clinical activities

The Tata Memorial Hospital continued its diagnostic, treatment services, research and educational activities to maintain the highest standard of patient care. During the year 23145 new cases were registered. In addition, 4745 Referral Cards were issued for certain investigations like Mammography, Pathological investigations etc.

Cancer prevention

Department of Preventive Oncology has arranged lectures and audio visual shows on the ill effects of tobacco and Cancer Awareness programmes at Municipal Schools, Colleges and also for General Population. Photo and Poster Exhibitions for the General Public were also conducted at 10 different locations viz. Chatrapati Shivaji Terminus, Churchgate Station, Mumbai University Kalina Campus etc.

The Department has conducted 14 screening camps in the community in collaboration with local organisations. An awareness campaign on breast cancer was conducted in the month of October, which is internationally recognised as 'Breast Cancer Awareness Month'. A total of 1231 new cases were registered for screening in the Preventive Oncology Dept. out of which 3 50 were pre-cancer cases.

Clinical research secretariat

The Clinical Research Secretariat (CRS) which was started in 1997 continued to assist clinical researchers in data management, data analysis and other aspects of research projects. During this year two new facilities have been provided. The 'Internet' for those who visit the CRS and 'an abstract service' to all the staff members which makes information available within three days of its publication. The CRS has offered infrastructural support for three randomised trials, four prospective studies from various departments. Data management and analysis have been carried out for 28 retrospective studies.

Academic activities

The Scientific Review Committee and Hospital Ethics Committee exhaustively reviewed and approved 11 new research projects in addition to, ongoing projects. Researchers of TMH published 92 scientific papers in international and national journals of repute. TMH conducted 19 Conferences/Workshops/Seminars during the year. Members of staff have attended several International/National Conferences/ Workshops / Seminars/Symposia etc., and have presented 60 scientific papers and delivered 67 lectures.

TMH is a postgraduate teaching centre and is affiliated to the University of Mumbai. During the year, it continued to conduct various postgraduate degree and diploma courses. The Hospital is a recognised training Centre for cancer education and research by national and international organisations such as WHO and IAEA.

Actrec project

All infrastructural development at site including 1st phase tree planting along the boundary and Project House, Guard House and 64 flats have been completed. An agreement has been signed with MSEB for supply of permanent power supply. Permanent connection for water supply is expected shortly.

Civil and electrical works of Research Centre Building are nearing completion. Civil and electrical works of Animal House have been completed. Service building has been completed. 80% work of the Ward Block is completed. The tenders for Clinical Research Centre has been invited.

Satellite extension of TMH at MGM hospital

An agreement between TMC and ESIC has been entered into to set up a Satellite Extension of TMH at MGM Hospital, Parel. Modification works in the Wards, Operation Theatres and ICU are being taken up in consultation with MGM authorities and CPWD Engineers.

Project "upgradation/modernisation of facilitates"

The Planning Commission had approved a one-time grant of Rs.25.00 crores for the Upgradation/ modernisation of facilities. The amount has been allocated for procurement of equipments for Labs/ Departments, Renovation of Wards and Setting up of new Library Complext. Renovation of Female Ward and Private Ward have been completed. 65% work in the

Semi Private Ward has been completed. Structural work of Library complex is expected to be completed by end of this month.

Epidemiological studies

TMH continued epidemiological studies in respect of Radiation Occupational Workers and their families at nuclear power stations sites in India. The report of the survey carried out at the TAPS was officially handed over to NPC. The survey at the KAPS is completed and the draft report was handed over to the NPC.

The data collection at RAPS and NAPS was completed and the report is under preparation. The data collection at MAPS is in progress. Epidemiological studies on cancer are also being carried out by the Department of Medical Records and Statistics. During the year studies on Colo-Rectal Cancers and Cervix Cancers were undertaken and results analysed.

Rural cancer centre at Barshi

TMC continued to extend its token grant-in-aid and other support to Rural Cancer Centre at Barshi.

Waste management and hospital infection control

The Dept. of Microbiology has been actively involved in setting up a tailormade system for handling the hospital's waste from "cradle to grave". The final plans of setting up the disposal technology are in progress. 'Infection Awareness Week' was organised during the year.

Computerisation and hospital information system

During the year 1998, one of the major activities of the Computer Department has been the installation and commissioning of the IBM AS/400 Server which makes use of OS/400 as operating system, DB2/400 as the RDBMS. Also, the entire campus was networked using structured cabling concept.

Patient rehabilitation

After Completion of Therapy (ACT) Clinic which was initiated in 1991 continued psychological support to patients and rehabilitation after receiving therapy. The patient clinics for Physiotherapy, Occupational therapy, Speech Therapy, Psychology etc., extended support to the patients with the ultimate goal of improvement in the quality of life of those unfortunate patients who are afflicted with disabilities.

The Stoma Clinic provided comprehensive care to patients with Stomas, Fistulas, Pressure sores, incontinence and would heating problems. Medical Social Service Department provided guidance to 13679 new patients and chemotherapy drugs at concessional rate were given to 3604 cases. Rail/Air/ST concession forms were issued to 71-782 patients. Accommodation was arranged for 3559 and transportation was provided to 1819 cases.

Cancer research institute

The major thrust of research work at the Cancer Research Institute continues to be on Head and Neck Cancer, leukemias and lymphomas. The potent transforming gene cloned from human oral cancer has been sequenced to a very large extent and its potential use for oral diagnosis is being evaluated.

In the studies on gene therapy of human oral cancers, after initial use of Hstk gene, new strategies for including cytokine, growth factor genes along with Hstk is being evaluated for obtaining higher cytotoxicity. These are being tested in the human oral cancer model developed in nude mice. Immunological studies on augmentation of tumour cell kill by the T cells have shown the involvement of gamma delta T cells in oral and esophageal cancers and this has been found to be dependent on stress protein—HSP-60 and ICE proteins.

Work has been undertaken to identify genetic factors responsible for susceptibility of oral cancer. Studies on genetic polymorphism at GST-M1 and GST-T1 and CYP-D6 gene loci on 300 patients and 450 controls by PCR RFLP have shown a significantly higher frequency of GSTM1 null alleles in oral cancer patients.

Combination analysis shows that individuals with CYP2-D6 wild type and GST-null alleles were at a higher risk for oral cancer than other allelic combination. Similarly, chromosomes 3p and 9p whose rearrangements are seen in oral cancer patients are being allelo-typed for microsatellite instability and loss of heterozygosity (LOH) for their potential use as susceptibility

Studies on workers occupationally exposed to tobacco have shown that tobacco exposure impairs xenobiotic detoxification mechanism via glutathione conjugation pathway and exposes the workers to higher genotoxic risk. Studies on multi-organ carcinogeneicity of pan masala in three different mouse models suggest that pan masala is a risk factor for cancer.

In the studies on chemo-prevention of cancer, circumin free extract of turmeric has shown strong chemopreventive activity. Immunological studies on leukemias and lympho mas show expression of TNF receptors ligand superfamily in patients with Hogkin's Disease. In 68 patients with lung cancer effector cell function was considerably reduced but could be partially augmented by treatment with IL- 1 and IL- 12.

Work has been initiated on developing retroviral vectors for gene transfer/gene therapy using HIV-2 viruses isolated at the Cancer Research Institute. Methods for collection, storage of umbilical cord stem cells have been fully standardized and the technology was transferred through the Department of Biotechnology to Armed Forces Medical College, Pune. Isolation of these cells by elutriation have yielded around 70% enrichment of pluripotent stem cells from the umbilical cord. Work is in progress to establish a Cord Blood Stem Cell Bank. The Institute has a larger programme on under-standing the basic mechanism of malignant transformation in CML. These include studies on chemotactic response, specific service proteins, modulated during leukemic transformation and activities of various tyrosine kinases and phosphates in these cells. The anti-metastatic role of drug pentoxyphyllin and related compounds is being investigated using mouse melanoma model.

Institute of physics

The Institute of Physics at Bhubaneswar is an autonomous research institution funded jointly by DAE and Govt. of Orissa for promotion of research in frontier areas of physics.

Research activities

The main areas of basic research comprise nuclear physics, condensed matter physics and high energy physics. However, experimental activities have also expanded considerably in recent years. The Ion Beam Laboratory with a 3 MV Pelletron Accelerator had user groups from within and outside the Institute.

The Accelerator Mass Spectrometry (AMS) project, funded jointly by the DAE, DST, DOS and CSIR, started augmenting the existing 3 MV accelerator facility for carrying out 14C and 10Be studies. A dedicated beam line for surface physics studies was setup using one of the beam ports of the Pelletron Accelerator. About 100 papers were published in referred international journals besides those presented in conference and symposia etc.

Collaborations

The ongoing projects include an Indo-US project on development of ion-microbeam facility and Indo-French project on "Clusters and Cluster Assembled Materials". The collaboration with CERN, Geneva or quark-Gluon Plasma work also continued.

Workshops, seminars and training

To keep scientists abreast with the frontline areas of research in physics, the Institute organised workshop schools etc. To encourage local college and university teachers as well as to Institute alumni, the Institute supports a short term programme during summer and other vacation periods. The Institute runs a regular programme in which physicists from within the country are abroad are invited to give talks are interact with the faculty and scholar The Institute also conducts Predoctoral and Doctoral research programmes.

Awards

The contributions of the physicists of the Institute have been recognised amply. The Institute bagged Shanti Swarup Bhatnagar award for Physical Sciences for the year 1998. The scientists of the Institute have also bagged an International award, an INSA young scientist award and several other national and state awards. One of the faculty members was awarded the Kamal Kumari National Award for Science & Technology, for the year 1996.

Metha Research Institute of Mathematics and Mathematical Physics

The Institute conducts investigations and research on problems in Mathematics and Mathematical Physics, Computer Science and related topics. During the year under report, research work continued further in Pure Mathematics including Number Theory, Algebraic Geometry, Coding Theory and Analysis as well as in Theoretical Physics in the areas of Mathematical Physics, High Energy Physics, Condensed Matter and

Astrophysics. Lectures and Seminars were organised during the year to the benefit of researchers whereby they were exposed to the latest ideas and achievements in the field of Mathematics and Theoretical Physics.

Several academicians from reputed institutions within the country and abroad visited the Institute and collaborated in research work with the members of the Institute. The members of the staff attended Conferences/ Workshop s/Symposia in India and abroad. The National Board for Higher Mathematics (NBHM) has selected the Institute for imparting training to the talented young students of Mathematics drawn through International Mathematics Olympiad-1995 (INMO-95) awardees. The second such course was successfully conducted during 1998.

The Institute will be hosting the second "National Conference on Commutative Algebra and Algebraic Geometry" from February 1-6, 1999. This is the second of a regular series of conferences to be held in India on this subject. The first such conference was held in March 98 at Kodaikanal. One faculty member of MRI was elected as a Fellow of the Royal Society and was nominated for R.D. Birla award. Computational facilities at the Institute were further strengthened.

Institute of Mathematical Sciences

The Institute of Mathematical Sciences (IMSc), which had its inception in 1962, is a National Institution of higher learning whose primary purpose is to foster high quality fundamental research in frontier disciplines of Mathematical Sciences. The Institute has programmes for doctoral degree, post doctoral work and the visiting scientists scheme. The Institute is presently in a phase of rapid growth. The three major groups of research areas of the Institute are:

Theoretical Physics, Mathematics and Theoretical Computer Science

The Institute has an excellent library, state-of-the-art computing facilities, very good communication systems and connectivity. To spot talent and nurture it, the Institute will conduct with conduct with Mehta Research Institute, Allahabad, National Centre for Radio Astrophysics, Pune, Inter-University Centre for Astronomy and Astrophysics, Pune, Indian Institute of Astrophysics, Bangalore, Institute for Plasrna Research, Gandhinagar and Physical Research Laboratory, Ahmedabad, a Joint Written Screening Test as a part of the selection process for Junior Research Fellows (JRFs).

The Institute faculty participated in several symposia and conferences both inside and outside India. Many internationally reputed scientists visited IMSc to collaborate with the scientists of the Institute and gave series of lectures, seminars and colloquial etc. The members of the Institute regularly published their research papers in international journals of repute in the areas of Physics, Mathematics and Theoretical Computer Science.

During the year, the following Training Programme, Workshop and International Conference were held in which a large number of academicians from within the country and abroad participated.

1. UNESCO-IMSc Regional Training Programme in Mathematics (November 9-21, 1998)
2. Quantum Chromo Dynamics Workshop (November 30 - December 8, 1998)
3. International Conference on Foundations of Software Technology and Theoretical Computer Science (December 14 - 19, 1998)

4. Third Workshop on Quantum Field Theory, Quantum Gravity and String Theory held at Puri. (December 11-20, 1998)

Major achievements during 1998 year are:

1. Developed and modernised the library into a definitive reference library in Mathematical Sciences, so that the library incorporates all aspects of information database (books, journals, preprints, pedagogic materials, CD-ROMS) and information dissemination (on-line access to libraries world wide).
2. Developed and augmented the computing environment so that IMSc become an important node for a supercomputing network. Developed both hardware and software so that the state of art computing as needed for the frontline research is provided.

Institute of plasma research

It has undergone significant upgrading during the last year with strengthening of the Ohmic heating coil system, integration of a large number of new diagnostics and introduction of the ICRF antenna and heating system. Aditya, a medium size tokamak, is being operated with the transformer-converter power system since September, 1989. 80-100 kA plasma discharges at toroidal field of 8.0 kG we studied.

RF heating system was tested separately and integrated to Aditya tokamak. In diagnostics, the installation of Aditya Thomson scattering system, based on ruby laser (10J,20 nsec) thermal lithium beam, laser blow off system were completed. The spectroscopic diagnostics were on Aditya augmented. Steadystate Superconducting Tokamak Experiment (SST- 1)

The SST-1 experiment is moving closer to fabrication. The engineering drawings and draft tender document for the vacuum vessel, cryostat, magnetic coil fabrication were reviewed by NPCIL. Order for fabrication and commissioning were in process. The contract for thermal and structural stress analysis of vacuum vessel, cryostat, magnetic coils and support structure was awarded. Efforts were made to resolve some of the uncertainties in the design of the first-wall (plasma facing components) and to advance the design concepts closer to the engineering design.

Preliminary experiments on heat flux testing were carried out at CAT, Indore. A contract to fabricate 15 km of Cablein-Conduit conductors (CICC) was also awarded. Tests on the Model coil was in progress. Various numerical codes were developed and adopted for design of the SST-1 subsystems. The main baffle shape was optimised for SST-1 using DEGAS. The DIVER code is developed for divertor erosion study. A closed cycle LHe plant was finalised. As a part of the technology development programme, designing 10 kA vapour cooled current leads, SHe/ LHe transfer line and superconducting bus line continued. A liquid nitrogen pump was indigenously designed and fabricated.

Three different schemes in RF heating and current drive for SST- I were in progress. Engineering of ion cyclotron heating to heat the plasma as an extension of the existing system on Aditya, continued. Feasibility of driving current using fast wave antennae was explored. Lower hybrid waves with asymmetric spectrum would be launched to drive plasma current during different operating scenarios. 1 MW of CW power would be supplied from two klystrons, to feed a grill.

The engineering design was completed and prototype testing of various crucial components was initiated. ECRF system will be used initially to preionize and startup of SST 1discharges the engineering design of which was completed. The engineering of the major components of the neutral beam injection system was taken up. The majority of this engineering activity was carried out on the cryo panel, heat transfer element, V-target, and the ion deflection magnet.

The critical design for the ion deflection magnet was that of shaping the soft iron profile to ensure that field within the iron core is maintained within 1.4 Testa. Major engineering efforts in the ion source was directed towards the fabrication of the back plate and the extractor grids. High voltage multimegawatt power supplies are used for certain applications. A Prototype (14kV 500kW) development project for these steady state power supplies, was started.

Feasibility of setting up of a charge exchange recombination spectroscopy, CXRS system for SST-1 was under study. A new design for ECE diagnostics and a suprathermal electron distribution diagnostics were proposed. At IPR, efforts continued on designing a high speed lossless data acquisition system for SST diagnostics for a shot duration 1000sec. New 12-pulse converter power supplies will be installed for various coils of the SSTI tokamak. A 10 kA dc power supply for the superconducting magnet test facility was ordered. System design and analysis of these schemes were completed and proto-typing work progressed.

Basic experiments

A Large Volume Plasma Device (LVPD) was installed for studies related to high temperatu re beta plasma. Initial experiments were focusing on issues related to excitation, propagation and linear and non linear interaction of whistler and helicon waves. Another major thrust will be on study of surface waves.

Theoretical and computational physics

The primary focus of the theoretical research programme continued to be on fundamental problems fusion physics and nonlinear phenomena in plasmas. There was also a broad range of work related to non-neutral plasmas, the neutrino problem and other exotic plasmas. Fluid / particle simulations and numerical modelling of nonlinear systems , constituted the major component of the computational programme.

The process of magnetic field generation in laser produced plasmas was re-examined. A Poynting like theorem for field generation was given. These results seemed to agree with some recent numerical simulations. Several nonlinear aspects of the Electron Magneto hydrodynamic (EMHD) model for plasma phenomena were studied.

These studies will be relevant for the description of experiments on a newly commissioned large volume plasma device (LVPD) at IPR. Using the Violation of equivalence principle (VEP), the solution to the solar neutrino problem and the atmospheric neutrino anomaly were studied. The VEP effect on laboratory neutrino oscillation experiment was also analysed.

Surface characterisation laboratory

Surface characterization facilities were made available to external users on a commercial basis. A few hundred Internal Samples were studied for different coatings and plasma modified surfaces of different steels alloys and powders were studied, which gave valuable inputs for improvement of plasma processes.

Plasma processing

The Facilitation Centre for Industrial Plasma Technologies (FCIPT) bridges the Institute for Plasma Research and the Indian industries. To promote the acceptance of plasma based technologies and to generate technocommercial data relevant to entrepreneurs, the job-shop of the centre executes job work for surface and material treatment on industrial scale. Work on plasma nitriding was extended to a variety of alloy steels and stainless steels. Feasibility of nitriding 17-4 PH SS used in solar array drives and other low speed mechanisms in space environment, was established in collaboration with ISRO Inertial Systems Unit.

A large capacity dual chamber plasma nitriding system was built and commissioned. A variety of components for a number of parties were successfully plasma nitrided. The list included major national and multinational organisations. Spherodization of irregular alumina particles in the 50 to 80 micron range using high enthalpy in-flight thermal plasma reactor was achieved with an efficiency of 98 %. Fully indigenous plasma ion implantation facility was setup at FCIPT. To demonstrate extended operation of the zircon dissociation process, a 2 - hour run at 50 kW was performed successfully.

Research performed under the IAEA Coordinated Research Programme concentrated on the performance of graphite electrode plasma torches under pyrolysis conditions. A compact plasma torch was designed and fabricated for experimental study.

Atomic energy education society

The Atomic Energy Education Society (AEES) manages 30 schools at 14 different places in the country, providing education to about 28,000 children of the DAE-employees. During the year 1998-99 a number of administrative and academic steps were taken to consolidate and improve the functioning of the schools as follows:

An Academic Unit was set up in the Central Office. A decision was taken to teach the use of computers and use them in teaching of prescribed subjects. Several measures were adopted to strengthen teaching of English language; special coaching in English and Mathematics was introduced for children from educationally weak background, and promotion norms for students were rationalised.

A horticultural programme, seeking to instil in students a greater awareness of environmental concerns was further expanded; assistance was provided to students appearing for Board Examinations; primary schools were placed in the charge of headmistresses, headmasters; a beginning was made in the preparation of special guide books in Mathematics for primary school teachers; primary school libraries were expanded. Vocational education for weak students was started in Anushaktinagar. A series of important personnel policy decisions were taken for better utilisation of the manpower available; Parents-Teachers Associations and School Management Committees were established.

Powers and responsibilities of the principal were further streamlined and a more scientific system to evaluate the performance of teachers was initiated. Special in-service orientation programmes were organised for about 500 teachers. The results in the Board examinations conducted in the year 1998 showed a significant improvement over the results in the previous year. 82% of the students passed the All India Secondary School Examination of CBSE as against 77% last year.